Spirituality and Holistic Spiritual Health

Spirituality and Holistic Spiritual Health makes the case for the key role that spiritual care and chaplaincy work play in healthcare.

Chapters articulate an innovative approach to spirituality, spiritual health, and spiritual care that integrates concepts from healthcare research, psychology, neuroscience, philosophy, theology, and religious studies. By engaging all these fields, this book offers a comprehensive understanding of spirituality and spiritual health while also describing clinical techniques and insights that can be used at the frontlines of care.

This book will be of interest to those researching chaplaincy and spiritual care practices, to professional Spiritual Care Practitioners/chaplains themselves, and to those who work in mental health and spirituality in healthcare more generally.

Simon Lasair is the Robert Steane Holistic Research Chair at St. Paul's Hospital in Saskatoon, Saskatchewan, Canada, and a Visiting Researcher/Research Associate at St. Thomas More College, also in Saskatoon.

SIMON LASAIR

Spirituality and Holistic Spiritual Health

Expanding Chaplaincy's
Theoretical Frame

Routledge
Taylor & Francis Group

NEW YORK AND LONDON

Designed cover image: Getty Images

First published 2026
by Routledge
605 Third Avenue, New York, NY 10158

and by Routledge
4 Park Square, Milton Park, Abingdon, Oxon, OX14 4RN

Routledge is an imprint of the Taylor & Francis Group, an informa business

© 2026 Simon Lasair

The right of Simon Lasair to be identified as author of this work has been
asserted in accordance with sections 77 and 78 of the Copyright, Designs
and Patents Act 1988.

ISBN: 9781032687490 (hbk)
ISBN: 9781032677873 (pbk)
ISBN: 9781003466147 (ebk)

DOI: 10.4324/9781003466147

Typeset in Joanna MT
by KnowledgeWorks Global Ltd.

To Spiritual Care Practitioners and chaplains
who must persistently justify their work
and whose ability to care becomes limited
by misunderstandings about who they are,
what they do, and why it might (or might not)
be important.

"*Spirituality and Holistic Spiritual Health* is an essential read for anyone invested in the future of spiritual care. With clarity and courage, Lasair shines a spotlight on the critical role of spiritual care in modern healthcare, bridging the sacred and the secular, and in doing so challenges the notion that it is merely an 'optional extra.' By addressing the difficult questions the profession has long avoided, Lasair offers invaluable insights and practical guidance for spiritual care providers, clients, scholars, and decision makers alike."

Shane Sinclair, PhD, University of Calgary, Canada

"*Spirituality and Holistic Spiritual Health* is an erudite and well-referenced work establishing an emergent theoretical foundation for contemporary spiritual care. It uniquely combines practical examples with theoretical insights, providing a comprehensive framework for understanding spirituality, needs, care, and development. This makes it invaluable for practitioners and researchers navigating both secular and religious contexts."

Richard Egan, PhD, University of Otago, New Zealand

"Lasair's book is masterfully written and is a must-read for spiritual care providers and students in secular and pluralistic contexts. Drawing on evidence-based, interdisciplinary research and case studies, Lasair provides theory for the therapeutic work of spiritual care. This book promises to inspire spiritual care practice for a new era!"

Pamela McCarroll, PhD, Emmanuel College, University of Toronto

"Lasair offers a critical and timely apologetic for the value of spiritual care as a profession in health institutions today. More than a convincing polemic, this book explores spirituality in fascinating and meaningful ways that enlarged my understanding and heart."

Wesley Fleming, DMin, BCC, hospital chaplain and author of
The Moral Injury Experience Wheel

"An essential read for spiritual care practitioners who are interested in taking a deep dive into the spiritual, psychological and holy layers that contribute to the formation of a life-enhancing appreciation of holistic health care."

Jody Clarke, DMin, professor of pastoral theology, Atlantic School of Theology

Contents

Acknowledgments

A project like this could not be accomplished without the support of many people and organizations. First, a huge thank you to St. Paul's Hospital in Saskatoon and the St. Paul's Hospital Foundation for providing the time and funding to make this project possible. A generous donation from the Robert Steane Foundation to the St. Paul's Hospital Foundation funded my role as the Robert Steane Holistic Research Chair, during which I was able to complete the writing of this book. The research chair's academic partners at St. Thomas More College, Saskatoon, also provided the setting for some very animated conversations regarding this book's content, so thanks are due to that institution for partnering with St. Paul's Hospital to make the research chair initiative possible.

The people I reported to at St. Paul's Hospital—Blake Sittler, Tracy Muggli, and Mary Heilman—each read different portions of this book and provided crucial feedback, and special thanks are due to Dr. Heilman, Francis Maza, and Loreen Rawlyk-Luby for reading the final version of the book in its entirety and for offering helpful suggestions for tweaking its presentation and argument. Wes Fleming read earlier versions of the chapters in their entirety, as did Meg Schmieder and Loreen Rawlyk-Luby, and all offered substantial suggestions for improving both the readability of the book as well as its content. Others who read portions of the book include Gina Camelia Adams, Richard Egan, Carmen Kampman, and Shanna-Lee Connell; all were generous in their feedback, and again the final result was much improved because of the insights they each shared. It really did take this community of thinkers and colleagues to make this book possible, so my gratitude to each person I've mentioned is deep, with an acknowledgment that whatever shortcomings remain in the book are due to my own limitations, not those of any of my colleagues.

My colleagues from the Canadian Association for Spiritual Care/ Association canadienne de soins spirituels (CASC/ACSS) have also been huge sources of support during this project. Special thanks are due to Brent Watts, Pam Driedger, Alida van Dijk, Andrea Thompson, and Matthew Heyn, all of whom I served alongside on the CASC/ ACSS Curriculum Development Working Group. All proved engaged and animated dialogue partners, especially as we worked together to set a new direction for CASC/ACSS's educational practices. Other CASC/ACSS colleagues who supported this work include Lynn Granke, Marvin Shank, Bob Bond, Heather Vanderstelt, Zinia Pritchard, Brian Walton, Tom Powell, Dale Nikkel, Pam McCarroll, and Don Cowie. Former CASC/ACSS Executive Director John Hayward also consistently affirmed this work, so thanks are due to him as well.

Academic colleagues from around the world have also contributed numerous conversations that helped to clarify many of the ideas contained in this book. Shane Sinclair has been a huge supporter of my work in this field for nearly ten years. It was Shane, George Fitchett, and Stephen King who paved the way for me to be brought onto the Joint Research Council for chaplaincy research. There I met Iain Telfer, Carmen Schuhmann, Simon Peng-Keller, Daniel Nuzum, Kate Bradford, Shelley Varner-Perez, Jaqui Tufnell, and others who have participated and collaborated in the work of the chaplaincy theory working group. Richard Egan from Otago University, Aotearoa New Zealand, has also been a close dialogue partner during this project, and our joint conversations with Sande Ramage have often brought together theoretical and frontline perspectives in some incredibly interesting ways.

The ideas for this book were first articulated during my time as Pastoral Associate at Emmanuel Anglican Church in Saskatoon. During my employment there I put together a series of workshops on spiritual health that were jointly provided by Queen's House Retreat and Renewal Centre and The Refinery Arts and Spirit Centre. Special thanks are due to Rev. Karen Sandell, Susan Pattison, Loretta Hartsook, Kathy Siemens, and Scott Verity for giving me permission to pursue this initiative while working at Emmanuel. Further thanks are due also to Sarah Donnelly at Queen's House and Janice Cook at The Refinery for providing the infrastructure to make these workshops possible. The participants in the workshops themselves also provided crucial feedback that helped me hone and refine the ideas herein while they were still in their infancy. While Queen's House has now shut its doors, my hope is that those who cherished the many programs there will be able to see this book as part of that center's legacy.

Springer Nature gave me permission to draw upon one of my publications with them in the development of Figure 2.1. At Routledge, Anna Moore, who supported this work from the time I contacted her, and Sophie Dracott have been wonderful resource people who have helped me navigate various editorial and technical questions connected to the publication process. Special thanks are also due to the two anonymous peer reviewers whose extremely helpful feedback informed the overall shape, structure, and content of the manuscript. In this case my experience has again affirmed my belief that when peer review processes happen well, the result is a much better end product.

My parents, Gord and Louise Adnams, and my in-laws, Gerry and Leda Halliday, have been extremely supportive of me and our family as we've lived through lots of ups and downs together. My wife, Bronwyn, and our children, Beth and Alex, have been constant supports throughout this writing process, and words can't express how important my relationships with each of them are, especially as we've worked hard to grow together as a family through all the ups and downs we've experienced.

Finally, as I've come to know many spiritual care colleagues in Canada and beyond, every day I'm impressed with what you do, especially in the face of many challenges to your funding and professional functioning. This book is for you.

List of Figures

CASC/ACSS	Canadian Association for Spiritual Care/Association canadienne de soins spirituels
CPE	Clinical Pastoral Education/Clinical Psychospiritual Education
SpC	Spiritual Care
IPNB	Interpersonal Neurobiology
R/S	Religion/Spirituality

About the Author

Simon Lasair is the Robert Steane Holistic Research Chair at St. Paul's Hospital in Saskatoon, Saskatchewan, Canada, and Visiting Researcher/ Research Associate at St. Thomas More College in the same city. Simon holds a PhD in Middle Eastern Studies from the University of Manchester, UK, and is also a Certified Spiritual Care Practitioner with the Canadian Association for Spiritual Care/Association canadienne de soins spirituels. Over his career, Simon has held a number of academic religious studies positions, and more recently, frontline and leadership roles in spiritual care. Simon has published widely in the field of theories of spiritual care, and when not working enjoys spending time with his family.

Introduction

Spiritual Care in Crisis

It was Wednesday, 22 March 2017. Two days before, I had returned to my work at the largest hospital in my city after taking a week off following the birth of my third child. My second child had been still-born at full term 18 months earlier. This third pregnancy had thus been very anxious for both my wife and me. Furthermore, only six months earlier, I had entered a leadership role with a spiritual care team consisting of several people working at three sites throughout my city, including at my hospital. Most members of this team had hoped someone else would get the job I now occupied. The previous six months had been very difficult on all fronts. Work was stressful, home was stressful, and I was often struggling to maintain my mental, emotional, physical, and spiritual wellbeing during it all.

That morning, I had been providing patient care. About mid-morning I received a page from the Spiritual Care Manager at the Roman Catholic hospital in our city. My boss was on vacation at that time. I was working for the public healthcare system, so it was unusual for me to receive calls from this manager unless patients who needed care were being transferred between our hospitals. In my province of Saskatchewan, public healthcare is owned and operated by our provincial government. Roman Catholic and other faith-based healthcare organizations have affiliate agreements with the provincial Ministry of Health. Like public healthcare, faith-based healthcare organizations in Saskatchewan receive most of their funding from the provincial government. Yet faith-based healthcare can maintain *some* independence regarding what services they might or might not provide at their sites. In contrast, public healthcare receives its mandates directly from the provincial Ministry of Health. Public healthcare organizations therefore often have little negotiating power when the provincial government implements various healthcare policies.

DOI: 10.4324/9781003466147-1

So, when I received the page from the Spiritual Care Manager at the Roman Catholic hospital, I didn't know what to expect. She told me that the CEO of her hospital wanted to meet with my entire team that afternoon. Our department reported to this CEO through my boss—the CEO was responsible for overseeing spiritual care in our local health authority on behalf of the Ministry of Health, but it was uncommon for us to have any direct interactions with her. I called all the members of our team, letting them know this meeting had been scheduled urgently. To say we were all feeling nervous would be a significant understatement.

When the time came for the meeting, both the CEO and the Spiritual Care Manager from the Roman Catholic hospital arrived. We sat down, and the CEO teared up and said, "This is the part of my job I always hate." She then proceeded to tell us that in the provincial budget that was being introduced in the legislature that very moment, all funding for professional spiritual care in Saskatchewan was being eliminated. Within a matter of months, all of us would lose our jobs. More importantly, after our jobs were terminated, there would be no one employed in our healthcare system to provide professional spiritual care to patients, families, and staff. We were devastated.

There is a lot that could be stated about what happened in the months following that announcement. I was appointed official spokesperson to the media for our provincial branch of the Canadian Association for Spiritual Care/Association canadienne de soins spirituels (CASC/ ACSS). I also participated in several meetings with government officials and provincial cabinet ministers, both before our jobs were eliminated and in the years following. Unfortunately, all our advocacy efforts were unsuccessful. There was one triumph, however. When the government initially announced its decision, it wanted to eliminate all funding for spiritual care in Saskatchewan, including in faith-based facilities. Yet as the political fallout of this announcement began to gain momentum, the government partially reversed its decision. Up to that point, some faith-based sites received lump sums of money from the government that they then allocated based on their internal programs and priorities. Other sites had their budgets established centrally by the Ministry of Health. Due to this variation in budgeting practices, the government felt it would create too significant an administrative burden to remove funds for spiritual care from all the faith-based sites. The faith-based sites, most of which were long-term care homes, could therefore maintain their spiritual care programs. Yet for those of us who worked in the public system, this change was small comfort. Funding for spiritual care in the public system would still be eliminated. The government's decision still meant that thousands in Saskatchewan would not receive good quality spiritual care, a form of care we believed significantly enhanced patients' healthcare experiences, as well as their paths to recovery.

As all this was unfolding, however, there was one crucial moment that occurred in the provincial legislature. At one point, when the opposition party called upon the government to defend its decision,[1] a former Minister of Health rose and responded by saying something to the effect of, "The government can't be in the business of funding Christian theology in public health care" (Lasair, 2018a, p. 5). From my perspective, this was precisely the position we needed to hear. As a Spiritual Care Practitioner, I knew my practices could be articulated in secular terms (Lasair, 2018a). However, I was also aware that the spiritual care research literature had yet to grapple seriously with how chaplains and other Spiritual Care Professionals might present their work in such a way. I knew that part of the problem was the (still) problematic distinctions between spirituality, religion, and the sacred (Swinton, 2012; Nongbri, 2012; Lynch, 2012; C. Taylor, 2007; Pargament, 2007). I also knew part of the problem was that secular approaches to reality differ significantly from those embodied in various religious and spiritual traditions (C. Taylor, 2007; Milbank, 2006, 2013; Habermas, 1992, 2008). I was therefore on the cusp of some huge philosophical, theological, and practical problems. How, then, to engage them productively?

In the years following, I wrote several philosophical research articles that appeared in the *Journal for the Study of Spirituality* (Lasair, 2018a), *Practical Theology* (Lasair, 2018b), the *Journal of Religion and Health* (Lasair, 2020a), and the *Journal of Pastoral Care & Counseling* (Lasair, 2019, 2020b, 2021a). Each of these articles sought to articulate different aspects of a theoretical approach to spiritual care grounded largely in secular thought. Given what happened in Saskatchewan, I knew I would need to acknowledge and engage the religious history of our profession (Lasair, 2020b, 2021a). But I also knew I would need to draw upon secular ways of knowing to position our work in the present

(Lasair, 2018a, 2018b, 2020a). Almost needless to state, this has been a challenging task that will no doubt be controversial for some. However, none of that diminishes the urgency of this work, especially given how chaplaincy and spiritual care services continue to be vulnerable, not only in Canada, but also internationally. This current book is the culmination of the work I've been undertaking since 2017, systematically presented in a single place for the first time. So, what are the basic concepts of my approach, and what is its overall trajectory?

THE CENTRAL PROBLEM

At the core of this book is an attempt to address a problem that became abundantly clear when meeting with officials from our provincial Ministry of Health. From the government's perspective, our province's healthcare system did not need in-house professional Spiritual Care Practitioners[2] because spiritual care also fell within nursing and social work scopes of practice. Furthermore, the government also felt that when nurses and social workers could not provide spiritual care, community clergy could be invited into healthcare facilities to offer their services. The Ministry of Health personnel did acknowledge there were challenges created by this new model in terms of how best to uphold privacy legislation. But there were also some parts of the province that had previously implemented something similar, and, from the government's perspective, this approach had worked quite well. Those of us who were losing our jobs, however, viewed the situation quite differently. Not only were we aware of the numerous policy and procedural issues that would emerge because of the government's new approach, but we were also convinced that we did our work very differently from social workers, nurses, and community clergy. But how best to articulate that difference?

As I've reflected on this question during the intervening years, I've become increasingly convinced that the solution can only be found in how we define and engage spirituality (Walton, 2012; Schuhmann & Damen, 2018; Lasair, 2020a). Nurses and social workers do indeed have their own understandings of spirituality (e.g., McBrien, 2006; Swinton, 2012; Lasair & Sinclair, 2018), yet they are also not specifically trained in this domain; it is only one of several areas in which they practice. During my Clinical Pastoral Education/Clinical Psychospiritual

Education (CPE)[3] training, in contrast, a recurring theme was that we were learning specifically to provide *spiritual* care through all our learning experiences. Somehow religious care was related to this, but we were learning to become *Spiritual Care Practitioners* and not faith-specific chaplains, at least not in the traditional *religious* sense. My CPE supervisor-educator generally acknowledged there was a connection between spirituality and religion, but he also admitted very few people knew how to articulate this connection while also differentiating between these two phenomena (see e.g., Pargament, 2007).

As I became familiar with the research literature after my CPE, I discovered this problem also pervaded the published work on this topic. Spirituality was often identified as an individual phenomenon whereas religion was defined in institutional, doctrinal, ritual, communal, and cultural terms (McBrien, 2006; Lasair & Sinclair, 2018; Swinton, 2012), yet both were somehow connected to questions of ultimate meaning, purpose, and reality. Given this situation, I didn't know how I could successfully define the territory that was unique to spirituality and hence to spiritual care. It also didn't help that much of the influential research literature coming out of healthcare, psychology, and psychiatry often conflated spirituality and religion using the technical term Religion/Spirituality (R/S) to designate this territory (e.g. Pargament, 2007; Puchalski et al., 2009; Puchalski, Vitillo, Hull, & Reller, 2014; see also Walton, 2012).

I also discovered that understandings of the sacred were similarly confused. Some researchers defined the sacred using concepts and terminology originating almost exclusively from traditional religious perspectives (e.g., Pargament, 2007). In contrast, other researchers were beginning to explore how the sacred could be territory encountered in secular settings as well (e.g., Lynch, 2012; M. C. Taylor, 2007)—hence sporting events, nature, secular social justice initiatives, and national holidays could be viewed as just as sacred to some as Easter, Ramadan, the Buddha's birthday, and other faith-based holidays are to people belonging to specific faith traditions. It was therefore becoming increasingly clear why spiritual care was so vulnerable to misunderstanding from people outside our profession. It was because we as Spiritual Care Professionals didn't have a good and clear way to articulate what we were doing either. It was upon this basis that I began my quest.

INITIAL DISCOVERIES

From the outset, I knew there were going to be several interconnected challenges bound up with defining the unique work of Spiritual Care Professionals. On the one hand, many Spiritual Care Professional organizations still require their members to receive formal education and spiritual mentoring within their specific faith traditions (e.g., CASC/ACSS, 2020). This requirement reflects the faith-based background of our profession. On the other hand, however, I also knew these faith-specific personal and professional formations often did not prepare individuals for work in highly professionalized environments like healthcare (Cadge et al., 2019). Yes, spiritual care personnel understood that CPE did do some work to prepare them for their clinical contexts. Yet because CPE was not well-equipped to offer its students comprehensive conceptual knowledge on any topic (Cadge et al., 2019; Ragsdale, 2018), it was becoming increasingly evident that Spiritual Care Professionals were receiving neither academic nor professional formations anywhere near similar to those working in other healthcare professions. As a result, there were (and are) some significant differences between the professional cultures of Spiritual Care Practitioners and those of other healthcare professionals (Cadge et al., 2019; Lasair, 2020b). These differences were (and are) in need of systematic engagement.

I was therefore grateful to discover there was a push in the research literature for chaplains and other Spiritual Care Professionals to become more evidence-based in their practices (e.g., Fitchett et al., 2014; Sinder et al., 2019). I was even more excited to begin exploring the rapidly growing body of research on spirituality in healthcare (e.g., Galek, Flannelly, Vane, & Galek, 2005; Hefti & Gomes Experandio, 2016; de Brito Sena, Damanio, Lucchetti, & Prieto Peres, 2021). Yet as I began deepening my engagement with this literature, I regularly experienced significant disappointment. Very little of it, from my perspective, was able to articulate an understanding of spirituality that could be successfully operationalized clinically (see Walton, 2012). There were some definitions of spirituality, like those articulated in Puchalski et al. (2009) and Puchalski, Vitillo, Hull, and Reller (2014) that were often quoted in the research literature, but when I reflected on these definitions, I found it difficult to connect them to my frontline practices (see Walton, 2012). In some ways these definitions were excellent in identifying the general territory of spirituality, but they were also not concrete enough to develop specific intervention strategies based upon them. Nor did they help to identify concrete outcomes patients might experience in response to receiving spiritual care. In other words, these definitions were limited in terms of how they might shed light on the specific practices of Spiritual Care Practitioners. For other healthcare professionals, for whom spiritual care was only a small part of their practices, it could be many of the already-established definitions of spirituality were adequate. For chaplains and Spiritual Care Practitioners, however, I was not sure these definitions got us much farther ahead. What, then, was going to be most helpful? From my perspective, a significant part of the answer lay in the nature of religious thought. This consideration invited me to reflect on one of the central learnings I received from my doctoral work.

In 2008 I completed my PhD at the University of Manchester, UK. During that degree I drew extensively on the fields of hermeneutics, linguistics, and narrative theory to study ancient Jewish Aramaic translations of the Hebrew Bible known as Targums.[4] In Judaism, Targums were used primarily in ancient Jewish synagogues to provide contact with the Bible for those who could no longer read nor understand Hebrew. However, because many Jews, both then and now, understand the language of the Bible itself as sacred, the Targums attempted to mirror the Hebrew text as much as possible, both in their sentence constructions as well as in their specific grammatical structures (Lasair, 2012). This was relatively easy because ancient Aramaic and biblical Hebrew are two closely related languages. Where things got interesting, however, was in the fact that some Targums inserted lengthy literary expansions into the narratives they were translating (Lasair, 2010, 2012). Often these expansions were constructed to address linguistic or exegetical issues from the source Hebrew text; they also often had the effect of changing the overall shapes of the narratives into which they were inserted (Lasair, 2010, 2012). The result was those who relied primarily on the Targums could potentially come away with very different understandings of the Bible compared to the understandings of those who were still able to engage the sacred text in Hebrew. In other words, the various sacred narratives presented in the synagogues—both biblical and Targumic—had the power to shape how ancient Jews, as individuals and as communities, perceived and engaged their religious realities, if not all of reality itself. I therefore came to understand that religion and spirituality are intimately connected to how people perceive and experience reality, in all its levels and dimensions (Lasair, 2012; Habermas, 2008; C. Taylor, 2007; Milbank, 2013). What does this have to do with spirituality and spiritual care?

On the surface, my intuition told me that the established healthcare definitions of spirituality and religion were at least partially correct: both were concerned with Ultimate Meaning or Ultimate Reality (McBrien, 2006; Swinton, 2012; Lasair & Sinclair, 2018; Lasair, 2020a). I also felt these definitions were likely correct to indicate that spirituality is an individual phenomenon whereas religion is collective or communal. But how to drive the distinction further? As I continued to explore it, it became evident that spirituality designates the individual *processes* that people use to interpret and engage reality, both lived and Ultimate (Lasair, 2020a). In contrast, religion, as a collective or communal phenomenon, provides the specific linguistic, conceptual, ritual, and behavioral *content* that individuals might use to assist them in their interpretations of and engagements with reality (see Swinton, 2012). This is true because religion can be seen as a macro-cultural phenomenon that uses symbols, metaphors, teachings, concepts, rituals, and practices as its main tools for engaging reality (Lasair, 2020b; Swinton, 2012; M. C. Taylor, 2007; Lynch, 2012). Many cultural and non-religious traditions can be understood similarly. Spirituality as an individual phenomenon, however, depends on a person's specific development, temperament, and life experiences to inform how they might configure reality and their engagements with it (Lasair, 2019, 2020a, 2020b; Culliford, 2012; Watts, 2017). Therefore, while there is often significant overlap between a person's spirituality and religion, culture, and traditions, there are also substantial portions of each that cannot easily be brought under the umbrella of the others. Religious, cultural, and traditional symbols, metaphors, teachings, concepts, rituals, and practices are integrated into individuals' lives. Yet the manner of this integration is entirely dependent on how that person perceives and engages reality *as an individual*—hence the need to understand their development, temperament, and life experiences when offering them spiritual care.

As I explored this territory further, therefore, it was evident my understandings of religion and spirituality were becoming increasingly anthropological, psychological, sociological, and philosophical in their orientations. This contrasted with my earlier understandings of these topics that were, in many ways, very faith-specific. In making this shift, I also came to understand that many secular, cultural, and various non-religious traditions could also have "religious" dimensions (Blankholm, 2022). What I mean by this is that often secular and other traditions provide the specific conceptual and linguistic content for many individuals' understandings of reality (C. Taylor, 2007; M. C. Taylor, 2007; Lynch, 2012). The processes by which secular people establish their understandings of reality are probably quite similar to those used by religious people. Consequently, the spiritualities of "secular" and "religious" people might be close cousins in terms of their constructions and functioning, but the *language and concepts* they use when speaking about their realities are likely much different one from the other. I did not find this discovery surprising. This was because I was aware that several religious studies researchers had begun to describe secular approaches to reality as highly "religious" and/or "spiritual" well before my own engagements with these topics (e.g., C. Taylor, 2007; M. C. Taylor, 2007; Schuhmann & Damen, 2018; van Dijke, Duyndam, van Nistelrooij, & Bos, 2022; Blankholm, 2022). As a result, I saw myself as venturing onto relatively firm territory, even if many of these ideas were not yet being considered by members of our profession, the general public, or even governments, for that matter. But what were some of the consequences of shifting my understanding in this way?

INITIAL CONSEQUENCES

First, it became clear that if Spiritual Care Professionals were going to offer *spiritual* care in contrast to *religious* care, we would need to establish much firmer understandings of the *processes* people use to interpret and engage reality. Yes, we would still need to have a secure understanding of the linguistic, conceptual, and ritual *content* of any person's specific understandings of their realities. But, because spirituality concerns

9 Introduction

these process-oriented questions, we, as chaplains and Spiritual Care Practitioners, needed to go deep in our understandings of how these processes might manifest in any person's life.

A second consequence of this approach, then, was the emerging insight that spiritual health or unhealth is directly dependent on how a person interprets and engages reality using the processes named above. Any person therefore manifests specific behavioral, emotional, and cognitive dynamics that are intimately connected to their spirituality. Consequently, I began considering whether there might be some overlap between spiritual care and spiritually integrated psychotherapy as offered by some counselors and psychologists (e.g., Pargament, 2007; Pargament & Exline, 2022; Béres & Crawley, 2023). However, I also felt spiritual care was different from psychology, in that, in my experience, Spiritual Care Practitioners were fundamentally concerned with the dynamics of a person's identity, not just disruptions or distortions in their behavioral, relational, emotional, or cognitive functioning (see Lasair, 2020a). If there was an affinity between spiritual care and psychology, then, it would most likely appear in the relationships between spiritual care and psychodynamic therapies (e.g., Schore, 2019). This would contrast with the relationships that might exist between spiritual care and more cognitively- or symptom-oriented modalities. Yet, in this insight, I still felt I had not identified spiritual care's truly distinguishing feature.

A third consequence was to see that our formations in our own faith traditions is a key feature of our profession's disciplinary identity (see CASC/ACSS, 2020). Because traditional religions are concerned with describing reality, not only according to what they have understood in the past, but also in conversation with contemporary life (Milbank, 2006; Habermas, 2008; C. Taylor, 2007), this means spiritual care practitioners relate very differently to clients than other types of healthcare practitioners. Most significantly, Spiritual Care Practitioners are uniquely positioned in healthcare and other environments to help their clients make sense of their realities (Lasair, 2019, 2020a). This is because, at least implicitly, we have some understandings of how people interpret and engage reality. We are also individually conversant with at least one (faith) tradition that can provide concepts, symbols, metaphors, rituals, and practices to assist in this interpretative work.

Where our field is lacking, however, is in its capacity to transform our implied understandings of these processes into thoroughly verified knowledge. It is this lack, in part, that is driving the current trend to make spiritual care and chaplaincy work more research-informed and evidence-based (Fitchett et al., 2014; Sinder et al., 2019). This book, as well, is attempting to address this lack, at least partially, but also in a somewhat preliminary philosophical sense.

The fourth and final consequence of my shift in understanding was to see that spiritual care would need to clearly articulate its own unique position in relation to other caring professions. This clear articulation would enable other professionals to identify explicitly what spiritual care can contribute to the care of patients and clients in various caregiving settings. To lay the foundation for this clarification, I knew I would need to draw upon other, well-established bodies of knowledge originating from numerous disciplinary contexts. This broad scope of engagement would help to identify both the connections and the distinctions between our work and the practices of other professionals. Religious studies, theology, philosophy, neuroscience, psychology, social work, and nursing research all seemed good candidates to offer useful perspectives. Insights from all these fields would assist in demarcating the territory I encountered daily in my frontline work, but bringing them together would also shed light on aspects of spirituality that had not yet been addressed in the research literature. Again, I knew I was venturing onto firm territory. I knew this because several researchers from a number of disciplines had issued calls for multidisciplinary approaches to spirituality and religion years before I began my own work in this field (e.g., Nongbri, 2012; Culliford, 2012; Watts, 2017; Oman, 2013). In the minds of these researchers, spirituality and religion are complex phenomena that cannot be fully understood using the concepts and methods of only one academic discipline. To truly grasp these phenomena, these researchers felt, it is necessary to function in multiple fields simultaneously—hence the challenge and opportunity of defining professional spiritual care. I therefore knew I had a big job in front of me, but I also knew that if I could do this job successfully, spiritual care might be positioned much more securely as a legitimate caregiving profession. How then does this book contribute to addressing this problem?

THIS BOOK'S CONTRIBUTION

At the core of this book's approach is the broad distinction between spirituality and religion: spirituality concerns the *processes* through which a person interprets and engages reality; religion, in contrast, concerns the specific *content* (i.e., concepts, ideas, theories, metaphors, symbols, rituals, practices, etc.) that a person assigns to reality when utilizing spirituality's interpretative processes. As stated above, cultural, secular, and other kinds of non-religious traditions can serve "religious" functions as well. In making this distinction between spirituality and religion, then, I am assuming two things:

1. that the dynamics of both religion and spirituality can be described in terms that are not exclusively dependent on the frameworks of specific faith traditions; and,
2. that despite the ostensibly "secular" approach of this book, reductionist approaches to spirituality and religion must be avoided as much as possible.

What do I mean by "reductionist"?

Unfortunately, many "secular" approaches to studying religion and spirituality, like the psychology of religion, the sociology of religion, the cognitive science of religion, and so on, tend to present religion and spirituality as if they exist only as functions of a person's neurology, social interactions, or mental capacities (e.g., Oman, 2013; de Cruz & de Smedt, 2015; Lynch, 2012). From my perspective, this kind of approach does an injustice to the depth of a person's experiences of spirituality and religion. As will be discussed below, spirituality and religion specifically entail the breakdown of any strong distinctions between internal and external realities. To describe spirituality and/or religion as things that manifest solely within a person's interior consciousness would therefore be a gross misunderstanding of these phenomena. Nevertheless, the approach I take herein will indeed assume that religion and spirituality can be described using immanent secular terms (see e.g., Lasair, 2018a). However, it will also be evident throughout my argument that none of spirituality's nor religion's dynamics can be completely captured by concepts and language, secular, reductionist, or otherwise.

The result is that this book will tread on the fringes of what some philosophers of religion call an "anti-realist" approach to religion and spirituality.[5] According to these philosophers, religion and spirituality are evident in systems of symbols, metaphors, concepts, theories, practices, and rituals, but whether someone can say in one case or another that any of these things is a clear manifestation of "religion" or "spirituality" is highly debatable. The emergence of various secular "spiritualities" like the so-called "wellness culture" is a suitable illustration of this point. Manifestations of this culture often draw upon the teachings of several traditions, but in doing so they blur the boundaries between religion, science, psychotherapy, and various other domains of human thought. The result is the terms *religion* or *spirituality* cannot be applied to many expressions of the wellness culture in any straightforward or conventional sense. From the perspectives of the philosophers of religion mentioned earlier, then, religion and spirituality may or may not actually exist in any concrete or easily identifiable sense—hence their anti-realist position in relation to religion and spirituality.

While I readily acknowledge the merits of this philosophical position, my approach indicates that regardless of what philosophers might think, each person's religion (traditional, secular, or otherwise) and spirituality are very real *to them*. This is because religion and spirituality are not just abstract concepts or beliefs. Rather, they are inscribed into our brains and bodies through the concrete processes of socialization, enculturation, and the accumulation of lived experiences (Ward, 2014; Lasair, 2021a). As a result, a person's religion and spirituality make distinct and concrete contributions to the social, political, and cultural spaces that person shares with others. These contributions are expressed in the person's behaviors, interactions, and interpersonal dynamics (Lasair, 2021a, 2021b). Therefore, religion and spirituality cannot be divorced from any person's relationships, politics, or cultural practices, simply because all people always express their inner dynamics outwardly in such contexts, in a variety of ways. Social, political, and cultural experiences also influence any person's internal dynamic (McGilchrist, 2009; Lasair, 2021b). As a result, there is always a reciprocal interaction between a person's inner experiences and their external contexts and vice versa. Therefore, one of this book's main contentions is that Spiritual Care Professionals are explicitly concerned with this reciprocal interaction, intervening in the dynamics of a person's interior experiences for the sake of transforming their understanding of and engagement with their external realities (Lasair, 2019, 2020a, 2020b).

Lest this idea be understood as reducing spiritual care to yet another kind of psychotherapeutic intervention, recall the key feature of a Spiritual Care Practitioner's professional identity identified above: their personal and professional formation in their own faith tradition. As already discussed, this formation enables Spiritual Care Practitioners to be conversant with at least one (faith) tradition that can orient the Practitioner to whatever conceptual, theological, or ritual content clients use when engaging their interpretative processes. This content is crucial when Practitioners work to access what I call a person's *frame for reality*.[6] This is because a significant part of a Spiritual Care Practitioner's role is engaging a person's frame for reality through the specific themes and content (religious, secular, cultural, psychological, or otherwise) manifest in their words, body language, behaviors, affect, gestures, and vocal inflections, etc. A Spiritual Care Practitioner's formation in their own and other faith traditions—in addition to their training in specific psychotherapeutic concepts and techniques—enables them to accurately identify the various themes in a client's frame (e.g., CASC/ACSS, 2019). Through such a baseline assessment, the Practitioner can then draw upon both their "religious" and psychological knowledge to identify any issues that might be affecting their client's spiritual health and wellbeing. Then, using their understanding of spiritual health, the Practitioner can engage their client's spirituality to facilitate growth and improvement in the client's overall spiritual health and wellbeing. What does this look like concretely?

THE BOOK'S OUTLINE

Due to the numerous challenges outlined above, this book's major task is to establish a system of vocabulary and concepts that can describe spiritual care in terms that can be understood by people who do not share Practitioners' faith or theological backgrounds. As such, the concept of a person's frame for reality is central to this book's trajectory. Not only does this concept identify and articulate the holistic concern that differentiates professional spiritual care from other caring professions, but it also provides the broad scaffolding for the understanding of spiritual health that will be explored in the chapters below.

Accordingly, the main contention of this book is that a person's spirituality is intimately connected to the frame they bring to reality. This frame is connected to a person's individual identity as much as it is connected to their religious/secular/cultural concerns. In fact, it depends precisely on the specific ways a person integrates their religious/secular/cultural concerns into their individual life narrative. Therefore, when a Spiritual Care Practitioner engages a client in a caregiving encounter, the Practitioner is assessing both their client's religious/secular/cultural beliefs and practices and how these beliefs and practices might—or might not—have enabled the client to navigate all their life's ups and downs (e.g., Lasair, 2018a, 2019, 2020a). If there are challenges in the client's current circumstances, then the Practitioner can explore how these challenges might or might not be bound up with specific dynamics within the client's frame. If the client's current experiences hold minimal challenges, then the Practitioner can explore how the client has been able to engage challenges in the past. In both scenarios, a review of past challenges can help to draw the client's past strengths and insights into conversation with their present experiences. The theory is that by drawing these strengths and insights into the present, clients will be better able to frame and engage whatever challenges their futures might hold (Lasair, 2018a, 2019, 2020a). Yet all of this depends upon a theoretical understanding of spirituality and spiritual health that has yet to be fully articulated. How will this book go about exploring this territory?

As implied by the former Minister of Health's remark recorded above, Western cultures have experienced some important shifts over the past five centuries (C. Taylor, 2007; M. C. Taylor, 2007; Lilla, 2007; Gillespie, 2008; Habermas, 1992; Milbank, 2006). While many of these shifts are often understood almost exclusively in terms of scientific, technological, and political advances, all of them have occurred due to significant changes in how Westerners understand the fundamental nature of reality. As a result, before exploring how individuals frame their specific realities, it is helpful to give an account of how the Western world now constructs its realities at a general, macro-cultural level. Chapter One will therefore trace some of the West's important cultural and philosophical shifts, bringing them to bear on Spiritual Care Practitioners' work at the frontlines. In doing so, this chapter will discuss how challenging it is to describe religion and spirituality within the current Western frame for reality. It will also offer a preliminary description of how Spiritual Care Practitioners can offer some descriptions of these phenomena, especially when engaging other professionals who may not share the Practitioner's understandings of them.

Chapter Two will then outline a broad theory of how a person's frame for reality is constructed through their enculturation, socialization, and accumulation of all their life's experiences. This chapter will explicitly discuss the *processes* by which individuals integrate the conceptual, ritual, and behavioral *content* from their cultural and religious traditions into their individual frame for reality. As such, this chapter will provide the most comprehensive account of how a person's spirituality functions within their daily life. Hermeneutic philosophy, as well as several emerging insights from science studies and neuropsychology, will play important roles in this chapter's argument. By drawing upon these seemingly disparate bodies of knowledge, this chapter will demonstrate explicitly how a person's spirituality is connected to reality writ large. At the same time, this chapter will acknowledge that a person's frame for reality naturally excludes multitudes of people, places, experiences, and various other phenomena. However, as this chapter will begin to reveal, spiritual health is in part dependent on how well-equipped a client's frame is to navigate and negotiate realities that are excluded from the client's explicit conscious awareness, at least initially. Therefore, Chapter Two will lay the broad framework that will be drawn upon in Chapter Three's preliminary discussion of what spiritual health looks like within this approach.

Chapter Three will begin with a discussion of how a client's frame for reality becomes manifest in specific clinical settings. Aspects of a client's frame are certainly evident in the themes contained in the stories they share with their Practitioner. However, this chapter will be concerned more specifically with perception. As in Chapter Two, Chapter Three will draw upon the insights of science studies, neuroscience, and psychology. Yet Chapter Three will also start to distinguish spiritual care from these disciplines by describing perception as a narrative phenomenon. In psychology and neuroscience, perception is often associated with a person's five senses. In contrast, this chapter will show how a client's perceptions emerge when they bring all their life's experiences into conversation with their current circumstances. In this process, a client's religious/cultural/secular symbols, images, rituals, concepts, and theories function as resources they can use to express what their experiences mean to them. Consequently, when a client articulates their perception in spiritual care encounters, the Practitioner can use them as entry points into the client's frame for reality. Using their clinical skills, Practitioners can then invite the client into further exploration of their frame. The goal of this exploration is to build the client's awareness of their frame's contours. This chapter will therefore argue that working with a client's awareness is a foundational move in facilitating their growth into greater spiritual health.

Chapter Four takes many of Chapter Three's insights regarding perception and begins to discuss how perceptions are brought into shared social, cultural, and political spaces. This information is particularly useful when clients are manifesting behavioral or interpersonal dynamics that are creating problems for them in relation to family members or other members of caregiving teams. Specifically, Chapter Four will explore a client case in depth to show how people can project their perceptions onto their lived realities. These projected perceptions can take various forms, from the subtlest of expectations to dramatic behavioral or interpersonal disturbances. This chapter will therefore discuss the intricacies of how perceptions are projected into the spaces a client shares with others, linking external expressions of projection to dynamics within a person's frame. In doing so, comparisons between spiritual care and some schools of psychotherapy will naturally arise. However, it will also become evident that part of a Spiritual Care Practitioner's role is not to diagnose and treat either behavioral, relational, or interpersonal disturbances, at least not in a formal psychotherapeutic sense. Rather, a Spiritual Care Practitioner's role is to begin fostering within their clients a capacity for openness. Openness, I will argue, enables a person to reflect on their frame from different perspectives. Initially the perspective of the Practitioner plays an important role in this regard. Later, perspectives of others take on greater importance. As such, openness enables a client to become increasingly aware of the contours of their frame; openness is the dimension of spiritual health that helps a person see that their frame does not encompass all of reality. Seeing the limitations of their frame then allows a client to have a greater appreciation of their unique identity and to take responsibility for whatever might be causing any behavioral or interpersonal disturbances. As with awareness, openness is understood in these pages as one of the fundamental building blocks for spiritual health—awareness cannot be built without openness, and openness cannot grow without awareness.

Chapter Five addresses situations when clients have built good capacities for awareness and openness. Specifically, this chapter will show how fulsome manifestations of these traits enable clients to experience themselves with relative objectivity. This is because their awareness and openness detach them (somewhat) from the cognitive and emotional investments they make in their perceptions and projections. The result is that such clients can view themselves from a stance of relative inner neutrality. This chapter will therefore discuss how such neutrality can be nurtured within a client. As a result, this chapter will explore some of the mechanisms bound up with a Practitioner's "non-anxious presence." Such presence, I will argue, helps clients to experience increasing freedom from their tendencies to automatically perceive their realities in certain ways and to project these perceptions into the spaces they share with others. This freedom allows clients to engage their lived realities more consistently on those realities' own terms. Freedom can therefore give rise to wisdom. In the theory being developed herein, wisdom is a multi-faceted phenomenon that is crucial for the integrity of any fulsome engagement with reality. Hence wisdom will be introduced in this chapter and the discussion of its dynamics will extend into the next.

Chapter Six argues that a client's growing capacities for neutrality, freedom, and wisdom enable them to see the truth of who they are, in relation to themself and in relation to others. This truth relies on the client's continuing work to render awareness and openness in themself. However, this truth is also encountered experientially when silence becomes a felt presence in a person's life. This chapter thus spends significant space exploring silence and how both clients and Practitioners can relate to it in caregiving contexts. Ultimately, nurturing a relationship with silence can assist contentment to emerge within the client. In these pages contentment does not mean that a client has finished growing or that all their concerns or issues are resolved.

Rather, contentment describes a client's ability to see the truth of who they are and use their wisdom to accurately identify what they need so they can move into the future with personal and spiritual integrity. Contentment thus grounds a client in the concreteness of their lived experiences as surrounded and framed by silence. Chapter Six will describe in detail how Spiritual Care Practitioners embody a relationship with silence that can assist clients in committing to truth and to building their capacity for contentment within clinical contexts.

Finally, Chapter Seven draws everything from the previous chapters into a fulsome picture of what spiritually healthy individuals can look like in clinical contexts. As such, human flourishing becomes a significant topic in this chapter's discussion. There will be some selective engagement with the research literature concerning human flourishing, but then the discussion will specifically address how flourishing can be understood from within the framework discussed herein. This chapter will conclude the book's formal argument by drawing some conclusions about the nature of spiritual care as a profession, pointing the way toward topics that can be investigated further.

Three appendices are found at the end of the book. Appendix A provides a brief exploration of questions that will need to be addressed should this book's conceptual framework be adapted for use in formal assessment measures. Appendix B discusses how this book's understandings of spirituality and spiritual health might be used long-term care contexts. And, finally, Appendix C outlines how this book's understandings of spirituality and spiritual health can best be integrated into mental health contexts. Finally, there is also a glossary after the appendices. I have provided the glossary mainly to offer formal definitions for the technical terms that are used in the progression of the book's argument.

HOW TO READ THIS BOOK

As readers are likely intuiting, this book takes an explicitly theoretical approach to describing spirituality, spiritual care, and spiritual health. This approach has been taken deliberately, mainly to meet the increasingly urgent need to provide robust theoretical engagements with each of these topics. Nevertheless, all the concepts explored in these pages can be connected to frontline realities. Each chapter therefore provides at least one lengthy clinical example. These examples illustrate how the concepts articulated herein can concretely manifest in the lives of clients. They also illustrate how Spiritual Care Practitioners might use these concepts in their own caregiving settings. Each of these clinical examples are based on real people I've encountered in my clinical work. However, to preserve the privacy and confidentiality of the individuals involved, I've often combined two or more cases into single clinical vignettes. I have also fictionalized these cases somewhat. Where verbatim accounts of interactions occur, these have been reconstructed in part from memory. As with the case examples, the verbatim accounts have also been somewhat fictionalized. Ultimately these case examples and verbatim accounts are intended give flesh and bones to the theory I'm articulating. They also show how employing these concepts requires some work from Practitioners so that Practitioners can recognize and engage them in clinical settings. To assist with some of this work, each chapter ends with some questions for reflection; Chapters Two to Six also include assessment and intervention questions that can help Practitioners integrate the concepts articulated herein into their frontline caregiving practices.

Due to the nature of this book's theory, some might argue that the concepts and practices herein are better suited for pastoral counseling or psychospiritual therapy contexts. There is some truth to these perspectives. Because I am articulating these concepts from within my own Canadian setting, I am aware that the CASC/ACSS is the professional body responsible for training and certifying both Spiritual Care Practitioners (formerly Chaplains and/or Pastoral Carers) and Psychospiritual Therapists (formerly Pastoral Counselors). As such, one of the emerging concerns for CASC/ACSS is how best to distinguish between these two professions, even when they share the same set of professional competencies.[7] This question becomes even more complicated when considering that more and more CASC/ACSS members are registering with professional colleges that also regulate psychotherapists or counseling therapists. Due to these realities, it is becoming increasingly evident that Spiritual Care Practitioners in Canada need to demonstrate how they align with psychotherapeutic thought and practices on the one hand, while also demonstrating their distinctiveness on the other. By defining and describing spirituality and spiritual health as the unique territory of spiritual care, then, this book is attempting to address concerns coming to Spiritual

Care Practitioners from multiple fronts: the regulatory bodies, the organizations that employ Spiritual Care Practitioners, and Spiritual Care Practitioners themselves. Whether this book sufficiently addresses these concerns will likely be judged best by people other than me.

However, what I am attempting to do in these pages is present a preliminary philosophical treatment of all these topics, namely through establishing a system of vocabulary and concepts that can provide a foundation for spiritual care practice somewhat independent from traditional religious thought. It may be, then, that this theory is better suited for Pastoral Counselors and Psychospiritual Therapists. Yet by mapping out the broad territory of spirituality and spiritual health, I believe Spiritual Care Practitioners will have a firmer foundation for assessing their clients and engaging them in conversations about spiritual health, no matter the spiritual concerns the clients are presenting. These assessments and conversations can then inform whether the Practitioner refers the client to a Psychospiritual Therapist or not. If the Practitioner does make such a referral, then their referral documents can use some of the concepts herein to communicate why the referral is being made. If the Practitioner does not make a referral, then the concepts and practices herein can form the basis of the Practitioner's case planning within the context of their workplace and its concerns.

Ultimately, my goal in articulating these concepts and practices is to assist Spiritual Care Practitioners to become more transparent with themselves regarding the nature and purpose of everything they do with their clients. To my knowledge, there has not yet been a fulsome attempt to give such a comprehensive theoretical treatment of these topics within the bounds of broadly secular thought. It is therefore my hope that this book will make a significant contribution in this rapidly emerging field. Perhaps in doing so this book might also contribute to preventing Spiritual Care Practitioners elsewhere from having their jobs eliminated or their funding reduced. Only time will tell.

Finally, I am keenly aware that I write as a white, Christian (Anglican), heterosexual, highly educated male of Western European (British) descent. While I believe I have done much work to account for the various kinds of privilege that are bound up with my identity, there will no doubt be blind spots and limitations that surface in this text due to my position in life and society. In the spirit of my profession, then, I invite readers to consider these limitations and blind spots as invitations for conversation. My desire is to learn as much as it is to describe and articulate. I therefore look forward to whatever fruitful and engaging conversations this book might produce between myself and its readers.

EPILOGUE

After the elimination of spiritual care funds was announced in Saskatchewan, it took the government six months to implement its plan to shut down all the spiritual care departments in publicly owned and operated healthcare facilities. When that shutdown occurred, several people retired, others relocated, and yet others moved on to find work in faith-based sites. For my part, I soon found work in a faith-based long-term care home. I worked there for over a year, but then it was clear life was taking me in a different direction. From there I moved into parish work for a time, but then, after about two years, I moved into the research role I currently occupy. I was also hired into a casual frontline spiritual care position at the same faith-based hospital where my research role is located. Through all the ups and downs I've experienced, I continue to find great joy in accompanying patients and their families through life's crises, joys, and griefs. My desire is that this book will support others involved in this work, bringing language and concepts to this form of care that offers hope and healing to so many.

Reflection Questions

- What organizational and/or political realities influence decisions regarding spiritual care/chaplaincy funding in your setting?
- What work have you or others done to advocate for maintaining or increasing spiritual care funding in your setting? How was this advocacy work received?
- What do you believe will be most helpful in strengthening spiritual care/chaplaincy services' position in your setting? Why do you believe this?
- How will you determine the likelihood of your idea being successful or not?

NOTES

1 As with Canada's federal parliament, provincial legislatures follow a Westminster parliamentary system. However, unlike Canada's federal government, the provincial governments do not have an upper house through which provincial legislations need to pass. All provincial legislative power resides in the House of Commons, more specifically in the hands of whatever party is governing at the time.

2 In this book I use the term *Spiritual Care Practitioner* to be consistent with the official nomenclature used by CASC/ACSS. In other jurisdictions such professionals are called Professional Chaplains, or simply Chaplains. CASC/ACSS adopted this terminology in 2016 to reflect the increasingly multifaith nature of chaplaincy work in Canada. It also reflects the increasing psychotherapeutic orientation of this work in Canada.

3 CASC/ACSS has recently adopted the nomenclature of Clinical Psychospiritual Education to designate what other jurisdictions call Clinical Pastoral Education.

4 This was published as Lasair (2012).

5 For two of several examples of this approach see Kearney (2001) and Caputo (2006).

6 I first began developing this concept in Lasair (2020a). In that publication I called a person's frame for reality their "metaphysical beliefs." I have since moved away from this formulation, due largely to the contentious nature of the term *metaphysics*. The use of this term in philosophical writings is controversial, to say the least. In theology it is given a very different meaning. And, again, in various spiritual traditions, it has yet another meaning. So, to use a more neutral term, I have adopted the idea of a person's frame for reality. This term more accurately captures both the ideological and psychological dimensions of a person's spirituality. It will be given a more comprehensive treatment in Chapter Two below.

7 For the CASC/ACSS competencies see CASC/ACSS (2019).

REFERENCE LIST

Béres, L., & Crawley, D. (2023). *The language of the soul in narrative therapy: spirituality in clinical theory and practice.* New York, NY: Routledge.

Blankholm, J. (2022). *The secular paradox: on the religiosity of the not religious.* New York, NY: New York University Press.

Cadge, W., Fitchett, G., Haythorn, T., Palmer, P., Rambo, S., Clevenger, C., & Stroud, I. (2019). Training healthcare chaplains: yesterday, today and tomorrow. *Journal of Pastoral Care & Counseling, 73*(4), 211–221. doi:10.1177/1542305019875819

Canadian Association for Spiritual Care/Association canadienne de soins spirituels (CASC/ACSS) (2019, June 19). *Competencies.* Retrieved October 14, 2022, from Canadian Association for Spirtual Care/Association canadienne de soins spirituels: https://spiritualcare.ca/explore-spiritual-care/cascacss_competencies/

Canadian Associaton for Spiritual Care/Association canadienne de soins spirituels (CASC/ACSS) (2020, December 24). *Index of the Manual.* Retrieved October 13, 2022, from spiritualcare.ca: https://casc-acss.wildapricot.org/resources/Documents/Index%20of%20the%20Manual%20Revised%20January%202%202021.pdf

Caputo, J. D. (2006). *The weakness of god: a theology of the event*. Bloomington and Indianapolis, IN: Indiana University Press.

Culliford, L. (2012). *The psychology of spirituality: an introduction*. London, UK: Jessica Kingsley.

de Brito Sena, M. A., Damanio, R. F., Lucchetti, G., & Prieto Peres, M. F. (2021, November). Defining spirituality in healthcare: a systematic review and conceptual framework. *Frontiers in Psychology*, 12, Article 756080. doi:10.3389/fpsyg.2021.756080

de Cruz, H., & de Smedt, J. (2015). *A natural history of natural theology: the cognitive science of theology and philosophy of religion*. Cambridge, MA: MIT Press.

Fitchett, G., Nieuwsma, J. A., Bates, M. J., Rhodes, J. E., & Meador, K. G. (2014). Evidence-based chaplaincy care: attitudes and practices in diverse healthcare samples. *Journal of Health Care Chaplaincy*, 20, 144–160. doi:10.1080/08854726.2014.949163

Galek, K., Flannelly, K. J., Vane, A., & Galek, R. M. (2005, March/April). Assessing a patient's spiritual needs: a comprehensive instrument. *Holistic Nursing Practice*, 19(2), 62–69.

Gillespie, M. A. (2008). *The theological origins of modernity*. Chicago, IL, and London, UK: University of Chicago Press.

Habermas, J. (1992). *Postmetaphysical thinking: philosophical essays*. (W. M. Hohengarten, Trans.). Cambridge, MA: MIT Press.

Habermas, J. (2008). *Between naturalism and religion: philosophical essays*. (C. Cronin, Trans.). Cambridge, UK: Polity Press.

Hefti, R., & Gomes Experandio, M. R. (2016, January/March). The interdisciplinary spiritual care model: a holistic approach to patient care. *Horizonte*, 14(41), 13–47. doi:10.5752/P2175-5841.2016v14n41p13

Kearney, R. (2001). *The god who may be: a hermeneutics of religion*. Bloomington and Indianapolis, IN: Indiana University Press.

Lasair, S. (2010). Targum and translation: a new approach to a classic problem. *Association for Jewish Studies Review*, 34(2), 265–287. doi:10.1017/S0364009410000346

Lasair, S. (2012). *Narratology and the pentateuch Targums: a methodological experiment*. Piscataway, NJ: Gorgias Press.

Lasair, S. (2018a). Spiritual care as a secular profession: politics, theory, and practice. *Journal for the Study of Spirituality*, 8(1), 5–18. doi:10.1080/20440243.2018.1431022

Lasair, S. (2018b). Understanding, assessing, and intervening in the spiritual nature of medical events: theological and theoretical perspectives. *Practical Theology*, 11(5), 374–386. doi:10.1080/1756073X.2018.1528749

Lasair, S. (2019). What's the point of spiritual care? a narrative response. *Journal of Pastoral Care & Counseling*, 73(2), 115–123. doi:10.1177/1542305019846846

Lasair, S. (2020a). A narrative approach to spirituality and spiritual care in health care. *Journal of Religion and Health*, 59, 1524–1540. doi:10.1007/s10943-019-00912-9

Lasair, S. (2020b). What's the point of Clinical Pastoral Education and pastoral counselling education? political, developmental, and professional considerations. *Journal of Pastoral Care & Counseling*, 74(1), 22–32. doi:10.1177/1542305019897563

Lasair, S. (2021a). HAVE-H: five attitudes for a narratively grounded and embodied spirituality. *Journal of Pastoral Care & Counseling*, 75(1), 13–22. doi:10.1177/1542305020965546

Lasair, S. (2021b). Truth in pastoral practice: a firmer foundation for contested territory. *International Journal of Practical Theology*, 25(2), 166–183. doi:10.1515/ijpt-2021-0004

Lasair, S., & Sinclair, S. (2018). Family and patient spiritual narratives in the ICU: bridging disclosures through compassion. In G. Netzer (Ed.), *Families in the intensive care unit: a guide to understanding, engaging, and supporting at the bedside* (pp. 289–300). Cham, Switzerland: Springer.

Lilla, M. (2007). *The stillborn god: religion, politics and the modern West*. New York, NY: Vintage.

Lynch, G. (2012). *The sacred in the modern world: a cultural sociological approach*. Oxford, UK: Oxford University Press.

McBrien, B. (2006). A concept analysis of spirituality. *British Journal of Nursing*, 15(1), 42–45.

McGilchrist, I. (2009). *The master and his emissary: the divided brain and the making of the Western world*. New Haven, CT, and London, UK: Yale University Press.

Milbank, J. (2006). *Theology & social theory: beyond secular reason* (2nd ed.). Malden, MA: Blackwell.

Milbank, J. (2013). *Beyond secular order: the representation of being and the representation of the people*. Oxford, UK: Wiley.

Nongbri, B. (2012). *Before religion: the history of a modern concept*. New Haven, CT: Yale University Press.

Oman, D. (2013). Defining religion and spirituality. In R. F. Paloutzian, & C. L. Park (Eds.), *The psychology of religion and spirituality* (2nd ed., Chapter 2). New York, NY: Guilford Press.

Pargament, K. I. (2007). *Spiritually integrated psychotherapy: understanding and addressing the sacred*. New York, NY: Guilford Press.

Pargament, K. I., & Exline, J. J. (2022). *Working with spiritual struggles in psychotherapy: from research to practice*. New York, NY: Guilford Press.

Puchalski, C., et al. (2009). Improving the quality of spiritual care as a dimension of palliative care: the report of the consensus conference. *Journal of Palliative Medicine*, 12(10), 642–656.

Puchalski, C., Vitillo, R., Hull, S., & Reller, N. (2014). Improving the spiritual dimension of whole person care: reaching national and international consensus. *Journal of Palliative Medicine*, 17(6), 642–656.

Ragsdale, J. R. (2018). Transforming chaplaincy requires transforming Clinical Pastoral Education. *Journal of Pastoral Care & Counseling*, 72(1), 58–62. doi:10.1177/1542305018762133

Schore, A. N. (2019). *Right brain psychotherapy*. New York, NY: Norton.

Schuhmann, C., & Damen, A. (2018). Representing the good: pastoral care in a secular age. *Pastoral Psychology*, 67, 405–417. doi:10.1007/s11089-018-0826-0

Sinder, E., St. James O'Connor, T., Dotzert, C., Hong, S., Smith, R., Dolson, L., & Foulger, M. P. (2019). Evidence-based spiritual care practice in the Canadian context: twenty years later. *Journal of Pastoral Care & Counseling*, 73(2), 88–95. doi:10.1177/1542305019843239

Swinton, J. (2012). Healthcare spirituality: a question of knowledge. In M. Cobb, C. M. Puchalski, & B. Rumbold (Eds.), *Oxford Textbook of Spirituality in Healthcare* (pp. 99–104). Oxford, UK: Oxford University Press.

Taylor, C. (2007). *A secular age*. Cambridge, MA: Belknap Harvard University Press.

Taylor, M. C. (2007). *After God*. Chicago, IL: University of Chicago Press.

van Dijke, J., Duyndam, J., van Nistelrooij, I., & Bos, P. (2022). "We need to talk about empathy": Dutch humanist chaplains' perspectives on empathy's functions, downsides, and limitations in chaplaincy care. *Journal of Pastoral Care & Counseling*, 76(1), 15–28. doi:10.1177/1542305021074271

Walton, M. (2012). Assessing the construction of spirituality: conceptualizing spirituality in health care settings. *Journal of Pastoral Care & Counseling*, 66(3), 1–16.

Ward, G. (2014). *Unbelievable: why we believe and why we don't*. London, UK, and New York, NY: I.B. Tauris.

Watts, F. (2017). *Psychology, religion, and spirituality: concepts and applications*. Cambridge, UK: Cambridge University Press.

One

INTRODUCTION

Spiritual care as practiced in Western contexts has to contend with several challenging cultural realities. These Western cultural realities therefore inform how Spiritual Care Practitioners practice their profession; they also inform how spirituality itself is understood in these settings. Building an explicit understanding of these Western cultural concerns is therefore foundational for describing how spiritual care might be practiced in Western healthcare. This chapter works to build such an understanding, drawing upon the insights of philosophers, social theorists, and neuroscientists to do so. By the end of the chapter it becomes apparent that, despite many conceptual and cultural challenges, spirituality and spiritual care are starting to be understood in new and invigorating ways in the West. This chapter points toward one such emerging understanding, entrusting its fuller articulation to Chapter Two's argument.

As with many emerging insights in spiritual care, this chapter begins with an encounter with a patient.

CINDY'S BELIEFS

As I've talked with many colleagues in chaplaincy and spiritual care, I've found all of us have had patients who stay with us. For whatever reason, they're the ones we remember years afterward. Something about them or their story speaks to us.

When I was working for the public healthcare system, the spiritual care office was responsible for offering care to patients who had no stated religious affiliation. If patients did have a religious affiliation, we assumed their clergy person could come to the hospital and provide care. However, on any given day, upwards of fifty percent of patients in our hospital were listed as having no religious affiliation. There were

DOI: 10.4324/9781003466147-2

many reasons for this. Yes, this reality reflected many demographic trends in Canada (see Bibby, 2011, 2017), but I also discovered that sometimes patients didn't want to state a religious affiliation when they came to hospital. Either they didn't want their faith community to know they were in hospital, or, if they felt they needed religious support, they would contact their clergy person on their own. Sometimes spiritual care staff would facilitate these contacts. In other cases, people from specific faith communities didn't feel comfortable talking with their clergy person about what they were experiencing. In those cases, Spiritual Care Practitioners provided a safe and neutral presence for people who were often facing very dark days. It was an honor to provide care for all these people. That's one reason why it hurt so much when our jobs were taken away.

One day when I was providing patient care, I encountered a woman in an observation ward on one of the units where I worked. Cindy was her name, and she had come to hospital requiring emergency surgery for a medical condition she had been living with for some time. The surgery had been successful, but there were several times when the surgeons wondered whether she would survive or not. Cindy was aware of this and was slowly working to integrate this experience into her self-understanding. As a self-described atheist, Cindy understood that death was part of life. She had also made her mind up long ago that there was no afterlife. In her view, nothing existed outside the physical universe; therefore she need not concern herself with things that were, from her perspective, ultimately inconsequential.

However, as we started exploring her experience together, there were several times when she teared up. One occurred when she described how the medical staff had shown her significant care and compassion. Something about that experience moved Cindy deeply, but she was not able to name what it was that so moved her. Cindy teared up another time when talking about her husband. Her husband belonged to a traditional religion, and it was clear that his beliefs had sustained him through Cindy's health crisis. While Cindy was very open about not sharing her husband's beliefs, she was moved deeply when she talked about the strength her husband's religion gave him.

Given how clear Cindy was about not sharing, nor wanting to share, her husband's beliefs, I didn't know how much I could invite her to explore her tears. However, when I did invite her to reflect on her emotions as she told this story, Cindy mentioned that she took courage from her husband's beliefs. Even though they did not make sense to her, somehow it was comforting for Cindy to know her husband had his beliefs, and that these beliefs consoled him. This was especially true as Cindy was beginning to realize that she herself could not console her husband in the same way, neither through her own beliefs, nor by offering him reassurance that her medical condition might get better. At that point, the doctors weren't sure what Cindy's recovery might look like. My contact with Cindy ended fairly soon afterward.

WHAT'S THE MEANING OF IT ALL?

I tell this story not to disparage Cindy nor other people like her who adhere to secular belief systems. Rather, I tell this story to illustrate how complicated matters of belief are in our contemporary Western context. Cindy had specific beliefs about the nature of reality—for her, nothing existed but the physical universe. However, her husband approached life from a very different perspective. Somehow, they had discovered a way to make their relationship work. Cindy clearly respected her husband's beliefs. I never met Cindy's husband, so I'm not sure what he felt about Cindy's self-described atheism. Nevertheless, it's likely this kind of relationship was extremely rare in the early- to mid-20th century. Five centuries ago, people like Cindy were scarcely imaginable. As Canadian philosopher and social theorist Charles Taylor puts it in the first chapter of *A Secular Age*,

> One way to put the question that I want to answer here is this: why was it virtually impossible not to believe in God in, say, 1500 in our Western society, while in 2000 many of us find this not only easy, but even inescapable (2007, p. 25)?

Taylor then spends over 800 pages exploring this question. To understand patients like Cindy, engaging with Taylor's thought is not only helpful, but also necessary—to date, his is the most thorough and authoritative account of Western secularity. Yet to engage this book comprehensively would require a much longer discussion than is available to me in these pages.

So, while I can only give this complex topic very superficial treatment in this chapter, it is helpful to remember how difficult it is to describe the current dynamics of Western religious and/or secular beliefs simply and succinctly. In fact, Taylor's book has been shown to contain several parallel and somewhat conflicting narratives concerning the West's general evolution into secular thought. Matters become further complicated when Anglican theologian John Milbank's perspectives are added to the discussion (see Milbank, 2006, 2013). And this does not even account for the ideas of German philosopher and social theorist Jürgen Habermas (Habermas, 1984, 1992, 2008), or Muslim American anthropologist Talal Asad (2003, 2018), or American political theorist Mark Lilla (2007), or American intellectual historian Michael Allan Gillespie (2008)! All these scholars (and more I have not named) have contributed significantly to the published discussions concerning the emergence of secularity in the West. All of them bring somewhat different perspectives regarding what moved us into the present, away from the social and cultural realities that existed five centuries ago. All their ideas are important, not only for understanding clients like Cindy, but also for engaging the current dynamics of Western cultures.

Now, it's fair to state that many of these authors made their main contributions to discussions about secularity between 15 and 20 years ago. Western cultures have again changed dramatically, even in the relatively short time of a decade and a half. Some scholars have thus begun to describe Western cultures as "post-secular" (e.g., Habermas, 2010; Graham, 2017). Similarly, others describe Western societies as being dominated by a "post-truth" approach to politics (Graham, 2017; Lasair, 2021). Both these dynamics can be seen in the current Western political and religious polarizations that often crystallize around issues of human sexuality, human reproduction, climate change, political correctness, debt cancellation, and taxing the wealthy, among others. While I will not take explicit positions regarding any of these issues in these pages, I will argue—very strongly—that all of them impact a person's spirituality, regardless of whether that person is a spiritual care client or not. So, to grapple with professional spiritual care in contemporary Western settings, it is impossible to avoid culture and politics, regardless of whether a Practitioner or client is religious, secular, post-secular, post-truth, or something else.

The irony is that clients like Cindy, and so many of the other clients I'll mention in these pages, are most likely unaware of how these macro-cultural and political dynamics affect their spiritualities. Instead, they probably see these dynamics as part of the overall cultural and political milieux in the contemporary West. To draw identifiable connecting lines between Western secularity (not to mention post-truth politics) and individuals' experiences of spirituality and religion could therefore be viewed as a very challenging task. Yet this is precisely the task I will be attempting in this chapter. To draw upon a familiar metaphor, Western secularity, politics, and culture are the waters in which we, in the West, all swim. To understand the conditions that make spirituality and religion possible in this context, it is necessary to engage each of these phenomena. Western secularity is my most suitable starting point.

HOW THE WEST BECAME SECULAR: IN BRIEF

Through his lengthy treatments of secularity in the West, Charles Taylor returns again and again to the secular's defining character-istic: viewing reality through a "purely immanent frame" (2007, pp. 539–593; Smith, 2014) What Taylor means by this is that prior to 1500, Europeans generally believed earthly realities were nested in an integrated cosmos (Taylor, 2007; Milbank, 2013). This cosmos contained varying levels of reality, with God and other divine beings at the top. From their position in the highest plane of reality, God and the other divine beings would engage lower planes through various kinds of causality (Milbank, 2013). God would issue a divine decree, then the decree would filter through reality's various levels before it became manifest on planes perceivable to humans. In this scheme it was impossible to trace events perceived by humans back to their divine source. However, people in Europe generally believed that whatever events they experienced had been ordained by divine decree and governed by divine Providence (Taylor, 2007; Milbank, 2013). European Christians could therefore trust that God's good intentions for the cosmos would ultimately be realized, and this was regardless of whether individuals or groups of people experienced their current circumstances as positive or negative or something else.

While elements of this perspective can still be detected in various forms of Western Christianity, most in the West would agree that they no longer see reality quite this way. Where prior to 1500, most Westerners approached reality in ways similar to the description in the previous paragraph, now most Westerners see reality through lenses constructed, at least in part, by empirical science (Taylor, 2007; Graham, 2017; Asad, 2003). Yes, there are variations in how specific Westerners use the concepts of science to describe their daily realities. However, most Western people rely on science's achievements simply to live their daily lives. Our homes are structured and function according to the discoveries of contemporary engineering. Our vehicles run on technologies developed in the 19th, 20th, and 21st centuries. Our food is grown and raised according to the practices of 21st-century agriculture. Much of our communication relies on computers and other digital devices that have emerged only within the past 40 years. None of these technologies, nor the science that enabled their development, were imaginable 500 years ago. To achieve all these things, the West had to shift how it viewed reality in some very significant ways. What does this look like in broad strokes?

Scholars who study secularity often describe what they call a "subtraction story" (Taylor, 2007, 2011a; Casanova, 2011). What they mean by this is that 500 years ago, Europeans saw the cosmos as permeated by God's Providence and the presence of other divine beings (Taylor, 2007). In short, Europeans lived in what these scholars call an "enchanted universe" (Taylor, 2007; Milbank, 2013). Spirits, sprites, and fairies were believed to cause a person's melancholy or rage, or strange coincidences that occurred in their life (Taylor, 2007). Yet due to a general desire for reform that emerged in both church and state during 14th-century Europe, matters began to shift (Milbank, 2006, 2013; Taylor, 2007). Where previously all of life was connected to God, the saints, spirits, sprites, and fairies, Europeans began to understand that there were some social domains separate from these various entities. Commerce, law, and the dealings of state were some of the first places where this understanding began to emerge (Taylor, 2007; Smith, 2014). Taylor calls this phenomenon "secular$_1$"—he calls it this not only to denote its relatively early emergence in European history, but also to indicate that this expression of secularity is but one of three he considers distinct in Western societies.

According to Taylor, secular$_2$ began to emerge when it became possible to imagine belief in God as one among several available options

(Taylor, 2007; Smith, 2014). Again, this contrasts with what Taylor describes as the situation prior to 1500. Historically, secular$_2$ began to emerge around the time of the European intellectual Enlightenment in the 17th and 18th centuries (Taylor, 2007; Root, 2017). This is when scientific thought began to present a compelling alternative to traditional Christian teachings. The result was that the views of reality traditionally articulated by the Christian church could no longer be assumed as true without question (Gillespie, 2008; Milbank, 2006). Instead, the evidence presented by empirical science began to undermine many Christian understandings of reality (Milbank, 2013, 2006). Over several centuries, then, scientific thought came to dominate Western approaches to reality (Taylor, 2007). The result was the emergence of secular$_3$. Taylor identifies secular$_3$ as encapsulating much of our current social and cultural condition. In this condition, belief in God is nearly impossible, mainly due to the dominant understanding that nothing apart from the physical universe exists—reality is generally viewed through a "purely immanent frame" (Taylor, 2007; Smith, 2014; Root, 2017).

Now, I fully acknowledge this brief summary is a drastic oversimplification of very complex and intricate historical processes, each of which, together with the others, brought us to our current moment in Western social and cultural history. However, it is not the precise details of these historical changes that are my primary concern. Rather, my hope is to illustrate—only generally—that our current social and cultural situation is the product of numerous cultural, philosophical, and ideological shifts and transformations. In doing so, I also want to indicate that Taylor's three manifestations of the secular are still evident today. Secular$_1$ is evident in how members of several religious traditions still configure their realities—they will talk about the distinctions between religious and secular lives. Secular$_2$ can be seen in situations like the one that existed between my patient Cindy and her husband—belief in God is but one of several possible options. Finally, secular$_3$ can be seen in the daily operations of governments, legal establishments, and healthcare organizations, among others. Individual members of these organizations may have private practices wherein they connect with God or other divine beings. However, these large Western institutions depend on a functional and procedural atheism, simply so they can carry out their daily operations (Williams,

2012; Habermas, 1992, 1984). If God or other spiritual beings were invoked every time these organizations began considering an initiative or needed to make a decision, each organization's perceived efficiency and effectiveness would be drastically affected. Consequently, at macro-cultural and institutional levels, the contemporary West has come to rely upon "rationalized" policies, procedures, and processes (Habermas, 1984, 1992). To achieve this goal, Western organizations and institutions have had to eliminate the "irrational" dynamics of religion, spirituality, God, angels, demons, spirits, sprites and fairies from their daily practices. In doing so, the West created several challenges for those who wish to maintain connections with these phenomena, regardless of whether these phenomena or entities actually exist or not.

CONTEMPORARY SECULARITIES

A good way to illustrate these challenges is to summarize some of the debates that have emerged between Charles Taylor and Jürgen Habermas (Habermas & Taylor, 2011). For those unfamiliar with his work, Habermas played a crucial role in shaping European politics through the late decades of the 20th century and up to our current time. Due to this influence, Habermas is widely acknowledged as one of the leading figures of Western secular political theory. It is therefore impossible to ignore his perspectives when considering contemporary social, cultural, and political expressions of secularity in the West.

One of Habermas' central social, political, and philosophical concerns is how best to engage diverse perspectives while also ensuring that political and institutional bodies can make decisions both efficiently and effectively. To accomplish this goal, Habermas constructed what he called a theory of "communicative action," wherein he laid out what he considered to be foundational principles for any person's participation in public decision-making processes (Habermas, 1984). One cornerstone of Habermas' approach is his understanding that before any organization can make any kind of decision, its members must first agree upon the processes and procedures by which decisions can be made (Habermas, 2003, 1992, 1984). For Habermas, this agreement concerns not only the procedural norms that will govern decision-making processes, but it must also determine what kinds of knowledge can inform the processes themselves (Habermas, 2003,

1984, 2008). On this latter point, Habermas is very clear: Western societies have largely adopted the truth-establishing procedures of empirical science (Habermas, 1992). As a result, any truth-establishing procedure that falls outside this empirical scientific norm ought to be excluded from public debate (Habermas 2003, 2008, 1992).

Not surprisingly, then, from Habermas' perspective, religious beliefs are prime examples of non-normative "truths" (Habermas, 2008). Habermas does admit that individuals who participate in decision-making processes may be privately motivated by religion (Habermas, 2008), yet religious beliefs, from Habermas' perspective, typically fall outside what can be empirically or rationally verified (Habermas, 1984, 2003, 2008). Consequently, Habermas argues religious justifications for action ought to be systematically excluded from decision-making processes in Western social and cultural settings (Habermas, 1992, 2003, 2008). However, because Habermas admits that individuals can be *privately* motivated by their religious beliefs, he does allow such beliefs to inform public decision-making processes, at least indirectly (Habermas, 2008). For individuals' religious beliefs and justifications to gain such influence, from Habermas' perspective, however, they must first be translated into terms that everyone can agree upon. For Habermas, such translation is necessary because, from his perspective, it is impossible to forge agreements on religious beliefs or motivations within the context of rational discussions or debates (Habermas, 2008).

Now, in his more recent publications, Habermas (2010) does see a potentially more public role for religious beliefs in Western societies In short, he comes to understand that secular belief systems lack the capacity to provide moral inspiration in the same ways that religious beliefs and practices often can and do (Habermas, 2010; see also Graham, 2017). From his perspective, there is a growing awareness that "something is missing" in purely secular approaches to reality (Habermas, 2010). Yet while Habermas acknowledges the moral value of religious beliefs and practices, he is not entirely certain that re-discovering religious beliefs will allow Western individuals to completely recover whatever was lost when the West became secular. Nevertheless, Habermas does continue to perceive "something" as "missing" in Western secular contexts. In response, Charles Taylor offers a striking alternative.

Where Habermas argues for a strictly governed procedural secularity, Taylor invites his readers to adopt a pluralistic approach to Western public life (Taylor, 2011b). From Taylor's perspective, Westerners should be competent enough to make sense of various approaches to reality, religious and secular. As a result, religious perspectives ought not to be excluded from decision-making processes (Habermas & Taylor, 2011; Taylor, 2011b). For Taylor, including such perspectives will enable Western institutions to make better decisions, mainly because they will begin to meaningfully engage people and groups that fall outside Western organizational secular norms (Taylor, 2011b). Demographically, such people and groups are reflective of the overall diversity present in Western societies and cultures. From Taylor's perspective, then, Habermas' procedural secularity excludes and oppresses such diversity, justifying itself solely on the assumption that secularity is the agreed-upon Western cultural norm. Taylor thus criticizes Habermas' assumption that secularity has been universally agreed upon in the West (Taylor, 2011b; Habermas & Taylor, 2011). From Taylor's perspective, this assumption is not borne out among many individuals and groups in contemporary Western settings—and it likely never has been (Taylor, 2011b; Habermas & Taylor, 2011). Yet secular approaches to reality do remain the current standard in many Western institutions. The result is that Habermas' and Taylor's distinct philosophical positions illuminate the dilemmas Spiritual Care Practitioners encounter daily, especially in such institutional settings as healthcare.

PROGRAMMATIC DILEMMAS: SECULARITY IN HEALTHCARE

When unpacking these dilemmas, former Anglican Archbishop of Canterbury and public theologian and intellectual Rowan Williams offers a helpful distinction. In his 2012 book, *Faith in the Public Square*, Williams explores the difference between what he calls "procedural secularism" and programmatic secularism. According to Williams, procedural secularism is manifest when groups or organizations do not invoke religious beliefs or practices when undertaking their various activities or initiatives. Such groups or organizations may in fact be affiliated with various faiths or cultural traditions. Yet, for whatever reason, they have decided not to include religious beliefs and practices as part of their standard operating procedures. In contrast, programmatic secularism is manifest when a group or organization requires that all its members must conform to the organization's secular approach to reality (Williams, 2012). In Taylor's terms, secular$_3$ is the only perspective held within such organizations, and such organizations require complete acceptance of secular$_3$ for anyone to become or remain a member. It should now be evident how Williams' distinction applies to Spiritual Care Practitioners, particularly those who work in healthcare.

It may be fairly argued that modern Western medicine is one of the crowning glories of secular$_3$ approaches to reality (see Taylor, 2007). It relies upon the biological, chemical, and physical sciences to undertake its daily work of bringing health and healing to humanity. As such, modern Western medicine embodies the humanist ideals of the European intellectual Enlightenment when it uses the tools of empirical science to eliminate disease and reduce human suffering (see Taylor, 2007; Smith, 2014). Few would deny the staggering achievements of modern Western medicine. However, in recent years patients and their families have increasingly reported feelings of dehumanization and alienation when receiving services in healthcare (Ho et al., 2017; Sinclair et al., 2016; Lasair & Sinclair, 2018; Timmins, Naughton, Plakas, & Pesut, 2015). Something about healthcare's ways of engaging patients and their realities gives patients and their families very negative experiences. Some researchers believe this may be due to the increasingly technical and technologically oriented nature of healthcare interventions (Timmins, Naughton, Plakas, & Pesut, 2015; Lasair & Sinclair, 2018; Ho et al., 2017). Others believe that healthcare practitioners have not been trained sufficiently to embody a compassionate approach to the care they provide (Sinclair et al., 2016). Consequently, medical personnel may be able to cure patients' physical diseases, but they are often less able to heal patients' wounded spirits or souls.

Now, it is worth noting that the idea of patients possessing spirits or souls does not conform to the norms of secular$_3$ understandings of reality. The existence of spirits or souls cannot be verified using the tools of empirical science, yet the research demonstrates that, in Habermas' phrase, "something is missing" in the provision of healthcare at the front lines (Habermas, 2010). It is for this reason that several researchers are calling upon healthcare practitioners to more consistently embody a compassionate approach to their care (Sinclair et al., 2017; Sinclair et al., 2016; Puchalski, Vitillo, Hull, & Reller, 2014). Other researchers are similarly urging healthcare practitioners to include patients' and families' religious and spiritual concerns as standard parts of their treatment plans (Puchalski et al., 2009; Puchalski, Vitillo, Hull, & Reller, 2014). Compassion, religion, and spirituality are thus beginning to be recognized as central to patients' and families' humanity. If Western medicine was created to help human beings, then each of these phenomena needs to be engaged by frontline service providers for healthcare to live up to its founding humanist ideals. Yet this perspective also raises several questions, particularly given that healthcare institutions often embody programmatic secular$_3$ approaches to reality.

Perhaps the most significant among these questions is, how permeable are healthcare approaches to reality? To clarify: to what extent do healthcare institutions grant the same powers and privileges to individuals and groups whose perspectives do not conform to healthcare's programmatic secular$_3$ norms? This question leads us directly to the heart of Habermas' and Taylor's debate. What does this look like concretely?

It is a commonplace that any treatment or practice in healthcare needs to be supported by empirical scientific evidence. If any treatment or practice is not supported by such evidence, then the belief is that such a treatment or practice ought not to be used. This is not just a matter of standard operating procedures. Rather, this understanding also has legal implications, in that healthcare practitioners can be subject to disciplinary or legal actions if they choose to use treatments or practices that are not supported by good scientific evidence. The result is that healthcare practitioners are systematically trained to exclude and stigmatize anything that does not conform to the empirically-driven scientific norms of their professions.

As hinted above, however, there is a mounting body of evidence that patients and their families benefit from having their spiritual and/or religious concerns somehow included in the care they receive in healthcare (Puchalski et al., 2009; Puchalski, Vitillo, Hull, & Reller, 2014; Lasair & Sinclair, 2018). Yet while there are growing numbers of researchers advocating for various approaches to meet this increasing demand, there continues to be a general lack of consensus regarding what this ought to look like concretely. For example, there was a landmark study published recently in the *Journal of the American Medical Association* arguing that professional spiritual care ought to be included as a standard part of the services offered by any healthcare organization (Balboni et al., 2022). While there is little with which I can argue in this idea, it still demands the question, how best to understand religion and spirituality in healthcare settings? And how best can Spiritual Care Practitioners be integrated into the overall provision of healthcare services? Again, there are a number of proposals emerging in the research literature (e.g., Stilos, Ford, Chakraborty, & Takahashi, 2021; Heard, Scott, & Yeo, 2022; O'Connor & Meakes, 2021; Visser, Damen, & Schuhmann, 2022). Yet there also continue to be a number of fundamental issues that need to be addressed, many of which much of this literature seems simply to be unaware.

A NEUROLOGICAL BASIS (AND CRITIQUE) FOR SECULAR THOUGHT

From my perspective, the most significant of these issues concerns a trend identified by British neuropsychiatrist and former Oxford University English literature professor Iain McGilchrist. In recent years, McGilchrist's neurological critiques of broad Western macro-cultural trends have become highly influential in multiple fields. Theologians, cultural critics, neuroscientists, psychotherapists, and spiritual writers have all found a wealth of insights in his magisterial treatments of brain hemispherality (e.g., Siegel & Solomon, 2013; Ward, 2014; Williams, 2014). For this book's argument, McGilchrist's thought offers a foundational neurological understanding for how spirituality and spiritual care might be approached within healthcare settings.

According to McGilchrist, Western cultures have come to rely too heavily on ways of perceiving and engaging reality associated with the left hemisphere of the human brain (McGilchrist, 2009, 2013, 2021). In making this argument, McGilchrist articulates his fear that Western approaches to reality are out of balance. He therefore argues that the West's survival depends on finding the right balance between the brain's two hemispheres. From McGilchrist's perspective, finding this proper balance individually is not enough. Rather, Westerners must also work to reintegrate a holistic approach to reality produced by finding this balance into our dominant cultural perspectives. While McGilchrist's clear demarcation of roles between the human brain's two hemispheres is contested (see below), his distinction between the hemispheres and their roles can be read as a heuristic that helps to describe several readily identifiable psychiatric and cultural trends.

McGilchrist draws upon a century's worth of neurological evidence to support his perspective. In doing so he shows evidence that suggests the brain's left hemisphere is concerned with bringing language to reality; hence the left hemisphere tends to categorize reality using linguistic and logical systems (McGilchrist, 2009, 2021). As such, its concern is with the conceptual coherence of reality, which means that the left hemisphere is very skilled in breaking various realities down into their distinct constituent parts. In contrast, McGilchrist demonstrates that the brain's right hemisphere is overwhelmingly concerned with engaging reality in a holistic and all-encompassing manner (McGilchrist, 2009, 2021). Spatial awareness is a high priority for the right hemisphere, in contrast to the left. Similarly, emotional and intuitive awareness are also greater priorities for the right hemisphere, again in contrast to the left. The result is that the right hemisphere of the brain is very skilled in rendering comprehensive pictures of reality. Consequently, when held in proper balance, the left hemisphere of the brain brings the perceptions of the right hemisphere into shared social and cultural domains by employing its capacity with language.

Based on this evidence, then, McGilchrist argues that, in healthy individuals and cultures, the right hemisphere of the brain is slightly dominant (McGilchrist, 2009, 2021). Through their right hemisphere's slight dominance, such individuals and cultures can maintain a holistic, emotional, intuitive, and systems-oriented approach to reality. In contrast, when an individual's left hemisphere is dominant, their perceptions of reality become fragmented. This is because such people cannot see the proverbial forest for the trees. The result is that left-hemisphere-dominant individuals tend to become fixated on small details that ultimately do not matter in the overall whole. From McGilchrist's perspective, this problem does not just plague select individuals. Rather, it dogs Western organizations and institutions as well, because, according to McGilchrist, this is a comprehensive macro-cultural problem in the West (McGilchrist, 2009, 2013).

Drawing out general themes in Western art and cultural history, McGilchrist therefore argues that since the medieval period, Western art, music, politics, and religion have become progressively more cognitive and conceptual in orientation (McGilchrist, 2009). In art, for example, medieval and renaissance paintings were highly representative and realistic when presenting their subject matter. In contrast, late 19th- and 20th-century art became increasingly abstract and conceptual in its approach. Pablo Picasso's cubist art is a paradigmatic example of this overall trend. Arnold Schönberg's serialist approach to musical composition is a similar example in a different art form. Moreover, from McGilchrist's perspective, these trends are not only evident in the arts, rather they are pervasive in all parts of Western life (McGilchrist, 2009, 2013). Western approaches to religion, for example, that judge people positively or negatively according to whether they hold "correct" or "orthodox" beliefs are another example of this trend. The over-valorization of science, technology, engineering, and mathematics (STEM) fields is yet another. Finally, McGilchrist sees the current polarizations in Western politics as yet another symptom of this overall problem. Why?

From McGilchrist's perspective, the Western over-emphasis of traits associated with the brain's left hemisphere has enabled Westerners to lose their capacity to tolerate ambiguity and disagreement (McGilchrist, 2013). The brain's right hemisphere is very skilled in maintaining relationships with all aspects of reality, regardless of whether they conform to our preconceived understandings of reality or not (McGilchrist, 2009, 2013). In contrast, the left hemisphere is quick to exclude perceived non-conforming aspects of reality, simply because it is not as sensitive to the emotional and intuitive connections that always exist between a person and every other part of reality. The result is that many of the ills present in Western cultures can be traced back to long-standing social trends that have had significant neurological consequences in the West—at least, this is McGilchrist's perspective.

Now, it is also necessary to acknowledge that McGilchrist's view is not universally shared among neuroscientists, nor even among all mental or spiritual health professionals (e.g., Cozolino, 2017; Hogue, 2003). Some would identify his distinctions between the brain's left and right hemispheres as polarizing, simplistic, and not reflective of the overall neural integration that makes all of human functioning possible (see e.g., Lombrazo, 2013; Shmerling, 2022;

Gamma, 2023). My desire in mentioning this counter-position is not to mount a comprehensive critique or defense of McGilchrist's (2009, 2021) argument. Nevertheless, it is worth noting, as I did above, that McGilchrist fears that Western cultural trends are actually heightening the polarities that his research evidence suggests are connected to how Westerners utilize traits associated with each of the brain's two hemispheres. So, in crafting his argument, McGilchrist is articulating the risk he perceives Western cultures are creating for all humanity: we are losing our holistic, emotional, and intuitive connections with all reality. From his perspective, these connections are often associated with the brain's right hemisphere. In losing these connections, we are no longer able to maximize whatever partnerships we might generate between ourselves, other humans, and the natural world. These partnerships are diminished because the left hemisphere, according to McGilchrist, tends to be more correlated with exploitative behaviors and reductive discourses (McGilchrist, 2009, 2021). McGilchrist can therefore be seen as teasing out the social and cultural implications of the views held by practitioners of Interpersonal Neurobiology (IPNB). According to IPNB practitioners, mental illness occurs when a person's neurobiology is not properly integrated (see Siegel & Solomon, 2013). The emerging correlation between McGilchrist's evidence and the overall Western trajectory toward secularism thus has far-reaching implications. The following paragraphs will directly explore this correlation.

In his most recent articulation of his theory, McGilchrist (2021) shows that when the brain's right hemisphere is dominant, everything seems alive. So, spirits are perceived in rocks and trees and birds and clouds and any other kind of physical entity imaginable. As a result, McGilchrist concludes that many traditional Indigenous and animist ways of engaging reality appear to be right-hemisphere-dominant. This is in contrast to modern, Western, European-originating ways of engaging reality; McGilchrist sees these as left-hemisphere-dominant. On this point McGilchrist and Charles Taylor agree: contemporary secular ways of engaging reality see the universe as a cold, hard place that operates only according to the rules of physical causality (McGilchrist, 2009, 2021; Taylor, 2007). Indigenous or pre-modern European ways of engaging reality, however, see the cosmos as full of life, with each part of reality communicating with everything else, because everything, *absolutely everything*, is interconnected (McGilchrist, 2021).

Now, it is interesting to note that in broad strokes Western medicine follows a similar trajectory away from holistic right-hemisphere priorities toward a more fragmented left-hemisphere approach to reality. In his classic genealogical exploration of modern Western medicine's emergence, French philosopher and historian Michel Foucault outlines a trajectory very similar to those described by Taylor and McGilchrist (Foucault, 1973). According to Foucault, in the 17th century, European medicine often diagnosed illnesses according to how human bodies had been influenced by such environmental factors as wind currents, tides, and other climactic events. As such, the causes of disease and illness were often attributed to how these various phenomena affected human bodies. The result was that if a specific individual experienced a certain kind of illness, a physician during this period would likely have instructed them to travel to a more health-supporting climate for a given period of time. If the ill person's health improved as a result of this trip, they could then return to the place where they fell ill and resume life as it had been prior to the illness's arrival. If the person did not recover from the illness, a longer period of time might be necessary in the health-supporting location.

As Western medical science developed, however, physicians became more aware of the distinct operations of human physiology. This new knowledge, combined with the discovery of microorganisms like bacteria and viruses, therefore shifted both the diagnostic and treatment options physicians used to cure illnesses. As a result, Foucault (1973) describes a long-term trend in medicine, up to the mid-20th century, wherein the human body gradually became the specific location of illness. This is in contrast to medicine's earlier position that viewed illnesses as largely caused by external environmental factors beyond a patient's—or a physician's—control. Due to this trend, according to Foucault (1973), modern Western medicine now typically focuses on anatomical or physiological pathologies that physicians work to cure, using medicines, surgeries, or other kinds of invasive treatments to do so. In this paradigm, the body is a purely physical object that can be physically or chemically manipulated for the purposes of rendering specific desired results. Not surprisingly, this approach embodies many of the typical hallmarks of secular, scientific, and left-hemisphere approaches to reality (see McGilchrist, 2009, 2021; Taylor, 2007). It is therefore also not surprising that patients and their families are increasingly describing their experiences in this kind of healthcare as dehumanizing and alienating, as discussed above; but it is also here that the push to include spiritual and religious perspectives in healthcare offers a compelling opportunity.

HOLISTIC APPROACHES IN SECULAR HEALTHCARE: INDIGENOUS PERSPECTIVES

As already mentioned, there is a mounting body of evidence indicating that patients and their families benefit from having their religious and spiritual concerns included in their overall care. In Canada, Australia, and New Zealand, for example, this work takes on some interesting nuances. In each of these contexts, significant work is being done to integrate Indigenous perspectives into healthcare policies and practices. While much of this work is occurring to correct devastating wrongs that were perpetrated against Indigenous peoples in healthcare and other settings, the fact this work is occurring indicates there is a growing openness to engaging right-hemisphere-oriented perspectives in healthcare. For example, an approach to medical care has been developed in New Zealand by Mason Harold Durie, a Māori researcher, to provide its guiding principles: Te Whare Tapa Whā, or the four sides of the house (whare) (Durie, 1985; Moeke-Maxwell et al., 2020). In this model, the four sides of the whare are as follows: Taha Hinengaro, or mental and emotional wellbeing; Taha Whanau, or family and social wellbeing; Taha Tinana, or physical wellbeing; and Taha Wairua, or spiritual wellbeing (Durie, 1985; Moeke-Maxwell et al., 2020, p. 180). According to this understanding, the four-sided house is also founded upon Whenua, the land, or a person's roots. This model was constructed to assist healthcare practitioners in New Zealand to become better attuned to Māori people's needs. New Zealand medical personnel are thus beginning to understand that each of these five domains needs to be addressed when they offer their services.

Such an approach therefore embodies what Indigenous researchers in Canada call "two-eyed seeing" (Peltier, 2018; Marsh et al., 2015; Martin, 2012). According to two-eyed seeing practitioners, both Indigenous and Western perspectives are understood as highly beneficial for patients and their families, both Indigenous and non-Indigenous alike. Accordingly, settings that practice two-eyed seeing strive to bring the best of both perspectives into conversation when delivering frontline services in healthcare. It almost goes without stating that much work still needs to be done to ensure two-eyed seeing is consistently implemented in contexts where healthcare practitioners have responsibilities for providing services to Indigenous peoples. Regardless, two-eyed seeing offers some helpful insights when considering how spirituality and spiritual care can best be integrated into healthcare.

To begin this discussion, it is worth observing the right-hemisphere orientation of all the domains identified in the Māori Te Whare Tapa Whā approach. Each domain describes a different relationship: the relationship between a person and themself (mental and emotional wellbeing); the relationship between a person and their social context (familial and social wellbeing); the relationship between a person and the earth; the relationship between a person and their body (physical wellbeing); and the relationship between a person and the transcendent (spiritual wellbeing). This approach therefore considers relational wellbeing as the primary concern of the care being provided. In doing so, it offers a striking contrast to typical Western approaches to healthcare that focus solely on the medical health of the body. Yet the Te Whare Tapa Whā approach to care is not incompatible with Western approaches; it still sees the medical health of the body as a significant concern for those receiving care. However, the Te Whare Tapa Whā approach also sees medical health as only one domain of five that contribute to a person's overall health and wellbeing. This Māori model therefore reorients the West's almost exclusive concern with the physical body; the Te Whare Tapa Whā model places this concern within the overall context of a much more holistic understanding of human health and wellbeing.

While it would be inappropriate to state that the Māori approach I have been exploring is exactly like other Indigenous approaches to health and wellbeing, it is worth noting the similarity between it and North American Indigenous teachings concerning the medicine wheel (e.g., Kimmerer, 2013). Like the Māori approach, these North American teachings understand health and wellbeing holistically, viewing physical wellbeing as only one part of the overall whole.

By engaging Indigenous perspectives, then, healthcare organizations in various settings are beginning to see the medical condition of the body as only one among several indicators of a person's overall health. As such, many of the assumptions that have typically been part of secular Western healthcare are being drastically reconfigured. What this reconfiguration will produce over the long term remains to be seen.

HOLISTIC APPROACHES IN SECULAR HEALTHCARE: WESTERN PERSPECTIVES

One way this reconfiguration is occurring is in the growing recognition that mental, emotional, and contextual factors can all affect physical health. One place this correlation has been observed is in trauma research (e.g., van der Kolk, 2014). According to many trauma researchers, there is a high occurrence of auto-immune disorders among people who experienced significant traumas early in life (van der Kolk, 2014). The explanation given for this phenomenon usually runs along these lines: when the brain's emotional centers are persistently over-activated, as they often are in trauma survivors, the adrenal glands consistently release adrenaline into the bloodstream, thus causing the body to experience states of stress long term. This stress is typically manifest in elevated heart and respiration rates, in addition to the narrowing of the perceptual field due to the so-called "fight, flight, or freeze" response. This response also causes the release of cortisol into the bloodstream; cortisol is typically known as the stress hormone. Now, because adrenaline and cortisol produce physical stress, the body's immune system often attempts to combat this stress by causing inflammation, particularly when the stress is ongoing. When left untreated, a persistent immune response like this can result in chronic illness because long-term inflammation can break down various tissues and disrupt several physiological processes in the body.

Epigenetics adds another dimension to these results (e.g., Lipton, 2016). It does so by showing how various environmental factors can negatively affect a person *at a genetic level*. Poverty, unemployment, and domestic abuse can all contribute to producing these genetic effects. Because of these effects, the body can experience the same kinds of inflammatory responses that are common in untreated cases of trauma. People who experience these kinds of environmental stressors can also become more susceptible to cardiac disease, as well as various forms of cancer. Such illnesses occur because of how these persistent stressors cause the activation of genes that are associated with each of these illnesses. Consequently, both trauma therapists and epigeneticists urge people to take a holistic approach to their health. From these professionals' perspectives, people should work to heal mental, emotional, and social/relational wounds at least as much as they ought to exercise their bodies to keep themselves physically fit and healthy.

Finally, human flourishing research, like the kind conducted by Tyler J. VanderWeele and colleagues at Harvard University, is beginning to see medical health as one domain among six that need to be experienced as "good" for someone to be understood as flourishing (see Höltge et al., 2023). The six domains that VanderWeele identifies are happiness and life satisfaction; mental and physical health; meaning and purpose; character and virtue; close social relationships; and financial and material security (see Höltge et al., 2023). VanderWeele does spend some time discussing religion and spirituality (see e.g., VanderWeele, 2017, 2020), but his approach is somewhat different than the one I take in the following pages. VanderWeele's contributions will be discussed more fully in Chapter Seven. Nevertheless, all this demonstrates that Western medical and mental health researchers are paying increasing attention to how non-physical dimensions of human existence can affect people's overall experiences of health and wellbeing. So, how does this book's approach to spirituality and professional spiritual care fit into all this?

DEFINING AND ENGAGING SPIRITUALITY

According to a definition established by international experts during two consensus conferences,

> Spirituality is a dynamic and intrinsic aspect of humanity through which persons seek ultimate meaning, purpose, and transcendence, and experience relationship to self, family, others, community, society, nature, and the significant or sacred. Spirituality is expressed through beliefs, values, traditions, and practices (Puchalski, Vitillo, Hull & Reller, 2014, p. 646).

I have chosen to engage this definition because it has gained increasing recognition in healthcare research as one of the most authoritative attempts to define spirituality (see e.g., Balboni et al., 2022). While it is necessary to state that this definition is conceptually dense and in need of significant unpacking, it does possess a number of key features worth noting. Of particular importance is its highly relational orientation: "Spirituality is… [an] intrinsic aspect of humanity through which persons… experience relationship to self, family, others, community, society, nature, and the significant or sacred." Based on the foregoing discussion, this portion of the definition suggests that spirituality is fundamentally right-hemisphere-oriented. This portion of the definition also indicates that many Indigenous peoples, when living according to their traditions, have an overwhelmingly spiritual orientation in their lives. It is therefore possible that, in the coming decades, Western medicine could shift away from its current fascination with technologically driven interventions, if spirituality, in the sense suggested by this definition, is systematically included in routine frontline care.

On the frontlines, however, it is also necessary to understand that many spiritual care patients, clients, and receivers might approach their spiritualities quite differently from the ways described by this definition. As discussed above, McGilchrist (2013, 2021) hints that, in many cases, Western religions also have become left-hemisphere-oriented. This phenomenon can be seen in the consistent need to define and defend perceived orthodoxies among various religious and secular groups. It can also be seen in the need among some of these groups to draw social boundaries around themselves based on what their perceived orthodoxies teach them. When considering such cases, it is helpful to highlight that, according to the consensus definition, spirituality is the phenomenon "through which" people experience the all relationships discussed above. This notion therefore suggests that any person's spirituality will always manifest a number of internal dynamics that will, without fail, inform how they engage all their lived realities. So, what does this mean for professional spiritual care?

As discussed in the introduction, the approach I take in this book argues that spirituality concerns the internal processes through which a person experiences and engages their lived realities.[1] Religion, culture, and tradition, in contrast, provide the specific conceptual and behavioral content that informs and structures any person's internal processes. It is therefore difficult to maintain a hard and fast distinction between religion and spirituality, except when done so along the lines I suggest in the following provisional definition of spiritual care:

> Professional spiritual care mobilizes the resources of religion or culture or tradition to assist clients in modifying their internal spiritual processes. This modification is done so clients can build, maintain, and enhance their relationships with all of reality. Professional Spiritual Care Practitioners therefore prioritize the affective, intuitive, and relational aspects of life.

Attentive readers may notice how this definition could bear some similarities to psychotherapeutic or social work approaches to care. This observation may arise in response to the definition's statement indicating that Spiritual Care Practitioners work to modify clients' internal spiritual processes. It could be argued that this statement has too much of a psychological overtone to clearly distinguish spiritual care from psychotherapy or social work. I agree this could be one way to read this statement. However, I formulated this statement this way intentionally. I did so because there is a significant amount of overlap between a person's individual psychology and their spirituality, yet the distinctions between the two begin to emerge when discussing the roles that cognition plays within each.

Much of contemporary psychology has become oriented toward understanding the processes that make cognition possible. Even in therapeutic circles, individual psychological pathologies are often defined according to a patient's or client's manifest cognitive distortions or disruptions (see e.g., American Psychiatric Association, 2013). The result is that approaches like cognitive behavioral therapy have achieved gold-standard status among many in the therapeutic community. Somewhat ironically, this emphasis on healthy cognition as the basis for psychological wellbeing again points toward the cognitive and linguistic (i.e., left-hemisphere) orientation that has come to dominate much of Western life.

Spiritual care, in contrast, flips this orientation on its head by approaching its caregiving work through a purely relational lens. Yes, this approach does reflect the significant influence psychologist

Carl Rogers had at earlier points in spiritual care's professional history (see Gerkin, 1986; Rogers, 1961), yet professional spiritual care does possess further distinguishing features. Of these, the mobilization of religious or cultural or traditional resources is most significant. Unlike many psychologists, Spiritual Care Practitioners are specifically trained in religious, cultural, or traditional teachings and practices. As such, they possess intimate knowledge concerning how various experiences in each of these domains can either improve or limit a person's overall holistic health and wellbeing. Moreover, Spiritual Care Practitioners understand holistic health and wellbeing through the relational focus that is so central to the consensus definition of spirituality quoted above. So, within the bounds of the relationships that Spiritual Care Practitioners share with their clients, Practitioners work to "build, maintain, and enhance [the client's] relationships with all of reality." The following section describes another way of understanding this idea.

SPIRITUALITY ON ITS OWN TERMS

Interfaith dialogue pioneer Raimon Panikkar believed that human spirituality is fundamentally concerned with what he called the "cosmotheandric" (2010). The word cosmotheandric combines three Greek words: cosmos, theos, and aner/andros. For Panikkar, cosmos refers to the physical universe, theos refers to the divine or transcendent realms, and aner/andros refers to the distinct domain of human consciousness. Panikkar firmly believed that humans uniquely bring all three domains together: human bodies belong to the physical world, and humans can be connected to the divine or transcendent realms through various phenomena in their consciousness.

Now, while it is true that Panikkar was trained philosophically and religiously in Western contexts, he was also fully immersed in Buddhist and Hindu thought. His mature philosophy thus provides a unique combination of Eastern and Western approaches to engaging reality. As such, it is helpful to draw attention to the similarities between his position and the Indigenous perspectives explored above.

Similar to Indigenous approaches, Panikkar's model describes a person's relationship with themselves in their mental and emotional wellbeing. It also describes a person's relationship with the physical universe as manifest in their body, and their relationship with the transcendent or divine realms as well. The only pieces missing in Panikkar's approach are a person's familial and social wellbeing and their relationship with Earth or the land. This may indeed be an expression of Panikkar's Western bias. However, the similarities between Panikkar's approach and the Indigenous perspectives discussed above are striking.

As a result, Panikkar's model will inform the descriptions of spiritual health that I will articulate in the following chapters. This is because, in broad strokes, Panikkar's approach was developed using a Western lens. However, in doing so, Panikkar also integrated Eastern thought, in addition to signaling his openness to traditional Indigenous perspectives. Consequently, Panikkar offers a compelling position in relation to both Western medicine and non-Western perspectives. Furthermore, while Panikkar himself may not have shared this view, his approach does not need to include only traditional religious understandings of reality. Rather, Panikkar's discussions of divine or transcendent realms are broad enough to also include emerging secular spiritualities. Some of these spiritualities are heavily influenced by quantum physics, neuroscience, and psychology, for example. As a result, atheists, agnostics, humanists, New Age practitioners, and adherents of many traditional religions and Indigenous spiritualities may find helpful insights in Panikkar's perspectives. This reality provides even more justification for taking Panikkar's approach seriously in the pages that follow.

Extrapolating from Panikkar's thought, then, I will argue that to be spiritually healthy, humans must find balance within themselves between the three domains he describes. If a person becomes overwhelmed by a physical experience (like a medical crisis that would bring them to healthcare), then such a person would need to recover their connection to their mental and emotional self. They would also need to re-engage those parts of themself that connect them to the divine or transcendent realms. Similarly, if a person becomes too overwhelmed by the divine or transcendent realms, they would need to ground themself again in their body, as well as in their own thoughts and emotions. Finally, if a person becomes too consumed by their own thoughts and emotions, then they would need to more fully engage with both the physical universe and the divine and transcendent realms. Familial and social wellbeing, as well as a person's relationship with the earth, provide some of the contexts that inform each of these domains.

SUMMARY AND CONCLUSION

This chapter began by recounting my encounter with a patient named Cindy. As a self-described atheist, Cindy indicated she believed that nothing apart from the physical universe exists. Due to this belief, her case raised some questions regarding how such beliefs became possible in the West. Charles Taylor's description of Western secularity's emergence provided some partial and initial answers. However, Taylor's account also highlighted some of the challenges experienced by Western Spiritual Care Practitioners. Of particular importance are the dilemmas produced by the programmatic and left-brain approaches to reality that are often dominant in Western secular healthcare settings.

However, because some Western healthcare settings are beginning to engage more thoroughly with traditional Indigenous perspectives (as well as emerging Western approaches to holistic care), space is beginning to emerge for spirituality in these settings. Yet to engage patients like Cindy, spirituality needs to be understood in terms that are not exclusively derived from traditional religions. This chapter therefore concluded that Raimon Panikkar's thought could offer at least some initial insights regarding how spirituality could be understood in this way. How, then, will this book's argument proceed from here?

Chapter Two will thus be consumed with bringing further definition to this understanding of spirituality, showing how spirituality is an intrinsic trait that all people share, through which they experience life's emotional, intuitive, and relational dimensions. As such, spirituality is a force that invites individuals to integrate all aspects of their identities into a holistic vision of reality. Spirituality thus draws a person into making sense of their life by coming to see and understand the distinct frame they bring to reality. Consequently, the processes by which people frame their various realities will be the focus of the next chapter.

The next chapter will therefore assume that, in many respects, the frame for reality explored here in Chapter One is inescapable for many in the West. Yet if this frame can be expanded to include realities that are, at this point, excluded from it, then perhaps some social and cultural healing can take place. When approached from this perspective, then, spiritual care is not just about specific therapeutic pathways or distinct treatment modalities. Rather, spiritual care is more fundamentally about inviting patients and clients to build and embody a holistic and inclusive frame for reality. By embodying this frame themselves, both in their presence and in their practices, Spiritual Care Practitioners can thus be significant forces for good in the world—in ways that extend well beyond their specific clinical contexts. The next chapter will therefore describe some fundamental concepts and principles that can help individual Spiritual Care Practitioners be and become just such a force.

Reflection Questions

- How do you see your setting manifesting secular approaches to reality? Are there some ways in which your setting differs from what was described in this chapter?
- To what extent do you agree with the approaches to spirituality and spiritual health described in this chapter? How might you describe them differently, if at all?
- How might the insights from this chapter help you position spiritual care/chaplaincy services in your workplace? What do you see as some strengths of that position? What do you see as some of that position's limitations?

NOTE

1 See the introduction, page 8.

REFERENCE LIST

American Psychiatric Association (2013). *Diagnostic and statistical manual of mental disorders: DSM-5* (5th ed.). Washington, DC: American Psychiatric Publishing.

Asad, T. (2003). *Formations of the secular: Christianity, Islam, modernity.* Stanford, CA: Stanford University Press.

Asad, T. (2018). *Secular translations: nation-state, modern self, and calculative reason.* New York, NY: Columbia University Press.

Balboni, T. A., VanderWeele, T. J., Doan-Soares, S. D., Long, K. N., Ferrell, B. R., Fitchett, G.,.. Koh, H. K. (2022). Spirituality in serious illness and health. *Journal of the American Medical Association,* 328(2), 184–197.

Bibby, R. W. (2011). *Beyond the gods and back: religion's demise and rise and why it matters.* Lethbridge, AB: Project Canada Books.

Bibby, R. W. (2017). *Resilient gods: being pro-religious, low religious, or no religious in Canada.* Vancouver, BC, and Toronto, ON: UBC Press.

Casanova, J. (2011). The secular, secularizations, secularisms. In C. Calhoun, M. Juergensmeyer, & J. van Antwerpen (Eds.), *Rethinking secularism* (pp. 54–74). Oxford, UK: Oxford University Press.

Cozolino, L. (2017). *The neuroscience of psychotherapy: healing the social brain* (3rd ed.). New York, NY: Norton.

Durie, M. (1985). A Māori perspective of health. *Social Science & Medicine, 20*(5), 483–486.

Foucault, M. (1973). *The birth of the clinic: an archaeology of medical perception.* (A. S. Smith, Trans.) New York, NY: Vintage Random House.

Gamma, E. (2023, May 1). *Left brain vs. right brain: hemispheric dominance.* Retrieved May 5, 2023, from Simply Psychology: https://www.simplypsychology.org/left-brain-vs-right-brain.html

Gerkin, C. V. (1986). *Widening the horizons: pastoral responses to a fragmented society.* Philadelphia, PA: Westminster.

Gillespie, M. A. (2008). *The theological origins of modernity.* Chicago, IL, and London, UK: University of Chicago Press.

Graham, E. (2017). *Apologetics without apology: speaking of God in a world troubled by religion.* Eugene, OR: Cascade Books.

Habermas, J. (1984). *The theory of communicative action* (Vol. 1: Reason and the rationalization of society) (T. McCarthy, Trans.). Cambridge, UK: Polity Press.

Habermas, J. (1992). *Postmetaphysical thinking: philosophical essays* (W. M. Hohengarten, Trans.). Cambridge, MA: MIT Press.

Habermas, J. (2003). *Truth and justification* (B. Fultner (Ed.) & B. Fultner, Trans.). Cambridge, MA: MIT Press.

Habermas, J. (2008). *Between naturalism and religion: philosophical essays* (C. Cronin, Trans.). Cambridge, UK: Polity Press.

Habermas, J. (2010). An awareness of what is missing. In J. Habermas, *An awareness of what is missing: faith and reason in a post-secular age* (C. Cronin, Trans., pp. 15–23). Cambridge, UK: Polity Press.

Habermas, J., & Taylor, C. (2011). Dialogue. In E. Mendieta, & J. van Antwerpen (Eds.), *The power of religion in the public sphere* (pp. 60–69). New York, NY: Columbia University Press.

Heard, C. P., Scott, J., & Yeo, S. (2022). Spiritual care professionals as unit-based interdisciplinary team members? Considering patient and staff perceptions in a forensic mental health care setting. *Journal of Pastoral Care & Counseling,* online pre-publication. doi:10.1177/1542050221092317

Ho, J. Q., & et al. (2017). Spiritual care in the intensive care unit: a narrative review. *Journal of Intensive Care Medicine,* online pre-publication. doi:10.1177/0885066617712677

Hogue, D. A. (2003). *Remembering the future, imagining the past: story ritual and the human brain.* Eugene, OR: Wipf & Stock.

Höltge, J., Cowden, R. G., Lee, M.T., Bechara, A. O., Joynt, S., Kamble, S.,.. VanderWeele, T. J. (2023). A systems perspective on human flourishing: exploring cross-country similarities and differences of a multisystemic flourishing network. *Journal of Positive psychology, 18*(5), 695–710.

Kimmerer, R. W. (2013). *Braiding sweetgrass: Indigenous wisdom, scientific knowledge, and the teachings of plants*. Minneapolis, MN: Milkweed Editions.

Lasair, S. (2021). Truth in pastoral practice: a firmer foundation for contested territory. *International Journal of Practical Theology*, 25(2), 166–183. doi:10.1515/ijpt-2021-0004

Lasair, S., & Sinclair, S. (2018). Family and patient spiritual narratives in the ICU: bridging disclosures through compassion. In G. Netzer (Ed.), *Families in the intensive care unit: a guide to understanding, engaging, and supporting at the bedside* (pp. 289–300). Cham, Switzerland: Springer.

Lilla, M. (2007). *The stillborn God: religion, politics and the modern West*. New York, NY: Vintage.

Lipton, B. H. (2016). *The biology of belief: unleashing the power of consciousness, matter, and miracles* (10th anniversary ed.). Carlsbad, CA: Hay House.

Lombrazo, T. (2013, December 2). *The truth about the left brain/right brain relationship*. Retrieved January 17, 2023, from NPR Cosmos & Culture: Commentary on Science and Culture: https://www.npr.org/sections/13.7/2013/12/02/248089436/the-truth-about-the-left-brain-right-brain-relationship

Marsh, T. N., Cote-Meek, S., Toulouse, P., Najavits, L. M., & Young, N. L. (2015). The application of two-eyed seeing decolonizing methodology in qualitative and quantitative research for the treatment of intergenerational trauma and substance use disorders. *International Journal of Qualitative Methods*, 14(5), 1–13. doi:10.1177/1609406915618046

Martin, D. H. (2012). Two-eyed seeing: a framework for understanding Indigenous and non-Indigenous approaches to Indigenous health research. *Canadian Journal of Nursing Research*, 44(2), 20–42.

McGilchrist, I. (2009). *The master and his emissary: the divided brain and the making of the Western world*. New Haven, CYT, and London, UK: Yale University Press.

McGilchrist, I. (2013). Hemisphere differences and their relevance to psychotherapy. In D. J. Siegel & M. Solomon (Eds.), *Healing moments in psychotherapy* (pp. 67–88). New York, NY: Norton.

McGilchrist, I. (2021). *The matter with things: our brains, our delusions and the unmaking of the world*. London, UK: Perspectiva Press.

Milbank, J. (2006). *Theology & social theory: beyond secular reason* (2nd ed.). Malden, MA: Blackwell.

Milbank, J. (2013). *Beyond secular order: the representation of being and the representation of the people*. Oxford, UK: Wiley.

Moeke-Maxwell, T., Collier, A., Wiles, J., Williams, L., Black, S., & Gott, M. (2020). Bereaved families' perspectives of end-of-life care: towards a bicultural Whare Tapa Whā olderperson's palliative care model. *Journal of Cross-Cultural Gerontology*, 35(2), 177–193. Retrieved from 10.1007/s10823-020-09397-6

O'Connor, T. S., & Meakes, E. (2021). Three emerging spiritual practices in the Canadian association for spiritual care (CASC): from pastoral care and counselling to multi-faith, evidence-based spiritual care and psycho-spiritual therapy. *Journal of Pastoral Care & Counseling*, 75(4), 278–283. doi:10.1177/15423050211036662

Panikkar, R. (2010). *The rhythm of being: the unbroken trinity—the Gifford lectures*. Maryknoll, NY: Orbis.

Peltier, C. (2018). An application of two-eyed seeing: Indigenous research methods with participatory research. *International Journal of Qualitative Methods*, 17(1), 1–12. doi:10.1177/1609406918812346

Puchalski, C., et al. (2009). Improving the quality of spiritual care as a dimension of palliative care: the report of the consensus conference. *Journal of Palliative Medicine*, 12(10), 642–656.

Puchalski, C., Vitillo, R., Hull, S., & Reller, N. (2014). Improving the spiritual dimension of whole person care: reaching national and international consensus. *Journal of Palliative Medicine*, 17(6), 642–656.

Rogers, C. R. (1961). *On becoming a person: a therapist's view of psychotherapy*. Boston, MA: Houghton Mifflin.

Root, A. (2017). *Faith formation in a secular age: responding to the church's obsession with youthfulness*. Grand Rapids, MI: Baker Academic.

Shmerling, R. H. (2022, March 24). *Right brain/left brain, right?* Retrieved January 17, 2023, from Harvard Health Blog: https://www.health.harvard.edu/blog/right-brainleft-brain-right-2017082512222

Siegel, D. J., & Solomon, M. (Eds.). (2013). *Healing moments in psychotherapy*. New York, NY: Norton.

Sinclair, S., Beamer, K., Hack, T. F., McClement, S., Raffin-Bouchal, S., Chochinov, H. M., & Hagan, N. A. (2017). Sympathy, empathy, and compassion: a grounded theory study of palliative care patients' understandings, experiences, and preferences. *Palliative Medicine*, 31(5), 437–47.

Sinclair, S., McClement, S., Raffin-Bouchal, S., Hack, T. F., Hagan, N. A., McConnell, S., & Chochinov, H. M. (2016). Compassion in health care: an empirical model. *Journal of Pain and Symptom Management*, 51(2), 193–203.

Smith, J. K. (2014). *How (not) to be secular: reading Charles Taylor*. Grand Rapids, MI: Eerdmans.

Stilos, K., Ford, B., Chakraborty, A., & Takahashi, D. (2021). Spiritual care as part of an interprofessional model for debriefing on an oncology unit. *Journal of Pastoral Care & Counseling*–75(3), 158–162. doi:10.1177/15423050211021387

Taylor, C. (2007). *A secular age*. Cambridge, MA: Belknap Harvard University Press.

Taylor, C. (2011a). Western secularity. In C. Calhoun, M. Juergensmeyer, & J. van Antwerpen (Eds.), *Rethinking secularism* (pp. 31–53). Oxford, UK: Oxford University Press.

Taylor, C. (2011b). Why we need a radical redefinition of secularism. In E. Mendieta & J. van Antwerpen (Eds.), *The power of religion in the public sphere: Judith Butler, Jurgen Habermas, Charles Taylor, Cornel West* (pp. 34–59). New York, NY: Columbia University Press.

Timmins, F., Naughton, M. T., Plakas, S., & Pesut, B. (2015). Suporting patients' and families' religious and spiritual needs in ICU—can we do more? *British Association of Critical Care Nursing*, 20(3), 115–117.

van der Kolk, B. A. (2014). *The body keeps the score: brain, mind, and body in the healing of trauma* (Kindle ebook ed.). New York, NY: Penguin.

VanderWeele, T. J. (2017). Religion and health: a synthesis. In M. J. Balboni & J. R. Peteet (Eds.), *Spirituality and religion within the culture of medicine: from evidence to practice* (pp. 357–401). New York, NY: Oxford University Press.

VanderWeele, T. J. (2020). Spiritual well-being and human flourishing: conceptual, causal, and policy relations. In A. B. Cohen (Ed.), *Religion and human flourishing* (pp. 43–54). Waco, TX: Baylor University Press.

Visser, A., Damen, A., & Schuhmann, C. (2022). Goals of chaplaincy care: a scoping review of Dutch literature. *Journal of Health Care Chaplaincy*, online pre-publication. doi:10.1080/008854726.2022.2080964

Ward, G. (2014). *Unbelievable: why we believe and why we don't.* London, UK: I. B. Tauris.

Williams, R. (2012). *Faith in the public square.* London, UK: Bloomsbury.

Williams, R. (2014). *The edge of words: God and the habits of language.* London, UK: Bloomsbury.

Framing Reality

Spirituality's Fundamental Processes

Two

INTRODUCTION

The last chapter argued that emotional, intuitive, and relational concerns are central to professional spiritual care. In practical terms, this means that Spiritual Care Practitioners are primarily concerned with assisting their clients to build, maintain, and enhance their relationships with all reality. Yet due to their professional training, Practitioners often use the language, concepts, images, theories, rituals, and practices of various religious/secular/cultural traditions to assist with this work. However, as I and many of my colleagues have experienced, it is possible to have deeply spiritual conversations with clients for whom God and other traditional religious themes are completely irrelevant. These kinds of experiences therefore demand the questions, what is spirituality, and how can it be distinguished from religion/culture/tradition? The previous chapter used the consensus healthcare definition as an initial entry point into this territory. In this chapter, the structures of human spirituality will be described in detail. Specifically, I will show how a person's religious/cultural/traditional affiliations are deeply connected to how they frame and experience their realities. A person's religion, culture, or tradition thus provides vocabularies, grammars, concepts, rituals, and practices that a person might use to explain how and why they experience reality in specific ways. However, a person is not their religion or culture or tradition. By exploring spirituality in depth, then, this chapter will show how spirituality integrates all dimensions of a person's identity, including their religion, culture, and tradition. Nevertheless, it will also be clear that a person's spirituality is not synonymous with their religion, culture, or tradition—spirituality includes much more than just a person's beliefs, concepts, rituals, practices, and so on.

DOI: 10.4324/9781003466147-3

To illustrate all this, this chapter therefore spends significant space engaging a single patient case. I will begin by describing how I came to know this patient, and then describe how I came to understand much of his spirituality over the course of our relationship. Consequently, the discussion will begin with a description of this patient and alternate between concrete details about his case and a general conceptual description of spirituality and its dynamics. As the discussion proceeds, spirituality will be shown to be deeply connected to an individual's experiences in time, particularly how they experience themself and their life's story in any given moment. I will also demonstrate that a person's spirituality is not just their abstract beliefs about the nature of ultimate reality. Rather, a person's spirituality is manifest in their behaviors, body language, actions, attitudes, and so on. Religious language and concepts can play specific roles in a person's spirituality, but this is not always the case. This chapter will show that whatever language a person uses to describe their daily events and experiences cannot be separated from how they perceive and experience reality. Therefore, religious, cultural, or traditional terms, concepts, and ideas are just as "everyday" as descriptions of whatever detergent or soap a person uses to wash their laundry. With all these things in mind, then, I now turn toward describing my encounters with my patient Jeff.

JEFF'S UNDERSTANDING OF REALITY

The first time I met Jeff, I was a CPE student. I was in my first unit of CPE and still working to find my way around the surgery unit in the hospital where I was doing my clinical placement. One day I was on this surgery unit and I saw a man rolling himself through the hallway in a wheelchair. My CPE supervisor-educator had always encouraged us to engage people when it seemed like no one else was paying attention to them, so I approached this man and introduced myself. The man introduced himself as Jeff and he agreed to have a conversation with me. As was my usual practice, I asked Jeff what had brought him to hospital, and he shared that he had a medical condition that often brought him to hospital. In fact, he had just received his fourth surgery to address some complications produced by his medical condition. Unfortunately, this condition was incurable, and Jeff knew he was living a life that would only proceed with increasing disability and illness. This reality weighed heavily on Jeff, and his affect reflected as much as I invited him to explore it with me.

Now, at the time, I would often ask patients directly what their religious affiliation was (I still do this in my practice, but only if it is evident that a patient's religious beliefs are important for them). When I asked Jeff this question, he hesitated for a moment, but then said he believed in fairies and earth spirits. I asked him how he came to see the world this way, and his response was non-committal, something to the effect of: "I just see it that way." I tried to explore these beliefs a bit more with him, and as I did so, I got the distinct impression that Jeff had not reflected much on his understanding of reality. Rather, it seemed his beliefs helped him to counterbalance his bleak medical future; they provided a magical view of the world that was in stark contrast to everything Jeff had come to expect about where his medical condition was going to take him. It was evident Jeff did not have personal relationships with fairies or earth spirits, but his belief that these entities existed permitted him to have at least a slim hope that reality might be drastically different from everything his physicians and surgeons told him. Jeff's cognitive beliefs about reality therefore helped him to find relief from the emotional turmoil he inevitably experienced in response to his incurable and degenerative disease.

Overwhelmed by this reality, I didn't know how best to respond. I soon brought the interaction to an end and spent a long time reflecting on it afterward. While I can't explicitly recall where my reflections led me in response to that initial interaction, all this came back to me when I met Jeff in hospital again, some years later. He had been admitted to hospital for yet another surgery, and it was clear his disease had indeed produced further disability in him. It was also clear Jeff's relationships with his wife and children were becoming increasingly troubled, in part due to how his disease was affecting his daily functioning. In response to all this, I remember asking Jeff what helped him get through his recurring hospital admissions and the progression of his disease. This time Jeff did not mention fairies or earth spirits. Instead, he stated he was simply curious to see whatever might happen to him next. This time I was able to engage this statement from Jeff better than I had navigated our previous interaction. I acknowledged the heaviness of his insight. After letting Jeff respond to this observation for a few minutes, I asked what supports he had to help him through the tough times. He named a few people, but he also said that talking with people like me helped him feel a bit better. I therefore asked whether I or someone else from the spiritual care team could connect with him again in the coming days. He said that yes, he would welcome that. I also asked whether it would be helpful for him to talk with a social worker who might be able to organize supports for him once he was discharged. Again, he agreed that that was probably a good idea. I therefore made a point of meeting with Jeff as often as I could over the six weeks during which he was in hospital; I also requested that a social worker consult with him. As will be shown below, during the time I worked with Jeff, I became quite familiar with his spirituality, and with what growth in spiritual health can look like.

Now, Jeff's story reminds me of how often Spiritual Care Practitioners encounter human tragedy when providing care in healthcare contexts. Whether it is due to significant illness or a sudden accident, death, disability, and sorrow can all be encountered daily in healthcare environments. Yet, amid it all, Spiritual Care Practitioners are called to engage patients and their families, no matter what they are experiencing, and somehow invite them to consider or engage their realities differently (see e.g., Cadge, 2023). Due to the significant life experiences through which these many individuals are living, this work needs to proceed gently and compassionately. Much of it therefore involves connecting with what I call a person's "frame for reality" and working within this frame's contours to invite that person toward personal integration rather than toward fragmentation. As discussed in the previous chapter, much of this work can often involve assisting clients to recover a proper holistic balance between various parts of themselves. More specifically, it is typically oriented toward assisting clients to incorporate whatever they are experiencing into the broader contours of their life's narrative (see e.g., Lasair, 2018b).

In the case being discussed in this chapter, Jeff had lived with his disease for so long it was an inescapable reality for him. In fact, his comments in our later encounters demonstrated how much his disease had come to dominate his lived experience. A recurring theme for Jeff during our relationship was that he was no longer able to work. So, when Jeff shared that the one thing keeping him going was his curiosity regarding what was going to happen to him next, this enabled me to understand that one of the few things occupying him was the question of how best to manage his disease. It was also evident that Jeff was having to actively engage some deep feelings of resentment directed toward him from his wife and potentially also his children. It therefore seemed Jeff's beliefs about fairies and earth spirits helped to distract him from his daily realities of living with chronic degenerative disease and the strains in his close relationships—I discovered as much during our first encounter. In other words, Jeff's beliefs provided some counterbalance to the despair he felt in response to living with his disease. But in terms of giving him some concrete tools for holding the realities of his disease in creative tension with a deeply examined understanding of reality, it was clear more work needed to be done.

Initially, Jeff seemed disinclined to undertake this work; during our first interactions he did not present like a highly reflective person. However, as I consistently made contact with him during his admission, I did build a trusting relationship with him. In that relationship, I used humor and other gentle ways of offering relief from the despair that was never far from his consciousness. This gentle use of humor enabled me to build good rapport with Jeff, and that rapport gradually helped us to get into deeper and deeper territory as our relationship progressed. Put in theoretical terms, this approach accepted Jeff's frame for reality for what it was, but then used various techniques to expand it into other experiential domains that were not accessible to him during our initial interactions. Over time I saw Jeff find several sources of joy and hope in his life. What, then, is a frame for reality, and how does it function in a person's life and spirituality?

JEFF'S FRAME FOR REALITY

As discussed in the last chapter, the consensus healthcare definition indicates that spirituality is a "dynamic and intrinsic aspect of humanity through which persons seek ultimate meaning, purpose, and transcendence, and experience relationship with self, family, others, community, society, nature, and the significant or sacred" (Puchalski, Vitillo, Hull, & Reller, 2014, p. 646). In my analysis of this definition in Chapter One, I suggested its key clause is "through which." By this I meant to show that "through which" indicates that spirituality is bound up with the various processes that enable an individual to "build, maintain, and enhance their relationships with all reality," as I suggested in my own definition of spiritual care. Spiritual Care

Practitioners specifically target this aspect of a person's being in their clinical work. However, this clinical work assumes that spiritual care clients already have pre-existing relationships with all reality (Lasair, 2021; McGilchrist, 2021; Panikkar, 2010; Puchalski, Vitillo, Hull, & Reller, 2014). It is therefore a significant part of a Spiritual Care Practitioner's role to assess the nature of these relationships and work with their clients to build, maintain, and enhance them, depending on the specific issues with which the clients are presenting.

As I worked with Jeff, it was clear his disease had affected all aspects of his life. A recurring theme for Jeff was that earlier in life he had enjoyed his career, yet now he was no longer able to work due to the progression of his disease. Jeff's relationships with his wife and children were also becoming increasingly strained. Before his admission to hospital, Jeff required more and more help with his daily activities, and Jeff felt his wife and children did not support him in the ways he needed. Jeff was therefore feeling more resentment toward them, and they were also feeling more resentment toward Jeff because of his physical needs and limitations. All these realities contributed to the feelings of despair that were so evident in Jeff's life.

Time-Bound Narratives

Now, as I talked with Jeff while he was in my care, I was aware I needed to understand his disclosures about his life as governed by time. As French philosopher Paul Ricoeur indicates (following St. Augustine), time is experienced in three different aspects: the present-past, the present-present, and the present-future (Ricoeur, 1984, 1991; Lasair, 2020).[1] The present-past is what is past for a person in this present moment; the present-present is what is present for a person in the present; and the present-future is what is future for a person given their present realities. According to this scheme, time moves linearly from the past, through the present, and into the future. Yet, whatever we perceive as past or future is always experienced in the present and needs to be understood as such. Therefore, I knew that whatever Jeff was experiencing when I met with him needed to be seen as products of his past as experienced by him in the present. This was particularly the case when considering his overwhelming feelings of despair. At the beginning of our work together it was at least partially unknown where Jeff's future might have taken him. Yet it was clear that Jeff's experiences of living with his disease and its social and relational consequences had affected him deeply.

Prior to his disease's taking an acute turn, Jeff felt he had had a promising career. From his telling of it, his relationships with his wife and children had also been happy and fulfilling at that time. Yet all that shifted once Jeff's disease took a turn for the worse. Now he had no career prospects, and his relationships with his wife and children were becoming increasingly strained. Jeff never shared this question with me explicitly, but I suspect that at some level he was asking what he might have done to deserve all this. Given this background and the prognosis for his disease, Jeff's feelings of despair were entirely understandable. Life had become very difficult for him, particularly after his disease began its downward turn. It was therefore not surprising that Jeff found little reason for hope amid his daily realities. This was especially the case given that Jeff perceived his life as having been mostly good prior to the change in his medical status. I was therefore able to assess that Jeff's present experience of limitation and disability was likely prompting him to idealize the parts of his past that were not so dominated by his disease.

Socially and Culturally Bound Narratives

Part of Jeff's despair was also linked to some of the social and cultural themes connected with his story. As I indicated in the last chapter, it is impossible for a person to experience their spirituality apart from their social, cultural, political, and linguistic contexts. In my Canadian context, it is common to receive economic updates in the news media; as a society we value a healthy economy. One indicator of a person's apparent social value, therefore, is their capacity to have gainful employment and to contribute to our society's economic well-being. This sense of value is further expanded to include a person's individual wealth or affluence, as measured by how much disposable income they earn. Western cultures generally value open displays of wealth or affluence to the extent that poverty and unemployment can often be stigmatized by politicians, policy makers, and news media, depending on their political orientations. Jeff's unemployability thus weighed heavily upon him. As a man who experienced his masculinity in fairly traditional ways, the fact that he could not work affected Jeff deeply. This was because Jeff's health prevented him from conforming to the traditional Western cultural expectation that men ought to be breadwinners for their families.

It was therefore not surprising that Jeff shared repeatedly that his unemployment was one of the main points of tension between him and his wife. She resented him because he could no longer work. Instead, she now had to work long hours simply to make ends meet. When Jeff was able to work, such long hours were not necessary. As a result, it was easier for their family to spend time together and enjoy one another's company before Jeff's health changed. Now, in contrast, Jeff's wife worked, their children had their own lives, and Jeff was "putting in time" managing his disease. So, in Jeff's own view, he could contribute neither to society nor to his own home. Consequently, the most significant feelings Jeff received from his family—and from himself—were frustration and resentment.

Narratively Bound Cognitive Beliefs about Reality

Under such circumstances, the possibility that beings might exist who could provide love and affection—and even magical cures for illness and disease—was very appealing. But this possibility begged the question, did Jeff have any experiential evidence for his beliefs in fairies and earth spirits? In all my interactions with him, Jeff did not present much information regarding any concrete experiences he might have had with fairies and earth spirits. I therefore needed to be cautious about how I engaged his beliefs regarding these entities. Nevertheless, as I hinted in the opening paragraphs in this chapter, Jeff's beliefs were only part of his spirituality. How best, then, to understand spirituality's structures and functions?

SPIRITUALITY'S SHAPES AND CONTOURS

Spirituality's Temporal Dimension

Based on the foregoing discussion, it is evident that a person's individual spirituality operates in multiple dimensions simultaneously (see Figure 2.1 for a visual representation of these dimensions; see also Lasair, 2020). In one dimension, spirituality is very attuned to the dynamics of time (Ricoeur, 1984, 1991; Lasair, 2020). In Jeff's life this was manifest in the differences between what his life looked like before his disease took a turn for the worse and what it looked like afterward. I could only meet Jeff in the present, but it was impossible to ignore the reality that, in many respects, he was still working through this change that had occurred long before even the first time I met him. Concretely, Jeff's experience illustrates something that Paul Ricoeur discusses at length: the competing forces of consistency and change (Ricoeur, 1984, 1991, 1992; Lasair, 2020). According to Ricoeur, these forces inform our movement through time. When life is mostly consistent, it can seem boring or stagnant. However, if we experience too much change at once, we can easily become overwhelmed because very little seems stable anymore (Lasair, 2020). So, any person must work toward achieving the right balance between consistency and change in their life.

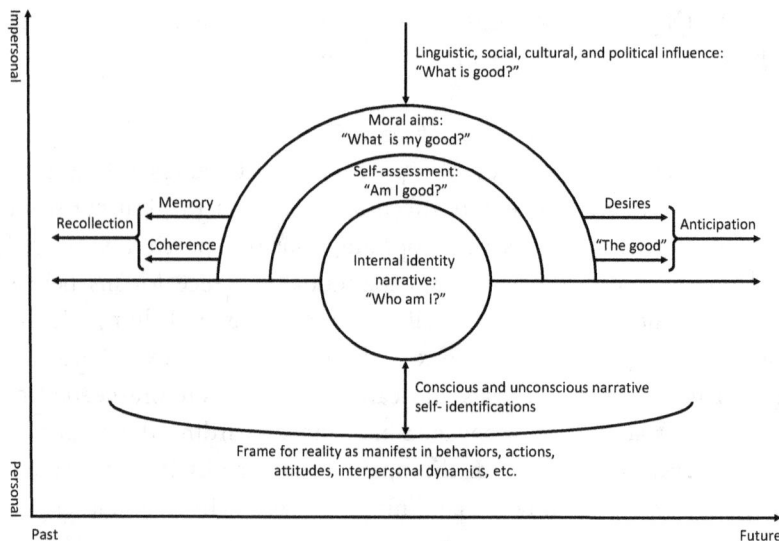

Figure 2.1 A Narrative Model of Spirituality

Source: This figure is modified from S. Lasair (2020). A narrative approach to spirituality and spiritual care in healthcare. *Journal of Religion and Health*, 59(3): 1532.

Unfortunately, there is no preset formula as to what this balance between consistency and change ought to look like. Finding the right balance depends, in part, on a person's temperament and their individual preference. At the beginning of our relationship Jeff perceived very few changes in his life, mainly due to the limitations caused by his disease. This reality was one of his main reasons for despair. The way Jeff's disease dominated his present experience also caused him to yearn for the past, when his disease was not such a significant part of his daily existence. Because Jeff's medical status had changed suddenly in the past, it seemed he still needed to grieve some of the losses this change had incurred. His yearning for the past was one expression of this grief, as was his perceived experience of stagnancy in the preset. As a Spiritual Care Practitioner, I addressed these dynamics by helping Jeff mourn some of these losses over the course of our work together. I also helped him to recognize how consistency and change were still both active in his life. I will describe how I did this below.

Spirituality's Impersonal to Personal Dimensions

In spirituality's other dimension, it is possible to identify various levels of impersonal and personal forces (see Figure 2.1). At the most impersonal level we find the cultural values that are prevalent in mass media, advertising, and cultural, philosophical, and political discourses. As these discourses become more personal, there is a mediating level where a person chooses what values they will pursue in life (Taylor, 1989, 2012; Lasair, 2018a, 2020). For many, these are very basic: earning a good income, establishing a good home, achieving a comfortable and enjoyable life for themself and their loved ones. In previous publications, I have called these goals a person's "moral aims" (Lasair, 2018a, 2019, 2020; see "Moral aims" in Figure 2.1). These aims are moral because they all embody ideas or objects that are considered good according to a person's social, cultural, political, and linguistic contexts; these concrete aims are different aspects of what might be called "the good life" (Taylor, 1989, 2012; Lasair, 2020). Now, these aims are so deeply embedded in our cultures, politics, and societies that it is almost impossible to question them. This is because these aims depict how any given culture, and individuals within that culture, understand what the good life ought to look like. In Jeff's life, his early promising career showed he was generally aligned with these cultural values. His enjoyable relationships with his wife and children at that time demonstrated similar alignment.

As we live our lives, however, all of us experience shifts in how our lives align or do not align with the cultural values we choose to pursue (see "Self-assessment" in Figure 2.1). Yet because we have internalized these values to greater or lesser extents, we are forced to choose how we assess our own personal value based on our perceived alignments with these broader cultural values (Taylor, 1989; Lasair, 2018a, 2020). It is often easy for those who experience their alignments as straightforward to assess themselves favorably (Lasair, 2018a). Those whose alignments have been persistently challenged, in contrast, often assess themselves less favorably (Lasair, 2018a; Madigan, 2019; Doehring, 2015). These self-assessments are less favorable because it is much more difficult for such people and groups to embody what the dominant culture presents as the good life (Doehring, 2015; Madigan, 2019). Consequently, when these people and groups do not feel capable of living in alignment with what the dominant culture says is valuable, it then becomes easy for them (and others) to question whether they do indeed have value (Lasair, 2018a; Madigan, 2019). In Jeff's case, this dynamic was evident in his experiences of illness and of being unemployable. This dynamic was also reinforced in the tensions between Jeff and his wife. Jeff's wife resented Jeff because he was not able to work, and Jeff resented his wife in part for persistently reminding him of this reality. As a Spiritual Care Practitioner, I addressed these dynamics indirectly, but over the course of our relationship Jeff learned how he could see value in himself. However, during our initial interactions there were also some other dynamics to consider.

As a person experiences themself as moving through life in a certain way, they begin to internalize the stories they receive from others and from the culture at large (White, 2007; White & Epston, 1990; Madigan, 2019; Lasair, 2020; see "Internal identity narrative" in Figure 2.1), and these stories can be either positive or negative. As discussed above, a person can assess themself as having either value or little value, both culturally and personally, depending on the stories they have internalized. In Jeff's case it was evident he had internalized the stories he received from our Canadian culture, and from his wife, both of which communicated to him that his current value was significantly less compared to the value he had before his disease took over. In fact, Jeff's feelings of despair could be directly correlated with how he currently perceived both his personal and cultural value.

However, depending on how a person responds to these internalized stories, one of several things can happen (see "Conscious and unconscious narrative identifications" in Figure 2.1). In one scenario, they can blame those around them, and even the rest of reality, for not taking care of them in the way they feel they ought to be taken care of. There were dimensions of this dynamic in Jeff's experience insofar as he felt resentment toward his wife and children for not supporting him in the ways he felt he needed. This resentment and blame fueled Jeff's despair because he could not see a way out of his situation. In another scenario, in contrast, a person can start to build beliefs around themself that offer some escape from their daily realities. Sometimes this dynamic is called "spiritual bypassing" (Masters, 2010). In these situations, people use their beliefs about reality (religious, secular, or cultural) to avoid dealing with whatever is causing them distress or disturbance. Again, there were elements of this dynamic in Jeff's situation: his beliefs in fairies and earth spirits were a mild form of this. I call Jeff's beliefs a mild form of spiritual bypassing because it did not seem he invested too much time or energy in using them to protect himself against his concrete experiences of reality. Finally, there is what I call an "integrative scenario." In this scenario people work hard to accept their current realities for what they are while also recognizing they are neither fully bad nor fully good. Instead, such people see there can be both gift and tragedy in their experience (Lasair, 2017). These people also see that whatever gifts and tragedies they experience need to be held in tension with one another so the people can recognize and embrace the fullness of whatever they are living through. In my work with Jeff, I was very intentional in inviting him to come to this place of recognition and embrace. I believe the goal of all spiritual care work is to invite clients into this place. In the chapters that follow, I will describe some concrete steps that can assist clients to arrive here. For now, however, there are a few more things worth mentioning.

Each of the dynamics I have been describing (i.e., the desire to blame, escape, or to integrate) are expressions of a person's frame for reality (see "Frame for reality..." in Figure 2.1). What the desires to blame or escape indicate is that there is something within such a person's way of engaging reality that prevents them from seeing how they might shape and influence their realities as they move into the future. In some ways, part of addressing how such a person engages such limitations begins with understanding how they perceive their realities—perception will be the topic of Chapter Three. At this stage, however, it is worth briefly considering how religious beliefs and religious language contribute to a person's frame for reality. Such beliefs and language are constituent components of a person's frame. Again, this topic will be covered in increasing depth in subsequent chapters.

RELIGION WITHIN THIS APPROACH

In the example discussed throughout this chapter, it is possible to describe how the resentments between Jeff and his wife manifested a dynamic similar to some Buddhist teachings about karma. In some popular understandings, karma is a metaphysical force that often informs how people move through various incarnations over several lifetimes. So, someone with bad karma might incarnate as a lesser being in their next lifetime; someone with good karma might incarnate as a higher being in their next lifetime. In contrast, for example, the well-known Tibetan Buddhist thinker Chögyam Trungpa (2018) taught that karma does not primarily manifest in the dynamics of reincarnation. Rather, according to Trungpa (2018), karma manifests in the concrete interactions people share with all other beings, human and non-human alike. Negative karma occurs when a person treats another being unkindly. This behavior then incurs a negative karmic debt wherein unkindness needs to be repaid with further unkindness. Similarly, positive karma occurs when a person expresses excessive kindness or goodness to another being. In these scenarios, a positive karmic debt is incurred wherein kindness or goodness needs to be similarly repaid. Now, somewhat surprisingly, Trungpa (2018) did not argue that people ought to live their lives incurring only positive karmic debts. Trungpa argued instead that people ought to live their lives incurring no karmic debts, neither positive nor negative. From his perspective, it is only in living life this way that people can become truly liberated from the throes of karma while also empowering others to do likewise. If Jeff were a Buddhist, this line of reasoning could have been one option to explore regarding how he might address his relationship with his wife.

From other religious perspectives, the wisdom writings of the Jewish Hebrew Scriptures (TaNaKh in Judaism, the Old Testament in Christianity) contain much advice regarding conflict. Particularly, readers are urged to maintain healthy relationships with their families and neighbors because this is what God intended (e.g., Leviticus 19:17–18; Psalm 133). Similar advice is offered in the Christian New Testament when St. Paul urges the members of the churches to whom he writes to maintain good relationships among themselves (e.g., Romans 14:1–12; 1 Corinthians 6:1–11). Paul urges these communities to do so because this is how they show the Christ to the world around them. Furthermore, when considering the mystical or contemplative traditions in both Judaism and Christianity, Jews might argue that conflict needs to be actively managed. When it is not, conflict brings too much divine wrath into the world (e.g., Scholem, 1954, 1991). Rather, from these Jewish perspectives, living in accordance with Torah and actively performing good deeds (mitzvoth) for one another helps to counterbalance divine wrath. In this way Jews can participate in tikkun 'olam, or the repairing of the world. Similarly, contemplative Christians might argue that conflict can be actively transformed into deeper manifestations of the Christ's presence within and between those directly involved in the conflict (e.g., Panikkar, 2004; Bourgeault, 2008). But this means that each person must let go of whatever is within themself that perpetuates the conflict—anger, frustration, impatience, resentment, etc. By coming to recognize that each person is an embodiment of God's image, contemplative Christians can imitate Jesus the Christ by emptying themselves of whatever might be preventing themselves or others from fully manifesting this image in relation to one another. In some cases, this process is characterized as letting go of the false self so the true self that is found in God can come to the fore (Merton, 2007). By living into this true self, contemplative Christians become channels for God's love to flow through them into the world. In doing so, they embody the Christ's presence for those around them (Panikkar, 2004). Contemplative Christians embody this presence by living a life characterized by death and resurrection (i.e., the death of the false self for the resurrection of the true self), as exemplified by Jesus the Christ (Panikkar, 2004; Bourgeault, 2008; Merton, 2007).

Because Jeff understood none of these beliefs as his own, it was difficult to introduce any of them as potential resources in his relationship with his wife. And, because Jeff's beliefs about fairies and earth spirits were under-developed, these quasi-neo-pagan beliefs did not provide him with much insight either. The result is that the interventions I initially used with him needed to be formulated in secular language. I did use some insights from my own Christian tradition to inform how I interacted with Jeff, but to use explicitly Christian language would have been inappropriate and perhaps alienating for him. Using such language would also have limited the impact of my interventions. My use of explicit Christian language could also have damaged the therapeutic relationship between Jeff and me. The result was that I worked hard to translate the religious teachings I drew upon into language and concepts that Jeff understood, somewhat similar to Jürgen Habermas' idea discussed in the last chapter. When I did this, it turned out my interventions with Jeff were quite successful. How to understand the nature of religious thought in such clinical situations? Canadian-British philosopher William Downes (2011) makes an important contribution in this regard.

According to Downes (2011), religious beliefs and language are deeply embedded in our daily realities. In fact, Downes posits that religious beliefs and language likely originated in humanity's capacity to apply a theory of mind to all sorts of natural objects at earlier stages of human evolution. According to Downes (2011), a theory of mind is a mental construct that allows those who possess it to ascribe consciousness to beings and objects outside themselves. So, as humans evolved, they ascribed consciousness to animals, rocks, trees, and all other beings they encountered daily (see also McGilchrist, 2021). Furthermore, as humans' cognitive capacities increased, they also began to ascribe consciousness to the cosmos and beyond. In making this argument, however, Downes (2011) is careful not to advocate strongly for or against the ultimate truth of such ascriptions. He rather indicates that human propensities to see God or other divine agents in daily events are as natural as any other part of human existence. Consequently, those who believe in God or other divine beings experience these entities as inextricable parts of their daily lives. To treat such beliefs as merely speculative propositions thus does a gross injustice to how such people live and experience their lives.

In light of these considerations, this last paragraph reveals why Jeff's purported beliefs in fairies and earth spirits were so unusual. They were not unusual simply because only a small minority of Canadians believe in fairies and earth spirits, which is statistically true. Rather, Jeff's beliefs were unusual because he had very little experiential basis for them. As Downes' argument indicates, beliefs in spiritual entities typically emerge when a person experiences something that suggests the existence of realities beyond the reach of their five bodily senses.

In contrast, as Jeff and I explored his beliefs over time, it became clear that fairies and earth spirits were more a matter of wishful thinking for him. It was therefore difficult to determine the extent to which Jeff considered fairies and earth spirits real entities with whom he might nurture significant relationships. As a result, it was initially difficult for me to establish what concrete differences Jeff's beliefs made in his daily experiences. It was for all these reasons that I assessed Jeff's beliefs as a potentially mild expression of spiritual bypassing when our work together began. At that point, Jeff's beliefs in fairies and earth spirits provided him the possibility that his lived realities might not conform to what his physicians and other caregivers were telling him. But, as the other parts of his story revealed, a larger part of Jeff was also very aware of the many difficulties contained within his daily life. As our work together continued, however, Jeff and I did explore how he might find beliefs that were more congruent with his daily experiences. In doing so, Jeff did begin to discover some more realistic hopes for his future. To discover these beliefs, Jeff needed to become more fully aware of his daily realities' shapes and contours, specifically how his own frame for reality contributed to them. He also needed to nurture openness to whatever insights this new awareness revealed to him. To accomplish all this, Jeff and I had to be very deliberate in engaging the temporal dimensions of his spirituality in greater depth.

FROM RECOLLECTION TO ANTICIPATION

Depending on what a person is experiencing in the present, it is possible for them to describe all their prior experiences as either positive, negative, or something else (Lasair, 2020; see "Recollection," "Memory," and "Coherence" in Figure 2.1). In other words, a person's current emotional experience can affect how they remember the past and even how they describe the sense of coherence they might or might not perceive in their life (Lasair, 2020). In Jeff's case, his feelings of despair at the beginning of our relationship dominated how he described his experiences of his disease. They also caused him to believe that everything in his life was good before his disease took its downward turn. However, as our work together unfolded, we discovered dimensions of his life that did not conform to this overall coherence he articulated for his story. Jeff and I therefore explored the various ways the coherence he articulated was grounded in his actual experience. As will be discussed in the next chapter, sometimes it is possible for people to become so attached to their stories about themselves that they cannot see how their actual lived realities transcend whatever stories might be told about them. Part of the integrative work Jeff and I did together was therefore to help him recognize that there were dimensions of his life that could never be fully captured in the stories he told about himself. Similar recognition can be accomplished even in brief encounters with almost any client. Techniques for accomplishing this goal will be described in more detail in Chapter Four.

Another way to see how a person's experiences are time-bound is to consider how they anticipate the future (Lasair, 2020; see "Anticipation," "Desires," and "The good" in Figure 2.1). Depending on what a person is experiencing in the present, they can anticipate the future with fear, apprehension, excitement, enthusiasm, or anxiety, to name but five possibilities. Part of Jeff's experience initially was the lack of consideration he could give to his future. His experiences at that point were so dominated by despair that he could not envision a future for himself that might be better than what he was experiencing currently. Jeff communicated this reality by indicating that the only thing keeping him going was his curiosity about what would happen to him next. Within the context of our interactions, I took this to mean that Jeff anticipated his disease would only produce increasing limitations and disability for him. According to the physicians who were overseeing his care, this expectation was reasonable given the normal trajectories of his disease. However, in my care for him, I invited Jeff to consider what he desired for himself, even within the context of what the physicians were saying about his disease. I then invited him to explore how these desires connected to his values regarding how he wanted to embody the good life. As with the question of how Jeff had been considering his past through his present perspective, this line of exploration invited him to detach himself from the coherence he had created for his life. In detaching himself from this coherence, it became possible for Jeff to consider different futures for himself (Lasair, 2020; Madigan, 2019; White, 2007). These potential futures did not involve a return to a past wherein his disease was not such a big part of his life. Rather, these futures still included his disease, given it was both incurable and progressive, but Jeff actively worked to envision realistic better-case scenarios for himself wherein he could meaningfully engage his family and his own sense of meaning and purpose, even within the confines of his limitations. All this growth was dependent on Jeff's capacity to work with his frame for reality and expand his explicit conscious awareness to include experiences that were not at that time part of this awareness. Drawing on Jeff's beliefs about the nature of reality was crucial in this process, to the point that he only partially maintained his beliefs in fairies and earth spirits. It therefore becomes possible to ask how best to understand what a trajectory toward improved spiritual health looks like in broad strokes. And how can Spiritual Care Practitioners assist their clients to move along such a trajectory, even when they may not see their clients beyond a single, 20-minute interaction, as is often the case in acute-care hospital settings?

INVITING CLIENTS TO RENEGOTIATE THEIR REALITIES

Each of the previous sections has been concerned with describing how a person's frame for reality manifests itself concretely. I have used the example of my patient Jeff to illustrate some of this concept's under-lying principles. However, these concrete descriptions are limited in the sense that they only partially reveal how a person can move toward greater spiritual health. For a fuller description of how a person can grow in their spiritual health, it is necessary to consider how frames for reality operate at more fundamental levels. This is because a spe-cific person's frame for reality informs and is informed by all the real-ities of which they are a part. The specific dynamics that substantiate this claim will be presented below. To describe these dynamics, it is helpful to draw upon the insights from science studies, particularly the writings of feminist physicist, philosopher, and social theorist Karen Barad (pronouns they/them).

Like few other theorists, Barad connects social phenomena to some of the fundamental physical realities of the universe. From Barad's (2007) perspective, physical realities inform social realities because our understandings of both kinds of phenomena are constructed pre-cisely by the various apparatuses we use to engage them. Electrons cannot be seen or measured without specifically designed scientific instruments and tools. Similarly, social phenomena exist precisely because of the physical, cultural, social, linguistic, and psychological factors that contribute to their varying emergences and preservations.

Now, Barad (2007) is very careful to state that this similarity between electrons and social phenomena is no mere analogy. Rather, from their perspective, this similarity illustrates the more fundamental reality that any specific phenomenon, whether it is physical or social or something else, can only be perceived and understood because of its relationships with absolutely everything else. Therefore, electrons could not be directly studied without specific social, scientific, philosophical, and technological advancements that enabled physicists to render these particles perceptible. Similarly, social and interpersonal phenomena cannot be engaged or transformed until they are also made perceptible for those who participate in them. Barad therefore describes what they call a process of intra-action wherein forces between various entangled phenomena act upon one another to produce systemic changes in how we perceive and experience reality. From Barad's perspective, these changes occur across all domains of reality, from physical to social, from religious to technological, and so on. For this reason, Barad's thought can be seen as an important source for the understanding of spirituality and spiritual care that is articulated in these pages.

In the case that has been explored in this chapter, one of Jeff's significant areas of distress was his relationship with his wife. She resented him for not being able to work, and Jeff resented her for reminding him of this reality and for not caring for him in the ways he thought he needed. As described above, this dynamic of blaming and resenting were two of several ways Jeff expressed his frame for reality in relation to his spouse; Jeff's frame for reality was built from all the emotional and cognitive dynamics mentioned above. Jeff brought his frame into his shared familial, social, and cultural spaces through his behaviors, actions, interactions, attitudes, body language, and so on. In this way, Jeff was connecting his internal world to his surrounding external physical, social, and cultural worlds through the medium of his body. Similarly, Jeff was interpreting the behaviors, actions, interactions, attitudes, and body language he received from his wife and children in various ways in his internal world. Again, Jeff received these dynamics from his wife and children through the medium of his body and its five senses. Jeff was therefore shaping his external environment through whatever dynamics were operational in his internal world. Jeff's internal world was likewise being shaped through whatever dynamics were operational in his external world, particularly in his interactions with his wife and children. Jeff's body was the concrete medium that allowed all these dynamic exchanges to happen.

To draw upon Barad's (2007) concepts, then, Jeff's relationship with his wife at the time I met him was a specific phenomenon that had emerged in response to their shared history together, the life they had created, Jeff's experiences of his disease, the changes his disease had rendered in his life and the lives of those who cared for him, and his resulting unemployability. In fact, this list expresses only very few of the various factors that enabled the challenging dynamics between Jeff and his wife to emerge—there were many more, most of which were impossible to name explicitly. All these factors, both those that could be named and those that could not, contributed to the relationship that Jeff and his wife shared. However, because Jeff was my patient in hospital, and because my spiritual care practice renders patients' frames for reality perceptible in clinical situations, my hypothesis was that if Jeff could learn to alter some of his frame's fundamental dynamics, that could potentially render positive benefit for his relationship with his wife, if not his overall situation in life.

To put all this concretely, as our work together progressed, it was evident Jeff had drawn specific conclusions about the characters of his wife and children. It was also evident that Jeff's dynamics in relation to his wife and children had changed based on how he assessed their respective characters. I therefore hypothesized that the wife's and children's dynamics in relation to Jeff had also likely changed in response to his new dynamic. Because Jeff's life was very much entangled with those of his wife and children, any change in his life would result in changes in their lives as well. Barad describes such dynamics using a metaphor from the physical sciences that they state characterizes the entire methodology underpinning their theory. This metaphor is diffraction.

According to Barad (2007), diffraction can be observed in nature when two rocks are dropped into water in close proximity to one another. Diffraction occurs when the waves from each rock's impact encounter one another. When a wave crest meets another wave crest, the resulting crest is higher than the two independent crests. Similarly, when a wave trough meets another wave trough, the resulting trough is lower than the two independent troughs. However, when a wave crest meets a wave trough, the two cancel each other. Barad (2007) uses this metaphor to describe the mutually entangled nature of all reality—a truth they indicate is confirmed by the findings of quantum physics. However, in describing diffraction, Barad also indicates that their use of this metaphor and methodology also necessitates that they account for meaningful differences between the various phenomena that contribute to an overall diffraction pattern. For example, if a larger and a smaller rock are dropped into a pond at the same time, the resulting wave pattern between them will be quite different from the wave pattern created by two rocks of relatively similar shape and size. Because Jeff was already feeling some resentment toward his wife when I began working with him, and because his wife was also feeling some resentment toward him, the meeting of these two feelings magnified what Jeff and his wife were already feeling about each other. To extrapolate from Barad's theory, therefore, if it might be possible for Jeff to generate a meaningful positive difference in his emotional responses to his wife's resentment, it might similarly be possible for the two of them to generate a different kind of diffraction pattern between themselves.

All this confirms what is becoming increasingly recognized in various quarters of healthcare research, namely that ill mental, emotional, and spiritual health can affect not only a person's own wellbeing, but also the wellbeing of others with whom they have contact. As mentioned in the previous chapter, this is one of the underlying principles of epigenetics, the emerging field that studies how environmental factors (physical, social, cultural, and interpersonal) affect individuals' medical health and wellbeing. As Hungarian-Canadian physician and thought-leader in the emerging healthcare paradigm Gabor Maté demonstrates (Maté & Maté, 2022), it is now becoming impossible to consider individuals as isolated from their social, cultural, political, familial, and interpersonal contexts. All these contexts can have significant effects on a person's physical, mental, emotional, and spiritual health. It is therefore necessary for individuals to work toward establishing and maintaining good mental, emotional, and spiritual health—their physical health depends upon it, as does the health of their families, workplaces, social networks, and cultural and political connections.

In Jeff's case, the fact that the diffraction pattern between him and his wife was initially so characterized by mutual resentment probably affected the overall interpersonal dynamic in their home. As Jeff himself put it, when he and his wife were in the same room together, their children often avoided them. Based on the last chapter's discussion, and the thoughts from Gabor Maté cited above, this interpersonal dynamic likely had negative effects for Jeff, his wife, and their children—in all aspects of their health. For Jeff to envision different futures for himself, then, his contributions to that diffraction pattern needed to change. If Jeff could accomplish such changes, it would likely be possible for everyone in the home, not just Jeff, to experience improvements in their overall health and wellbeing.

Now, it is worth acknowledging that when providing spiritual care in an acute-care hospital, it is unlikely that spiritual care clients in these settings will accomplish changes of the magnitude described in the previous paragraph (Lasair, 2021). The duration of the interactions between Practitioners and clients is often too short. Similarly, the number of interactions between Practitioners and specific clients is often too few. However, in the case of long-stay patients or in cases when patients are especially receptive to the Practitioner's care, much more can be accomplished. Because Jeff's stay in hospital was longer than average, we were able to accomplish much more than what would typically be possible. When a Practitioner is employed in contexts where longer-term relationships are more the norm, like in long-term care homes or parish, military, corporate, or correctional settings, even greater results can be possible (Lasair, 2021). Regardless of the Practitioner's workplace, it is helpful for Practitioners to keep the overall trajectory I am about to describe in mind, simply because a well-placed question or strategic turn of phrase can produce long-lasting positive consequences for clients, even after a single interaction.[2]

Within the framework being proposed herein, a turn toward greater spiritual health involves bringing together Barad's ideas and some from Iain McGilchrist, as explored in the last chapter. According to McGilchrist (2009, 2021), one of the significant challenges currently facing those who live in the global West is the overwhelmingly cognitive orientation of Western societies. From

McGilchrist's perspective, this orientation has resulted in significant fragmentation in our affective and intuitive connections with the rest of reality, to the point that we are losing much of our social and cultural cohesion. At this point I will not rehash the major points of McGilchrist's (2009, 2021) argument, because I covered many of them in the last chapter. However, I will state here that McGilchrist does point the way toward the kind of intra-action, to use Barad's term, that has the capacity to render significant social and cultural change; his strong advocacy for the reclamation of traits he associates with the human brain's right hemisphere is particularly salient in this regard. If his argument is accepted, such reclamation will produce better neuro-integration and mental and spiritual health at individual levels, in addition to greater social and cultural cohesion at collective levels. As I suggested in my definition of professional spiritual care in Chapter One, Spiritual Care Practitioners work directly with the emotional and intuitive dimensions of their clients' lives, precisely for the sake of helping clients experience better neuro-integration, as well improved senses of connection with the rest of reality. Because the West has by and large neglected these emotional and intuitive dimensions of both individual and collective experiences, engaging them therapeutically thus bears the potential to change the diffraction patterns built between individuals and created by Western societies as a whole. Furthermore, engaging clients' emotions and intuitions also bears the potential for Western individuals and societies to regain a healthier balance between the physical, divine/transcendent, and human domains of Panikkar's (2010) cosmotheandric principle. This balance can be regained because the human and divine/transcendent domains have typically been neglected in Western contexts due to the hegemonic secular$_3$ perspectives in such settings.

While this conclusion may seem obvious for various reasons, its importance for how spiritual health is explored in this book cannot be overstated. This is because the picture of spiritual health described below requires that spiritual care clients consciously understand and embody their particular ways of being in holistic, affective, intuitive, and cognitive relationships with the rest of reality. Concretely this means a person does not claim to know or understand things that are beyond the scope of their awareness. It also means that a spiritually healthy person is open to whatever might be beyond their awareness's current scope. This openness applies to such a person's internal realities, as well to as those realities that are external to them. Moreover, because all people are finite, spiritual health also considers a person's individual interests, aptitudes, and situation in life. In other words, a person's relative spiritual health cannot be divorced from the contours of their specific narrative. Working to improve a person's spiritual health therefore also invites them to reconnect with their particular senses of ultimate meaning, purpose, and transcendence. As suggested by the consensus definition of spirituality (Puchalski, Vitillo, Hull, & Reller, 2014), such connections with meaning, purpose, and transcendence can also help a person interact in healthy ways with all the other entities, both human and non-human, with whom they share relationships. The coming chapters will describe what this looks like explicitly and concretely.

Jeff worked hard to shift the diffraction pattern of resentment between him and his wife. He did this by starting to change his own dynamic in relation to her by attending more fully to what they were both feeling in relation to each other and working to respond differently to both his and his wife's resulting interpersonal behaviors. This then enabled Jeff's wife to start manifesting different ways of interacting with him. She began to do this because Jeff's changes in behavior, actions, interactions, attitudes, and body language demonstrated to her that Jeff did not always conform to the stories she was telling herself about him. Likewise, as his wife's way of interacting with him started to respond to the changes he was making, Jeff too began to see that his wife's ultimate character transcended the stories he told himself about her. As a result, a diffraction pattern still existed between Jeff and his wife, but it began to take on quite a different shape from before. No longer was it characterized by the resentments Jeff and his wife harbored against each other. Instead, Jeff and his wife began to consciously choose what emotions they wanted to experience within themselves and between each other. If Jeff and his wife were able to sustain this change, who knows what other shifts might have happened in the mental, emotional, spiritual, *and physical* health of everyone in that home!

To conclude this section, then, none of the results described in these paragraphs can be manifest in shared realities without first understanding that a person's spirituality is connected to their fundamental frame for reality. Neither can these results be accomplished without first seeing how any person's reality frame informs absolutely everything they engage with and experience in life. When considering the implications of these last two statements, it is furthermore evident that the interplay between any person's inner and outer realities can be quite individually specific. Let's bring all this together to start better articulating a theory of spirituality and point the way toward a better understanding of spiritual health.

FRAMING REALITY: IMPROVING SPIRITUAL HEALTH

At this point, it is helpful to recall in greater depth Raimon Panikkar's (2010) concept of the cosmotheandric as explored in the last chapter. To briefly recap that discussion, the word cosmotheandric puts together three Greek words cosmos (this refers to the physical universe), theos (this refers to transcendence, the divine, and the infinite domains), and aner/andros (this refers to the unique domain of human consciousness). According to Panikkar, humans bring together these three domains; their bodies belong to the physical domain, and humans can come into contact with transcendence, the divine, or the infinite domains through the unique medium of human consciousness.

My approach expands on this framework to state that each person constructs relationships with the physical universe, other human beings, and the divine, the infinite, and the transcendent through their frame for reality. In other words, every person's frame for reality mediates all the relationships they share in each of these domains! A person's reality frame therefore informs how they relate to their memories and their feelings just as much as how they relate to the people and various physical objects in their life. A person's frame even informs how they understand ultimate realities, as was illustrated above in my discussion of Jeff's beliefs about fairies and earth spirits.

To enhance a person's spiritual health, then, it becomes necessary for Spiritual Care Practitioners to facilitate the emergence and growth of six specific traits or characteristics within a person's frame.[3] These traits are awareness, openness, freedom, wisdom, contentment, and flourishing. Each trait also has a specific relationship with an identifiable phenomenon within a person's consciousness. There are five such phenomena: perception, projection, neutrality, truthfulness, and conscious interconnectedness. In the system described in the following chapters, each trait emerges in response to at least one of these experiential phenomena; it is a Practitioner's role to facilitate the emergence of these traits, mainly by working directly with clients' awareness of the phenomena that precede them. The rest of this book will therefore be occupied with describing both the experiential phenomena and the traits of spiritual health that emerge from them. Each of these descriptions will also provide specific spiritual caregiving techniques that can facilitate growth in each trait of spiritual health.

CONCLUSION

This chapter spent significant space exploring my patient Jeff's spirituality. Even though his case was somewhat exceptional in that I shared a caregiving relationship with him that lasted longer than those I share with many in hospital, I did get a good sense of Jeff's frame for reality and the overall dynamics of his spirituality. Clinically, such information is crucial, as it opens up a number of avenues that Practitioners can explore in their interactions with their clients; in the preceding pages I hinted at several of these. Now, in response, the coming chapters will discuss how Practitioners can mobilize such information so clients can begin to experience specific therapeutic outcomes. As discussed in the previous paragraphs, a crucial building block in a client's growing spiritual health is their capacity to increase their awareness, so it is toward this topic that the next chapter now turns.

Reflection Questions

- How does the approach to spirituality articulated in this chapter resonate with your own clinical experience? Is there anything you might add or remove?
- If you were to summarize the key concepts of this chapter, what would be some of the main takeaways?
- How might you integrate these main takeaways into your own clinical practice?

Clinical Assessment and Intervention Questions

- How would you describe this client's notions of the good, their self-assessments, and their internal sense of identity?
- Have any of the items in the last question been affected by the client's experiences of consistency and change?
- How does the client recall the past and anticipate the future? Are there any aspects of their recollections or anticipations that might require clinical intervention?
- What kind of diffraction pattern does the client manifest through their body language, affect, actions, behaviors, and attitudes? What insights might this diffraction pattern render about the client's overall frame for reality?
- What role(s) do religious, spiritual, cultural, and/or scientific concepts, rituals, theories, and practices play in the client's frame for reality? How might these concepts, rituals, theories, and practices be mobilized to provide positive clinical benefit for the client?

NOTES

1 Paul Ricoeur is being invoked here because his narrative understanding of identity has been influential in several generations of spiritual care thinkers and psychologists (e.g., Gerkin, 1986, 1984). His thought has also played a significant role in the construction of the theory being articulated in these pages. See Lasair (2020) in particular.

2 For example, a former patient recently contacted me about six years after I had seen her only once in hospital. She told me that something I had said in a prayer for her significantly changed how she approached her life afterward. She was contacting me to express her gratitude for that interaction and to share with me how even that single encounter had made a big difference in her life.

3 See Lasair (2021) for initial definitions of these traits and phenomena.

REFERENCE LIST

Barad, K. (2007). *Meeting the universe halfway: quantum physics and the entanglement of matter and meaning.* Durham, NC: Duke University Press.

Bourgeault, C. (2008). *The wisdom Jesus: transforming heart and mind: a new perspective on Christ and his message.* Boston, MA: Shambhala.

Cadge, W. (2023). *Spiritual care: the everyday work of chaplains.* Oxford, UK: Oxford University Press.

Doehring, C. (2015). *The practice of pastoral care: a postmodern approach* (Revised and expanded ed.). Louisville, KY: Westminster John Knox.

Downes, W. (2011). *Language and religion: a journey into the human mind.* Cambridge, UK: Cambridge University Press.

Gerkin, C. (1984). *The living human document: re-visioning pastoral counseling in a hermeneutic mode.* Nashville, TN: Abingdon Press.

Gerkin, C. V. (1986). *Widening the horizons: pastoral responses to a fragmented society.* Philadelphia, PA: Westminster.

Lasair, S. (2017). Reconciliation through narrative: toward a theology of spiritual care in public health care. *Practical Theology*, 10, 160–173.

Lasair, S. (2018a). Spiritual care as a secular profession: politics, theory, and practice. *Journal for the Study of Spirituality*, 8(1), 5–18. doi:10.1080/20440243.2018.1431022

Lasair, S. (2018b). Understanding, assessing, and intervening in the spiritual nature of medical events: theological and theoretical perspectives. *Practical Theology*, 11(5), 374–386. doi:10.1080/1756073X.2018.1528749

Lasair, S. (2019). What's the point of spiritual care? A narrative response. *Journal of Pastoral Care & Counseling*, 73(2), 115–123. doi:10.1177/1542305019846846

Lasair, S. (2020). A narrative approach to spirituality and spiritual care in health care. *Journal of Religion and Health*, 59, 1524–1540. doi:10.1007/s10943-019-00912-9

Lasair, S. (2021). HAVE-H: five attitudes for a narratively grounded and embodied spirituality. *Journal of Pastoral Care & Counseling*, 75(1), 13–22. doi:10.1177/1542305020965546

Madigan, S. (2019). *Narrative therapy* (2nd ed.). Washington, DC: American Psychological Association.

Masters, R. A. (2010). *Spiritual bypassing: when spirituality disconnects us from what really matters.* Berkeley, CA: North Atlantic Books.

Maté, G., & Maté, D. (2022). *The mythe fo normal: trauma, illness and healing in a toxic culture.* Toronto, ON: Knopf Canada.

McGilchrist, I. (2009). *The master and his emissary: the divided brain and the making of the Western world.* New Haven, CT, and London, UK: Yale University Press.

McGilchrist, I. (2021). *The matter with things: our brains, our delusions and the unmaking of the world.* London, UK: Perspectiva Press.

Merton, T. (2007). *New seeds of contemplation.* New York, NY: New Directions.

Panikkar, R. (2004). *Christophany: the fullness of man* (A. DiLascia, Trans.). Maryknoll, NY: Orbis.

Panikkar, R. (2010). *The rhythm of being: the unbroken trinity: the Gifford lectures.* Maryknoll, NY: Orbis.

Puchalski, C., Vitillo, R., Hull, S., & Reller, N. (2014). Improving the spiritual dimension of whole person care: reaching national and international consensus. *Journal of Palliative Medicine*, 17(6), 642–656.

Ricoeur, P. (1984). *Time and narrative* (Vol. 1) (K. M. Laughlin, & D. Pellauer, Trans.). Chicago, IL: University of Chicago Press.

Ricoeur, P. (1991). Life: a story in search of a narrator. In M. J. Valdes (Ed.), *Paul Ricoeur: reflection and imagination* (pp. 425–437). Toronto, ON: University of Toronto Press.

Ricoeur, P. (1992). *Onself as another* (K. Blamey, Trans.). Chicago, IL: University of Chicago Press.

Scholem, G. (1954). *Major trends in Jewish mysticism.* New York, NY: Schocken.

Scholem, G. (1991). *On the mystical shape of the godhead: basic concepts in the Kabbalah* (J. Chipman, Ed., & J. Neugroschel, Trans.). New York, NY: Schocken.

Taylor, C. (1989). *Sources of the self: the making of modern identity.* Cambridge, MA: Harvard University Press.

Taylor, C. (2012). Perils of moralism. In K. L. Grasso, & C. R. Castillo (Eds.), *Theology and public philosophy: four conversations* (pp. 1–20). Lanham: Lexington.

Trungpa, C. (2018). *The future is open: good karma, bad karma, and beyond karma* (C. R. Gimian, Ed.). Boulder, CO: Shambhala.

Vernon, M. (2022). *Spiritual intelligence in seven steps.* Winchester, UK: Iff Books.

White, M. (2007). *Maps of narrative practice.* New York, NY: Norton.

White, M., & Epston, D. (1990). *Narrative means to therapeutic ends.* New York, NY: Norton.

Three

INTRODUCTION

The previous chapter discussed all the processes through which a person constructs their frame for reality. In that context, I explored the everydayness of spirituality and religion, insofar as both these phenomena are embedded in a person's way of engaging their daily realities. One person may therefore see the hand of God or other divine beings amid their daily events; others will see only the influences of physical entities or forces, similar to what was revealed concerning the purely immanent frame of secular$_3$ in Chapter One. Regardless, Spiritual Care Practitioners are called to provide care for all people, no matter how they might describe their realities. In Chapter Two I hinted at some caregiving techniques that can be useful in some situations. In contrast, in this chapter I will begin to explore how frontline spiritual care practices can help to produce client outcomes that are grounded in a comprehensive understanding of spiritual health. As I discussed at the end of the last chapter, awareness is the first outcome I will consider. Before I begin addressing that topic explicitly, however, it is beneficial to engage some of the processes I described in Chapter Two in greater detail. Specifically, it is helpful to consider perception.

NEUROLOGY AND PERCEPTION

At the end of the introduction, I indicated that after my Canadian province eliminated its spiritual care funds, I worked for some time in a faith-based long-term care home. In this setting I learned much about the fragility of human existence that I scarcely could have imagined when I was working full-time in the hospitals. One significant question I faced daily was how it might be possible to offer people with very fragile health good quality of life, no matter the time they might have remaining among us physically. Almost needless to state, this question demanded a great deal of creativity from all of us

DOI: 10.4324/9781003466147-4

who worked in that home. We worked hard to respond to it meaningfully. Many times, we were successful in doing so. In other cases, we could probably have done better.

Now, anyone who has worked in long-term care knows that one significant challenge in such settings can be managing the behaviors of residents living with various forms of dementia (e.g. Swinton, 2012). Not all people living with dementia manifest challenging behaviors, but some do. As a result, when residents moved into our long-term care home, part of the documentation that accompanied them was a behavioral assessment. This assessment would measure the extent to which the resident was at risk for exhibiting behaviors like wandering or striking out physically at caregivers. At our site, the people assessed as being at high risk for wandering, in particular, had their private rooms in secure parts of the building. To go in or out of these parts of the building, it was necessary to enter a code on an electronic keypad next to the door. These keypads prevented the residents from leaving of their own accord. If these people were somehow able to exit the secure areas on their own, they could easily get lost or experience various kinds of harm. To keep these residents safe, the only times they could leave the secured areas were when they were accompanied by someone who could supervise them. We would try to include these people in communal events as much as possible, but they still required supervision for both family and internal recreational events alike. These residents could therefore still participate in collective fun, yet we as staff also had to put appropriate precautions in place, mainly to ensure their wellbeing and safety.

Most of the time, staff were able to manage the behaviors of these residents quite well. It helped that the staff responsible for these residents' care had generally worked with them for some time. They were therefore able to recognize when each resident was at risk of becoming agitated. Staff had also all received specialized training that helped them de-escalate residents' agitation before the residents' behaviors became unmanageable. On several occasions while I worked at this long-term care home, however, one or another resident's behavior did become unmanageable, and these situations did require more significant interventions.

While I won't go into detail, these situations were high-risk for everyone involved. Because the agitated residents were living with reduced cognitive capacities, they could not be reasoned with. Moreover, because dementia can affect a person's perceptions of reality (sometimes in the form of visual or auditory hallucinations), in addition to their ability to communicate using language, it could be quite difficult to help them calm down. It was therefore necessary for those of us involved to remain outwardly as calm as possible. Yet we also needed to gently but firmly invite the agitated residents to come somewhere away from the other people housed in the secure areas. Once the agitated resident was away from the other residents, medical staff could administer medications that would help calm them. But this was a less preferable option for us. Most times, we would play quiet music the resident liked, offer them food, or put calming, familiar images on a television for them. Because such residents' capacities with language were often significantly impaired, our most effective communication with them was non-verbal. Learning to understand and work with residents' perceptions of reality was therefore crucial for this work.

In all these scenarios, part of this learning was to build an understanding of how various disease processes were affecting the brains of these residents living with dementia (Swinton, 2012; Cozolino, 2017). Because each kind of dementia affects brains differently, the symptoms each person experienced varied according to the specific disease operating in their brain (Swinton, 2012; Cozolino, 2017). For some, their capacities with language were deeply affected. People in these situations might therefore experience neurolinguistic conditions like aphasia. Other residents might lose their social inhibitions, and this caused them to enact behaviors that most people would consider wildly inappropriate. For example, some such residents would unexpectedly shout profanities at no one in particular, without any seeming provocation. Yet others would lose their capacities for higher reasoning and executive functioning. Such individuals would act impulsively and be driven by their emotions and physical needs. They behaved this way because they could no longer reflect upon their actions and whatever consequences might result from them. In many cases, residents manifested varying combinations of all these symptoms and behaviors.

Drawing upon the language of the previous chapter, then, all these individuals' frames for reality were becoming drastically altered, primarily due to the disease processes that were operative in their brains. Nevertheless, our role as staff members was still to achieve a good understanding of what each resident's frame for reality entailed. Somehow we needed to work within each resident's frame to help them have good quality of life—and this was regardless of whatever behavioral challenges their diseases might be producing in them! Almost needless to state, this was very challenging work, but it could also be very rewarding.

Now, all this illustrates something Iain McGilchrist discusses at length in his two books on brain hemispherality (McGilchrist, 2009, 2021): the intimate connection between our perceptions of reality and our neurobiology. From McGilchrist's perspective, our perceptions of reality are not just connected to our five senses. Rather, our perceptions are also very connected to how each region of our brain receives and processes whatever our five bodily senses are bringing to us (McGilchrist, 2009). McGilchrist therefore draws upon over a century's worth of studies to explore how strokes or lesions in various regions of the human brain affect both perception and cognition (McGilchrist, 2021, 2009). His results are striking. While space does not permit me to go into the details of his argument, in *The Master and His Emissary* McGilchrist (2009) states at one point that the reality a person perceives is the reality they experience. Concretely this means that the five bodily senses in combination with the specifics of any person's neurobiology create perceptions of reality that can be highly individualized. As a result, each person's experience of reality is unique. This is because no person's sensory acuity nor neurobiology are 100 percent identical to those of others. Now, a few caveats are in order.

To interpret McGilchrist as arguing there is no such thing as "objective" reality would be a significant misreading of his argument. McGilchrist's ongoing psychiatric practice and its reliance on the findings of neuroscience demonstrate his commitment to realities that can be measured and studied empirically. My position is similar. However, my response to a naïve empiricism is to introduce some thoughts from Karen Barad (2007). Drawing upon Niels Bohr's philosophy-physics, Barad indicates that human perceptions and concepts are very much parts of reality, but our perceptions and concepts are also limited by various physical, psychological, social, and cultural factors that are largely beyond our control. This *does not* mean it is impossible to discover at least parts of what lies outside our current perceptions and understandings of reality. To believe as much would undermine the fundamental principles of both theoretical and empirical science, not to mention individuals' potentials to grow in insight and knowledge. However, Barad's (2007) interpretation of Bohr *does* suggest that human consciousness actively constructs its realities through the relationships it shares with all other entities, human and non-human, material, organic, social, and spiritual alike—even within the context of scientific thought. Consequently, the realities we are able to understand and engage in any moment are only those that our individual human brains are capable of processing (Barad, 2007; Cozolino, 2017; Swinton, 2012; McGilchrist, 2009, 2021).

Hence, when a person's brain is damaged or experiencing some disease, like when a person is living with dementia, the realities they understand and experience are vastly different from those understood and experienced by those of us not affected by these conditions (McGilchrist, 2009, 2021; Cozolino, 2017; Swinton, 2012). The current drive to recognize some astounding social, cultural, and scientific achievements from neurodivergent individuals also teaches the same lesson. People living with autism spectrum disorder, attention deficit and hyperactivity disorder, and all other forms of neurodiversity, perceive and experience reality in ways that can differ significantly from people belonging to so-called "neurotypical" populations (McGilchrist, 2021). All this indicates that any person's specific frame for reality is very much bound up with their particular neurobiology. It furthermore demonstrates, again, that a person's frame for reality also has concrete consequences for the realities they share with others. This is not only true regarding a person's behavioral and interpersonal dynamics, but it is also true in relation to whatever any person devotes their life to. Whatever any person might accomplish through such devotion is also dependent, at least in part, on their individual neurobiology.

When working with people living with dementia, then, I was keenly aware that the disease processes in these individuals' brains could alter their internal sense of identity, in many ways and at many levels (Swinton, 2012; Cozolino, 2017). These processes also changed how these individuals' identities manifested in the world around them. Part of the challenge in working with these people was thus to discern what had remained consistent for them in their sense of identity and what had changed as their disease progressed. Working with residents' families or other loved ones was therefore crucial.

When the residents themselves could no longer recall many of their lives' events due to their dementia processes, family members or other caregivers were able to share numerous insights regarding who these people had been in the past. They could also provide explanations concerning what historical factors might be contributing to residents' behaviors in the present. If, for example, a resident had previously experienced interpersonal trauma or abuse, this might explain why undressing for bathing was something that would cause the resident to lash out physically at their caregivers. Information like this would give staff caregivers important insights regarding the residents' prior experiences. This information would then enable the staff caregivers to brainstorm with families about what could help the residents feel safe and secure in situations where they might otherwise perceive threats.

Some cases like this were particularly memorable. In a couple of examples, residents with traumatic histories had never manifested violent behaviors previously. These behaviors only emerged once their dementia processes were well underway. Somehow these residents' diseases had unearthed symptoms of trauma that the residents had suppressed for most of their adult lives. This is not surprising, given that trauma can produce long-lasting neural pathways in the brain (van der Kolk, 2014; Treleaven, 2018). When their brains are functioning normally, however, many people can mitigate against some of the more disturbing symptoms of trauma; when their brains are affected by dementia, such internal mitigation becomes more difficult (Swinton, 2012). As a result, when a person is living with dementia, behaviors can emerge that are products of a traumatic past, rather than simply part of a typical dementia-related disease process. Once staff at the long-term care home were informed of these specific residents' histories of trauma, they were then better able to provide care that reduced the residents' tendencies to exhibit violent protective behaviors. The staff were able to do this by creating physical and emotional environments that allowed the residents to feel safe and secure while, for example, bathing with staff assistance.

From my perspective, these were excellent examples of assessing a person's frame for reality, inhabiting that frame, and providing care from within that frame. It was also possible to see changes in the frame dynamics of the residents involved, even though they were living with dementia! These expansions occurred because the residents learned to trust their staff caregivers to the extent that they began to allow the staff to assist them with previously difficult tasks like bathing. Consequently, I believe the staff caregivers were, in fact, providing a form of spiritual care. I believe this because trust is one phenomenon that helps humans feel connected to the rest of reality. Furthermore, because trust is an emotional phenomenon, it transcends whatever a person's thoughts or perceptions might tell them about the nature of their various realities. If a person is able to trust their realities, they are less likely to rely upon aggression or manipulation to help them in life. Concepts or ideas cannot provide such emotional connections on their own. Trust in any dimension of a person's life can therefore offer at least a partial measure of their overall spiritual health, but there are more fundamental measures of a person's spiritual health. To describe one of these I now turn to how perception can occur in populations not affected by various cognitive or neurosensory impairments.

PERCEPTION, NEUROBIOLOGY, AND BIOGRAPHY

In the last chapter, I explored how a person constructs their frame for reality in response to many, if not all, of their life's events. Drawing upon my work with my patient Jeff, I showed how Jeff's experience of living with a long-term degenerative disease contributed not only to his internal experiences, but also to his interpersonal dynamics in the familial, social, and cultural spaces he shared with others. In light of the discussion in the previous paragraphs, then, it is possible to see how Jeff's prior experiences had produced specific neurological structures in his brain and body (Cozolino, 2017; Graziano, 2019; Seth, 2021). As a person moves through life, everything through which they live produces corresponding neural pathways. The more significant an event is emotionally, the longer-lasting the neural structures and the more likely a person is to generate patterns of thought and behavior that are somehow rooted in such events (Graziano, 2019; van der Kolk, 2014; Zimmerman, 2018). The discussion of the long-lasting effects of trauma in the previous paragraphs can be seen as one demonstration of this reality (van der Kolk, 2014; Treleaven, 2018).

In addition to the neurological structures produced in response to significant life events, psychologists and neuroscientists also indicate that a person's baseline temperament can affect how they perceive and experience reality (Cozolino, 2017; Graziano, 2019; Seth, 2021). Not only can a person's temperament affect the attachment patterns they manifest in relation to parents and other caregivers early in life, but a person's temperament can also influence the choices they make in terms of career, leisure activities, friendships, romantic partners, etc. (Cozolino, 2017; Aron, 1997; Granneman & Sólo, 2023). As indicated above, all these choices are connected to a person's neurobiology. Hence, a person's temperament and disposition are two additional concrete manifestations of how their neurobiology affects the way they move through life (see also Ward, 2014). Within the context of spiritual care, part of the work Practitioners undertake is to assess and engage the specific dynamics bound up with a client's temperament and disposition—both are further aspects of the client's frame for reality.

A person's cognitive beliefs can also play various roles in their frame's dynamics (Downes, 2011; de Cruz & de Smedt, 2015). In my experience, for example, some clients will often foreground their religious beliefs when I encounter them clinically. Other clients, again in my experience, tend to be more reserved when discussing their faith and its teachings. Within the system being discussed in these pages, these dynamics, too, can be expressions of a person's frame for reality. Those who are more reserved may consider their religious beliefs to be private matters that do not deserve much explicit attention outside specific social settings like faith community gatherings or intimate family interactions. In contrast, those who are more forthright in expressing their beliefs may do so because they view their beliefs as holding the key to understanding reality as it truly is. For some such clients, others must learn to share these beliefs so they, too, can experience the joy of encountering reality and its truth (at least this may be one perspective held by these kinds of people).

In either kind of case, a client's relationship with their religious/secular/cultural beliefs can provide insights into how they construct their relationship with the rest of reality (Downes, 2011; McGilchrist, 2021; de Cruz & de Smedt, 2015). Those who foreground their beliefs may have a slightly more cognitive relationship with the rest of reality.

Such people's explicit discussions of their beliefs may help to orient them conceptually in relation to the realities they encounter. Those whose beliefs are more reserved, in contrast, may construct their relationship with reality primarily through their emotions and intuition. If this is the case, such people may not need to use concepts and propositions to describe how they relate to reality. Instead, they may simply enjoy the connections they experience in relationships without feeling any particular need to express the cognitive meanings of those relationships in language.

However, part of a spiritual care assessment is to determine the extent to which a client's cognitive beliefs are products of their lived experiences (LaRocca-Pitts, 2024; Lasair, 2018a, 2018b). This last statement gives substance to some things I hinted at in Chapter Two. Because a person's religious beliefs are deeply embedded in their daily experiences (Downes, 2011; McGilchrist, 2021; Lasair, 2020), maintaining an experiential focus is crucial when providing spiritual care. Clinically it is therefore often helpful to explore how a client's experiences are connected to their tradition's wisdom teachings (for examples of wisdom approches to faith, see Bourgeault, 2003, 2008; Barnhart, 2018). Such teachings are often more useful for exploring the meaning(s) of a client's experiences than are abstract propositional and/or dogmatic statements concerning the nature of reality. I do not mean that propositional or dogmatic statements ought to be excluded completely from a Spiritual Care Practitioner's clinical work. Rather, I am attempting to indicate that such teachings need somehow to be connected to a client's life in terms of providing potential lenses through which they might interpret their experiences. Such use of a client's tradition can, in fact, deepen that client's connection to its teachings. Clients can experience these deeper connections because they can begin to see how they experience the tradition's teachings in their own life. There will be more to say on this topic in the coming pages. In the case of my patient Jeff, it was clear his cognitive beliefs about fairies and earth spirits were not grounded in his lived experience to any great extent. So, as I indicated in the last chapter, I needed to draw upon other resources to assist in my care for him.

Now, all this has been stated for the sake of demonstrating that a client's personal narrative; temperament and disposition; body language, actions, behaviors, and attitudes; and cognitive beliefs and capacities with language all give Practitioners good indications of the dynamics of their frame for reality. Such indications are valid for people belonging to so-called "typical" populations, as well as for those who live with various conditions that can affect both their perceptions and cognition. Consequently, effective Practitioners use whatever communicative means they have to connect with a client's frame for reality, establish its general contours, and work within those contours to assist the client to experience improvements within their overall spiritual health and wellbeing (Doehring, 2015; Scheib, 2016; Lasair, 2019). As implied in my discussion above regarding my work with people living with dementia, body language, a felt sense of emotional connection between Practitioner and client, and the Practitioner's conscious choices about the language and concepts they use all assist in this work. As American psychotherapist Allan N. Schore indicates in his book *Right Brain Psychotherapy* (2019; see also Rogers, 1965), the effectiveness of a therapist's work depends on the shared sense of emotional resonance between the therapist and the client. Likewise, everything a Spiritual Care Practitioner does in relation to a client needs to build and enhance a similar shared sense of emotional resonance. This resonance is the main tool Practitioners have to assist clients to build, maintain, and enhance their relationships with the rest of reality. As a result, building such shared resonance is foundational to the practice and goals of spiritual care; as psychologists and social workers often express it, shared resonance is one indication of a good therapeutic alliance between Practitioner and client (Rogers, 1965; Schore, 2019). At this point it is helpful to recall what I stated in Chapter Two about diffraction patterns.

BUILDING RESONANCE, WORKING WITH PERCEPTIONS

To this point, I have been following McGilchrist's (2009) argument that what a person perceives is what they experience. Yet, according to McGilchrist and others, most of perception—sensory, neurological, and autobiographical—occurs below the threshold of a person's conscious awareness (Cozolino, 2017; Graziano, 2019; McGilchrist, 2009, 2021; Seth, 2021). Concretely this means that no one will completely understand the contributions that they or others make to the diffraction patterns of which they are part. For most people, perception is automatic (Hogue, 2003; Graziano, 2019; Seth, 2021), therefore very few are consciously aware of how their perceptions influence their behaviors, interactions, interpersonal dynamics, body language, etc. Yet everyone contributes to emotional and spiritual diffraction patterns in the familial, social, cultural, and political environments they share with others, regardless of whether they are aware of it or not (Schore, 2019; McGilchrist, 2009, 2021). Spiritual Care Practitioners, however, know how to limit and strategically mobilize their contributions within these shared diffraction patterns. Practitioners do this by observing whatever emotional dynamics their clients contribute to the diffraction patterns of which they are part. To draw upon Allan Schore's language, Practitioners can perceive and observe their clients' contributions to diffraction patterns by synchronizing their brains' right hemispheres to the right hemispheres of their clients' brains (Schore, 2019).[1] Because the human brain's right hemisphere is very sensitive to emotional and intuitive phenomena (McGilchrist, 2009, 2021; Schore, 2019), this synchronization enables Practitioners to perceive and understand many of the unspoken dynamics contained within their clients' frames for reality (see Schore, 2019). Consequently, a Practitioner's interactions with the diffraction patterns they share with their clients enables the clients to become at least partially aware of their frames' particular dynamics. I will discuss awareness in greater depth below. Yet to give some greater context for Schore's approach, it is helpful to explore his understanding of the psychoanalytic phenomena of transference and countertransference (Schore, 2019). Schore himself is one of the leading figures in the IPNB school of psychotherapy (Siegel & Solomon, 2013; Schore, 2019; Cozolino, 2017), to which Iain McGilchrist is also a significant contributor (McGilchrist, 2013). Due to the general alignment between Schore's and McGilchrist's positions, Schore's thoughts are helpful to consider at this point.

From Schore's (2019; see also Pedhu, 2019) perspective, *transference* refers to whatever feelings a therapist themself elicits from within their client. Often these feelings are connected to the client's prior experiences in ways that the client typically has some difficulty naming. Schore (2019) therefore indicates that part of a therapist's role is to guide the client into a deeper experience of these feelings so the client can re-experience and heal some of the emotional structures that are contributing to their emotional and behavioral dynamics in the present. Schore (2019) calls this a "regression process," and he believes that much psychotherapy in both the psychoanalytic and Rogerian traditions is oriented toward guiding clients through such processes. From Schore's (2019) perspective, therapists guide clients through regression processes so they can experience improvements in their overall psychological wellbeing. Schore (2019; see also Pedhu, 2019) thus understands countertransference to be the feelings that the client themself elicits from within in the therapist. As with the client's experiences of transference, countertransference can be an indication that something from the therapist's past is being invoked by whatever the client is exploring (Schore, 2019; Pedhu, 2019). However, unlike with the client's experience of transference, the therapist can use their experiences of countertransference as a therapeutic tool in relation to the client (Schore, 2019). According to Schore (2019), the feelings the therapist experiences through countertransference can mirror whatever feelings the client experiences in certain circumstances. As a result, if a therapist is able to skillfully mobilize whatever occurs for them through countertransference, the client can potentially experience significant therapeutic benefit.

Now, it is worth stating that Schore's (2019) regression process and his acute awareness of the intricacies of transference and countertransference require specialized training. Such training typically extends far beyond what Spiritual Care Practitioners receive in CPE (CASC/ACSS, 2019; Ragsdale, 2018). However, I have gone into relative depth in my description of these dynamics to illustrate that when a spiritual care client perceives reality in a particular way, they typically do so because of some prior experience. Therefore, just as prior experiences can produce neurological structures in a client's brain and body (Hogue, 2003; Cozolino, 2017; Seth, 2021; Ward, 2014), so too can prior experiences produce specific tropes or themes in the stories the client tells about themself (Lasair, 2020; Scheib, 2016; Doehring, 2015; Zimmerman, 2018). Nevertheless, because there is also a correlation between the stories the client narrates about themself and their neurobiology (Zimmerman, 2018; Ward, 2014), Practitioners need to be attentive to how the client's words correspond or do not correspond with all the other data that emerges as the client tells of their experiences (Schore, 2019). As mentioned before, body language, actions, behaviors, attitudes, tone of voice, temperament, and disposition all communicate as much, if not more, about a client's experience as do their words. All these things allow Practitioners to assess the fundamental dynamics of the client's frame.

Whatever a client says about their experience is therefore of crucial importance. This is because a client's words reveal how they make cognitive and conceptual sense of their experience (Williams, 2014; White & Epston, 1990; Madigan, 2019). Words are what most people use to communicate the meanings of their experiences (Williams, 2014). Within this approach, whatever a person says about their life and its events is the product of some sort of interpretative process (Lasair, 2020, 2019; Madigan, 2019). Yes, a person's emotions, temperament, and disposition play important roles in how a client might assign meanings to specific events, or to their life as a whole. This is why it is so important for Practitioners to attend to these unspoken dimensions of their clients' stories. However, the client's words give the Practitioner insights into the *cognitive value* the client is assigning to their life and its events (Schore, 2019; McGilchrist, 2009). This cognitive value may or may not correspond to what the client's non-verbal cues might be communicating. As indicated above, non-verbal cues can render insights about how the client's neurobiology might interpret the value of the client's experiences (Schore, 2019). The result is the client's cognitive perceptions might or might not align with the non-verbal or pre-verbal (i.e., neurobiological) dimensions of their experiences (Schore, 2019; Cozolino, 2017; Graziano, 2019; Seth, 2021). Part of the Practitioner's role, then, is to intentionally explore with the client the origins of the client's cognitive perceptions of their life and its experiences. As this exploration proceeds, the Practitioner is actively assessing the alignment between the client's words and the client's non-verbal communication. By naming what is happening non-verbally for the client, the Practitioner can thus begin to draw the client's attention to the full emotional breadth and depth of their story, of which the client may only be partially aware. This is part of how the Practitioner uses language to start building an understanding of the client's life and experience that is shared between themself and the client (Zimmerman, 2018; White & Epston, 1990; Madigan, 2019).

A Practitioner therefore consistently draws attention to whatever might be emotionally or narratively implied by the client's words; the client may or may not mention these things explicitly. As Canadian social work professor and narrative therapist Laura Béres (2023) indicates, Michael White, one of the first developers of narrative therapy, late in his life became increasingly concerned with such so-called "absent but implied" material in client narratives. White believed this material required explicit attention in therapeutic processes. This material requires such attention because it can often provide context for whatever the client might be expressing to their therapist. This context can render crucial data for the therapist insofar as it will often offer clues as to how a client's healing journey might unfold. For example, if a client does not talk about a significant event that occurred for them in the past, then inviting the client to tell more about this event can help to uncover how this unexpressed reality might be affecting the client in the present. The fact the client excluded this event from their initial telling of their story might also indicate that the client themself does not yet fully recognize its importance. By inviting a client to explore such absent but implied material, then, a skilled therapist can assist a client to become aware of various factors that might be shaping their experience in the present. The same is true in spiritual care contexts.

Yet in engaging clients this way, Practitioners are also aware that there are always dimensions of the clients' experiences that can never be captured in words (Zimmerman, 2018; White & Epston, 1990; Madigan, 2019). So, the Practitioner understands that whatever shared understanding they build regarding the client's narrative is highly provisional. Ultimately, clients typically experience themselves as the protagonists in their own narratives, in addition to being the narratives' first-person narrators. Therefore, the Practitioner's role is to assist the client to come to an understanding of their narrative that makes sense *to them*, given all the concerns bound up with their life and how they experience those concerns (Lasair, 2019; Madigan, 2019; White & Epston, 1990; Zimmerman, 2018). Relating to clients in this way can help clients grow their awareness of their own frame's dynamics. Awareness of their frame's dynamics also helps clients to see how these dynamics contribute to the diffraction patterns of which they are part. This discussion therefore now turns explicitly toward awareness.

AWARENESS

At the outset, it is fair to state that the term *awareness* is used with different meanings in different contexts. Often it is associated with consciousness, particularly with a person's capacity to place their attention upon specific objects within their consciousness (Cozolino, 2017; Graziano, 2019; Hogue, 2003; Seth, 2021). These could be external objects, thoughts or ideas within their mind, or simply specific feelings within their body. In this sense, awareness denotes the neurological and psychological structures that enable a person to place their attention on whatever is rising in their mind.

Now, some spiritual and religious traditions expand on this definition to state that *consciousness* is pure awareness (Godman, 1985; Aurobindo & Mother, 1998; Trungpa, 2018). Such traditions teach that when people reach a high level of spiritual development they often have the capacity to register almost everything that arises in their consciousness/awareness. As a result, these people typically experience deeply felt senses of connection between themselves and whatever comes into their consciousness (Wilber, 2017). People who have these experiences thus frequently describe feelings of "oneness," "non-duality," or "union" as features of this all-encompassing awareness (Wilber, 2017). Yet these feelings are usually held in tension with the stance of detachment that these people typically embody at the same time (Wilber, 2017; Trungpa, 2018). Detachment means these people do not attempt to grasp or capture whatever arises in their consciousness. Those who experience such oneness, non-duality, and union are consequently "aware of being aware," but their ability to approach other beings on their own terms also frees them from any internal or external dynamics that might otherwise imprison them or those with whom they interact. A prime example of this understanding is articulated in Chögyam Trungpa's (2018) discussions about how to free oneself and others from the throes of karma, as discussed in Chapter Two.

While the previous paragraph may describe a very accomplished manifestation of awareness, the approach taken in these pages begins with awareness's more basic elements. This approach is taken deliberately, in part to ground awareness in realities that can be readily observed in clinical settings. Hence when Practitioners assess the concrete manifestations of a client's frame, this process offers some information that can assist clients to build their awareness. But all this begs the question, why is awareness so important for clients when working to build their spiritual health?

In Chapter One I highlighted the relational nature of the consensus definition of spirituality (see Puchalski, Vitillo, Hull, & Reller, 2014). Based on my analysis of this definition, I indicated that spiritual care seeks to build, maintain, and enhance a client's relationship with all reality. In Chapter Two I spent an extended amount of space discussing the processes through which a person constructs their frame for reality. Over the course of that discussion I indicated that a person's frame is the basis upon which they relate to the rest of reality. I used the case of my patient Jeff as an example to demonstrate how frames function both in our internal dynamics and in the spaces we share with others. All this was discussed to show how the frames we bring to reality can either help to connect us with all reality or create barriers between ourselves and reality. The current chapter's discussion of perception was articulated to show how our perceptions are concrete manifestations of our frames' inner workings, both in terms of the themes and tropes in our personal narratives and in terms of how these themes and tropes might or might not correlate with our neurobiology. Building awareness, then, is an initial process that Practitioners can use to assist clients to understand at least some of their frames' dynamics. Once this awareness is built, both client and Practitioner can start to determine which of these dynamics have been helpful in the client's relationship with the rest of reality and which have not been helpful. There will be more to discuss on this topic in the coming chapters.

Now, building such awareness typically entails the client gaining some understanding of why they experience and engage reality in their distinctive ways. Hence, in their interactions with a client, a Practitioner will often share observations with the client regarding the client's responses to various topics that come up within the interaction (see Lasair, 2019). Such observations can then lead to explorations as to the origins of the client's response. These explorations are crucial in uncovering various aspects of the client's frame. However, it is worth noting at this point that the kind of in-depth exploration that occurred in the last chapter is often beyond what a Spiritual Care Practitioner can undertake with their clients, particularly in acute-care settings. In settings where Practitioners are able to form longer-term relationships with their clients, such in-depth work might be more possible. To illustrate what a process of building awareness might look like in a short-term interaction, it is helpful to explore a clinical example.

Ernest

I encountered Ernest some time ago on one of the surgery units where I work. At that time Ernest was in his early 50s and had worked most of his career as a first responder. He had been brought to hospital with severe abdominal pain, and at the point I shared this interaction with him the physicians were unable to provide a conclusive diagnosis. As I began my interaction with him, I observed that Ernest manifested an intensity that was uncommon in many other patients. The way he explained this was that he knew how things ought to go in the healthcare system, and things weren't going that way for him. Given Ernest's intensity and frustration, I felt these topics warranted further exploration. Here's what part of this interaction looked like:

SpC: You seem pretty frustrated with how things have been going for you in the hospital. Can you tell me a bit more about that?

E: It's all about how things oughtta be done. I know, because when I'm called to a situation you get in there, you see what needs to be done, and you do it. You know that people are in a world of shit, and your job is to get them out of it. So now I'm here [in the hospital], no one seems to know what's going on, and I'm left here to do what? Just fuck around? No way! I'm not having any of this!

SpC: You seem pretty angry.

E: You bet I am!

SpC: And this is because you feel this is not the way to do things, that things should be moving faster.

E: You got it!

SpC: So, what would happen if I told you that in my experience patients often tell me of having to wait a long time for the doctors to figure out what's going on for them?

E: I'd probably say that's bullshit. No one should have to wait for days so the doctors can tell them, "We need to do more tests!" Can't people see we need to get moving on this? I'm getting really fucked up with all this waiting!

SpC: Fucked up ... what do you mean?

E: I'm just having too much time alone with my thoughts. You know, I need to get things done ... that's how I know I'm doing good ... I get shit done!

SpC: You get shit done ...

E: Yeah, you know, I help people. That's why I got into my line of work ... I wanted to help people.

SpC: But now it feels like no one's helping you ...

E: (tears up) ... That's right ... (long pause. Ernest's tears continue for a while, but then he composes himself) ... You know, you spend your whole life helping people, then you wind up in hospital, and ... I dunno ... shit ...

SpC: Sounds like this is a new experience for you.

E: Yep ...

SpC: And part of that newness is that you like to be the person helping people, but now you're the one needing help.

E: Yep ...

SpC: Wow. How would you say that's sitting with you?

E: Not good.

SpC: Not good ... why's that, would you say?

E: It's because I know how bad things can be. I told you, I see all sorts of crazy shit almost every day. But I know how to deal with that. I go in there, I do my thing, I get out. Yeah, there's some stuff that sticks with you, but you move on. You have to, otherwise you can't do your job.

SpC: But with this there's no moving on ...

E: That's right.

SpC: You can't move on because it's you, and at this point you don't know how bad things are ...

E: You got it!

SpC: Seems pretty scary ...

E: (tears up again) ... Yep ...

Analysis

In this interaction Ernest initially articulated that he was angry due to how he felt he was being treated by the system. In having to wait for more and more tests, Ernest was not able to maintain the fast pace of life he was accustomed to as a first responder. As we explored his story further, it became evident that Ernest was experiencing his own health situation with the same kind of intensity he typically brought to his job. Earlier in our conversation Ernest had described the pain that brought him to hospital as "insane." While the physicians and nurses had immediately put him on pain medications and his pain was now under control, Ernest also experienced the need to wait as similarly intolerable. As I was assessing him in our conversation, it seemed the high level of intensity at which Ernest lived his work life translated into other domains for him as well. For Ernest, intensity was a way of being, and this way of being gave him a sense of urgency in much of his life, particularly now, when he needed answers regarding what was going on for him medically.

As we explored his intensity further, Ernest articulated that "get[ting] shit done" was his way of monitoring his own wellbeing. In his own words, "that's how I know I'm doing good, I get shit done." It was therefore evident that Ernest's forced slowdown due to his hospital admission was affecting his psychological and spiritual wellbeing as much as his medical emergency was causing him physical distress. As Ernest articulated it, the waiting was giving him too much time alone with his thoughts, and that was causing him to "get all fucked up." All this made me wonder if Ernest maintained his high intensity at work so he could cope with some traumatic events from his past. Unfortunately, our interaction did not render much opportunity to explore this together. It was clear, however, that Ernest built his relationship with the rest of reality around his deeply felt need to help people. If Ernest was intense when helping people, why couldn't his caregivers care for him with similar intensity and urgency? In response to this implied question, I offered my perspective as a person who had cared for many people who had experienced long waits in hospital. Again Ernest's anger surfaced in his naming of the long waits as "bullshit," but it was also here that Ernest's dynamic began to shift, in that he named that his psychological and spiritual wellbeing were being affected by his experience of now being a patient himself. In his own words, he was getting "all fucked up."

An unexpected byproduct of all this was now Ernest was the one needing help. As a result, a large part of his identity needed to shift. While Ernest never articulated this explicitly, there is a power dynamic bound up with being a person who always helps other people: it offers a sense of control. Ernest hinted as much later in our conversation when he said, "… I see all sorts of crazy shit almost every day. But I know how to deal with that. I go in there, I do my thing, I get out." In his current situation, Ernest was no longer in control. There was nothing he could do to fix his medical situation himself. Neither could he speed up the process through which the healthcare system was engaging his situation. This loss of power and control therefore struck at the core of the person Ernest had experienced himself to be up to that point. It was not surprising, then, that Ernest teared up so many times when I brought this dynamic to the surface of our conversation. As Ernest himself said, "You know, you spend your whole life helping people, then you wind up in hospital, and … I dunno … shit …" Ernest's loss of words likely signaled how overwhelming he found this experience. As I articulated in my next sentence, this experience was "new" for him, and it was evident that Ernest felt this newness at all levels of his being.

Put into the language that has been built to this point in this book, Ernest experienced his frame for reality as being predicated on his capacity to help people. It was this capacity that gave Ernest his sense of overall health and wellbeing, but it was also this capacity that gave Ernest a sense of power and control in his life. Ernest's hospital admission was the first time in his life he had been in a position of receiving care himself. Up to this point, it did not seem such experiences had played significant roles in shaping Ernest's frame, or, if they had, Ernest's frame had taken on a dynamic that was specifically oriented toward ensuring he would never feel powerless or out of control again. It was this dynamic that made me wonder whether there was something traumatic in Ernest's past that might need to be addressed at some point. The result was that Ernest initially interpreted the delays and waits he experienced in hospital as failures of the system. To interpret the delays and waits as such enabled Ernest to maintain his sense of power and control. However, his admission that he was getting "all fucked up" through all the waiting indicated that his sense of power and control—indeed, his entire frame—was being threatened at some fundamental levels. When I drew attention to the fact that now Ernest felt like no one was helping him, my statement enabled him to get in touch with the deep fear that lay behind his feelings of threat that presented themselves as anger. In other words, Ernest's conscious awareness of his frame's dynamics was starting to expand to include experiences that he had previously worked very hard to exclude from it (see Chapter Two).

There is a lot that could be stated regarding all the work that would be involved in helping Ernest expand his frame in a gentle and holistic way. However, for the purposes of this chapter I want to focus on how crucial building Ernest's awareness was. Over the course of the interaction documented above, it is possible to see Ernest's awareness shift. Initially, in his blaming of the system, Ernest was remaining within the confines of the automatic perceptions he was accustomed to generating within the already-established dynamics of his frame. These automatic perceptions enabled him to maintain the senses of power and control that were fundamental to his sense of identity as a first responder who helped people. However, early on in our interaction there were already signs that these perceptions did not accurately reflect what was actually going on for Ernest in this experience. In his admission that he was getting "all fucked up," Ernest hinted that his impatience and intensity were not just about the system failing to do its job. Rather, they were more about how difficult it was for Ernest to be in this situation, both emotionally and spiritually. Ernest wanted to get back to life as usual as quickly as possible, but the delays and waits were preventing this from occurring in ways he thought were timely. So, when I indicated to Ernest that delays and waits are often part of being in the hospital, it prompted Ernest to become aware of his own inner dynamic, namely that he was "getting all fucked up."

As we explored this statement further, Ernest's awareness grew to realize that his characterization of his inner dynamic was inadequate to express what was actually going on for him. So, as our conversation proceeded, Ernest articulated how his feelings were connected to his own sense of wellbeing: Ernest knew he was "doing good" when he was helping people. Now that he was no longer able to help people, Ernest was getting "all fucked up." Furthermore, when I was persistent in articulating the absent but implied material in Ernest's next few disclosures, it became clearer that Ernest's distress was particularly centered on his perceived losses of power and control in his current situation. These losses produced great fear in Ernest, as he acknowledged in response to my articulation of this reality. As our conversation continued beyond what was recorded above, Ernest and I therefore explored the themes of power and control explicitly. We also began to identify various ways Ernest could re-establish feelings of control in his current situation. Ernest did hint at the possibility that he had experienced some past events as traumatic, but given it was unlikely I was going to encounter him much after this initial interaction, I did not delve too deeply into this dynamic; I sensed it would take much more work for Ernest to sort through whatever traumas he might have experienced.

Nevertheless, in all our subsequent interchanges I was careful to draw upon Ernest's identity as a first responder. I took this approach because Ernest's professional identity was so central to how he configured his relationship with the rest of reality. It was also necessary to explore dimensions of this identity that were, at that point, unfamiliar to Ernest. Specifically, we explored how he was able to keep a cool head in the midst of crises. These new explorations were necessary because the urgency and intensity Ernest previously foregrounded had been revealed as unhelpful for him in this situation. The result was Ernest's awareness of the depth and breadth of his identity grew in response to our work together. And, most importantly, he was able to draw upon the resources contained within this identity to help make his time in hospital more manageable.

IMPLICATIONS FOR SPIRITUALITY

When drawing out the theoretical implications of the case just discussed, the following is perhaps the most significant: as Ernest's awareness grew through our encounter, the boundary between what was initially included in his awareness and what was excluded from it became reconfigured. Previously, Ernest had worked hard to keep his feelings of powerlessness and being out of control at bay, but now those feelings were unavoidable. Because Ernest's identity (and frame for reality) had been predicated on maintaining of his senses of power and control, he consequently experienced his identity in the midst of his own crisis as untenable. He initially expressed this lack of tenability through his anger and blaming of the system. Nevertheless, as he began to get in touch with his fear toward the end of the excerpt above, he took one first step toward re-imagining how he might reconfigure his frame, his identity, and, indeed, his fundamental relationship with the rest of reality.

The process through which I led Ernest can therefore be described as deeply spiritual (LaRocca-Pitts, 2024; Lasair, 2020, 2019). It can be described this way because it invoked various aspects of Ernest's relationship with the rest of reality: his needs for power and control; his perceived identity as a first responder who helped people; and his need to reconfigure the dynamics of his frame to make his hospital experience more bearable. While Ernest himself did not use traditional religious language or concepts, his identity as a first responder did seem sacred to him. I saw this sacred value in how deeply Ernest held his sense of identity, particularly how he predicated his mental, emotional, and spiritual wellbeing on helping people.

Ernest's awareness expanding to engage the greater depth and breadth of his identity, then, can be described as a kind of spiritual transformation (e.g., LaRocca-Pitts, 2024). Not only did Ernest view himself as a first responder who helped people—he was still this—but now he also began to understand himself as someone who had tremendous emotional resources. These resources assisted him to engage crises in his work every day that few would ever encounter in their lives. During our work together, Ernest thus began to bring these resources to bear in his own crisis, and they served him well. Specifically, once he more consistently engaged his own feelings and kept a cool head in his own situation, Ernest was able to smooth over his relationships with his various caregivers. These caregivers had initially been the targets of his anger and intensity. The result was that, by the time he was discharged, Ernest was able to express deep gratitude for the care he received while in hospital. All this was accomplished largely because Ernest's awareness grew to include parts of his identity that had previously been hidden outside his explicit consciousness. There were additional traits of spiritual health that Ernest needed to build during our work together, but these will be discussed more in the chapters below.

Drawing the theoretical threads together, then, the initial process Ernest used to describe his situation drew upon his automatic perceptions concerning his identity. These perceptions about his identity informed how Ernest related to his lived realities. Specifically, Ernest's automatic perceptions and felt sense of identity caused him to create an emotional and spiritual diffraction pattern between himself and his caregivers that was characterized by animosity and intensity.

However, during our encounter Ernest became aware of his automatic perceptions, particularly how they did not accurately reflect the realities of his situation. He therefore started to acknowledge and become further aware of what he was experiencing in deeper parts of himself. Initially this deeper awareness manifested itself as Ernest's explicit naming of and engaging with his fear. As our work proceeded, he became further aware of more nuanced dimensions of his identity, namely the significant emotional resources he brought into to his work. Furthermore, Ernest also started to bring these resources to bear on his life a whole. In light of this new awareness, Ernest could intentionally shape his inner emotional and external interpersonal dynamics. Ernest therefore began to build better rapport and trust with his caregivers. In other words, through his increased awareness, Ernest was able to enhance his relationships with the people with whom he shared his lived realities. Ernest was able to do this because he was no longer governed by his previously automatic perceptions.

Placed in the context of how spirituality was defined in previous chapters, then, Ernest's medical condition caused a physical crisis in his body, but because of how he had predicated his identity on power and control, Ernest had neglected the emotional and intuitive dimensions of himself. Once he began to reconnect with his emotions, Ernest was able to regain a healthier balance between the human and physical dimensions of Raimon Panikkar's *cosmotheandric* principle within himself (see Panikkar, 2010). Furthermore, when he made greater contact with deeper dimensions of his identity, Ernest was able to get in touch with something that transcended the previous contours of his frame. This contact signaled that Ernest was encountering at least a small part of the divine/infinite/transcendent realms that again were so central to Panikkar's (2010) understanding of spirituality. While Ernest did not describe this transcendence in traditional religious terms, there was something sacred about his contact with it. This sacredness was evidenced by the tears Ernest displayed when he began to consciously recognize the richness of the emotional resources he brought to bear on both his work and his life. The process that Ernest and I undertook together therefore enabled Ernest to regain a healthier balance between all dimensions of his *cosmotheandric* identity. The tangible results of this work were the significant changes Ernest was able to make in the diffraction patterns he shared with his caregivers as initially expressed through his body language, actions, behaviors, interpersonal dynamics, and attitudes.

CONCLUSION

This chapter began by discussing how a person's frame for reality is deeply connected to their neurobiology. Not only does a person's neurobiology affect their cognition, but it can also affect their temperament, disposition, and how they interpret and engage many of their life's events. I therefore highlighted how important it is for Spiritual Care Practitioners to assess not only their clients' words, but also the neurobiological dimensions of their clients' experiences as shown in their behaviors, body language, affect, and interpersonal dynamics.

Throughout this discussion, perception was a crucial theme, in that a person's sensory neurobiology, previous experiences, and temperament and disposition can all affect how they perceive and experience their realities. By discussing my encounter with my patient Ernest, I demonstrated how a person's perceptions can affect their engagements with their realities in ways that can be unhelpful in certain circumstances. An initial step Practitioners can take is thus to help their clients build their awareness regarding the various dimensions of their perceptions. Practitioners can then assist their clients to reconfigure the contours of their frame by specifically engaging the client's awareness. Practitioners do this in the hope that clients might begin to experience their current circumstances differently. Ultimately I argued that all this work is deeply spiritual. I argued as much by showing how this work invokes the definitions of spirituality that were explored earlier in this book. Ernest's transformation from a person who expressed anger and intensity to someone who could articulate deep gratitude helped to illustrate the spiritual nature of this work.

However, because professional spiritual care, as I am working to articulate it, is a complex practice, this chapter's discussion of perception and awareness only provides part of the overall picture. At various points above I stated that Ernest and others needed to build several traits of spiritual health to experience lasting transformation and change. In particular, Ernest needed to become open to the new information that his expanded awareness was bringing to him. To continue describing how Spiritual Care Practitioners can contribute to clients' growth into greater spiritual health, then, Chapter Four will begin by focusing on how people project their perceptions onto reality. After that, Chapter Four will address how Spiritual Care Practitioners can assist clients to overcome their projective tendencies by helping them build openness.

Reflection Questions

- How do you understand the connection between a person's neurobiology and how they perceive and experience reality? Would you add anything to this chapter's discussion?
- In your clinical context, how have you seen people's automatic perceptions operating? What effects have these perceptions had on your ability to provide care?
- How have you worked with clients' awareness in the past, even if you haven't called it that? What outcomes did these clients experience because of how you worked with them?

Clinical Assessment and Intervention Questions

- To what extent is the client aware of their automatic perceptions? Are the client's automatic perceptions helpful or unhelpful in this situation?
- To what extent is the client capable of exploring the origins of their automatic perceptions? What intervention strategies might be needed to help the client in such explorations?
- What dynamic in the client's diffraction pattern seems most in need of expanded awareness? How does this dynamic fit within the client's overall presentation of their spirituality?
- As the client's awareness expands, what dynamics can be observed in their body language, actions, behaviors, and attitudes? Is there anything in any of these domains that might require follow-up, either now or in a subsequent interaction?

NOTE

1 As indicated regarding McGilchrist in Chapter One, Schore may be using his distinctions between the brain's two hemispheres heuristically.

REFERENCE LIST

Aron, E. N. (1997). *The highly sensitive person: how to thrive when the world overwhelms you*. New York, NY: Harmony.

Aurobindo, S., & the Mother (1998). *Powers within* (A. S. Dalal, Ed.). Ojai, CA: Institute of Integral Psychology.

Barad, K. (2007). *Meeting the universe halfway: quantum physics and the entanglement of matter and meaning*. Durham, NC: Duke University Press.

Barnhart, B. (2018). *The future of wisdom: toward a rebirth of sapiential Christianity*. Rhinebeck, NY: Monkfish.

Béres, L. (2023). *The language of the soul in narrative therapy: spirituality in clinical theory and practice* (Kindle ebook ed.). New York, NY: Routledge.

Bourgeault, C. (2003). *The wisdom way of knowing: reclaiming an ancient tradition to awaken the heart*. New York, NY: Jossey-Bass.

Bourgeault, C. (2008). *The wisdom Jesus: transforming heart and mind: a new perspective on Christ and his message*. Denver, CO: Shambhala.

Canadian Association for Spiritual Care/Association canadienne de soins spirituelle (CASC/ACSS) (2019, November 26). *CASC/ACSS manual Chapter II, Sections I–VIII, v6 191021*. Retrieved May 2020, from Canadian Association for Spiritual Care/ Association canadienne de soins spirituelle: https://spiritualcare.ca/download/ casc-acss-manual-chapter-2-sections-i-vii-revised-april-2019/

Cozolino, L. (2017). *The neuroscience of psychotherapy: healing the social brain* (3rd ed.). New York, NY: Norton.

de Cruz, H., & de Smedt, J. (2015). *A natural history of natural theology: the cognitive science of theology and philosophy of religion*. Cambridge, MA: MIT Press.

Doehring, C. (2015). *The practice of pastoral care: a postmodern approach* (Revised and expanded ed.). Louisville, KY: Westminster John Knox.

Downes, W. (2011). *Language and religion: a journey into the human mind*. Cambridge, UK: Cambridge University Press.

Godman, D. (Ed.). (1985). *The teachings of Sri Ramana Maharshi: be as you are*. London, UK: Penguin.

Granneman, J., & Sólo, A. (2023). *Sensitive: the hidden power of the highly sensitive person in a loud, fast, too much world* (Audiobook ed., narrated by P. Nieman). New York, NY: Random House.

Graziano, M. S. (2019). *Rethinking consciousness: a scientific theory of subjective experience* (Kindle ebook ed.). New York, NY: Norton.

Hogue, D. A. (2003). *Remembering the future, imagining the past: story ritual and the human brain*. Eugene, OR: Wipf & Stock.

LaRocca-Pitts, M. (2024). The bidimensional spirit and mattering: a continuum of spiritual care interventions. *Spirituality in Clinical Practice*, online pre-publication. doi:10.1037/scp0000377

Lasair, S. (2018a). Spiritual care as a secular profession: politics, theory, and practice. *Journal for the Study of Spirituality*, 8(1), 5–18.

Lasair, S. (2018b). Understanding, assessing, and intervening in the spiritual nature of medical events: theological and theoretical perspectives. *Practical Theology*, 11(5), 374–386.

Lasair, S. (2019). What's the point of spiritual care? A narrative response. *Journal of Pastoral Care & Counseling*, 73(2), 115–123. doi:10.1177/1542305019846846

Lasair, S. (2020). A narrative approach to spirituality and spiritual care in health care. *Journal of Religion and Health*, 59, 1524–1540. doi:10.1007/s10943-019-00912-9

Madigan, S. (2019). *Narrative therapy* (2nd ed.). Washington, DC: American Psychological Association.

McGilchrist, I. (2009). *The master and his emissary: the divided brain and the making of the Western world*. New Haven, CT: Yale University Press.

McGilchrist, I. (2013). Hemisphere differences and their relevance in psychotherapy. In D. Siegel, & M. Solomon, *Healing moments in psychtherapy*. New York, NY: Norton.

McGilchrist, I. (2021). *The matter with things: our brains, our delusions and the unmaking of the world*. London, UK: Perspectiva Press.

Panikkar, R. (2010). *The rhythm of being: the unbroken trinity: the Gifford lectures*. Maryknoll, NY: Orbis.

Pedhu, Y. (2019). Efforts to overcome countertransference in pastoral counseling relationships. *Journal of Pastoral Care & Counseling*, 73(2), 74–81.

Puchalski, C., Vitillo, R., Hull, S., & Reller, N. (2014). Improving the spiritual dimension of whole person care: reaching national and international consensus. *Journal of Palliative Medicine*, 17(6), 642–56.

Ragsdale, J. (2018). Transforming chaplaincy requires transforming clinical pastoral education. *Journal of Pastoral Care & Counseling*, 72(1), 58–62.

Rogers, C. R. (1965). *Client-centered therapy*. Boston, MA: Houghton Mifflin.

Scheib, K. (2016). *Pastoral Care: Telling the stories of our lives*. Nashville, TN: Abingdon Press.

Schore, A. N. (2019). *Right brain psychotherapy*. New York, NY: Norton.

Seth, A. (2021). *Being you: a new science of consciousness* (Kindle ebook ed.). New York, NY: Dutton.

Siegel, D., & Solomon, M. (2013). Introduction: Interpersonal neurobiology and psychotherapy. In D. Siegel, & M. Solomon, *Healing moments in psychotherapy*. New York, NY: Norton.

Swinton, J. (2012). *Dementia: living in the memories of God*. Grand Rapids, MI: Eerdmans.

Treleaven, D. (2018). *Trauma-sensitive mindfulness: practices for safe and transformative healing*. New York, NY: Norton.

Trungpa, C. (2018). *The future is open: good karma, bad karma, and beyond karma* (C. R. Gimian, Ed.). Boulder, CO: Shambhala.

van der Kolk, B. A. (2014). *The body keeps the score: brain, mind, and body in the healing of trauma* (Kindle ebook ed.). New York, NY: Penguin.

Ward, G. (2014). *Unbelievable: Why We Believe and Why We Don't*. London, UK: I.B. Tauris.

White, M., & Epston, D. (1990). *Narrative means to therapeutic ends*. New York, NY: Norton.

Wilber, K. (2017). *The religion of tomorrow: a vision for the future of the great tradition: more inclusive, more comprehensive, more complete* (Audiobook ed.). Denver, CO: Shambhala.

Williams, R. (2014). *The edge of words: God and the habits of language*. London, UK: Bloomsbury.

Zimmerman, J. (2018). *Neuro-narrative therapy: new possibilities for emotion-filled conversations*. New York, NY: Norton.

Four

INTRODUCTION

The last chapter concluded with an in-depth discussion of my encounter with a patient, Ernest. While the last chapter focused on how I worked with Ernest to increase his awareness of his own inner dynamic, it also made evident that his perceptions of his situation in hospital were causing difficulties for him and for the staff who were providing him care. In short, Ernest's perceptions were causing difficulties because he was projecting them into the spaces he shared with others. This dynamic was preventing him from building an understanding of how his care would proceed that aligned with the understandings of his caregivers. Part of the work Ernest and I did together was therefore to facilitate growth in Ernest's openness to perspectives other than his own, even though I did not explore this topic explicitly in my discussion of Ernest's case in the previous chapter.

In contrast, this chapter covers the dynamics of projection explicitly, showing how this common human dynamic can create problems for some individuals. By exploring my work with a patient, Bonnie, in depth, this chapter illuminates some of the intricate dynamics that can often be bound up with projection, while also suggesting specific techniques that can be used to address them. In the process, openness is revealed to be a trait of spiritual health that is closely connected to awareness, as discussed in Chapter Three. This chapter concludes by drawing together many of the theoretical themes that are emerging in this book's pages, pointing the way toward Chapter Five's discussion, which will again assume a largely theoretical register.

PROJECTION, AWARENESS, AND HEALTH

One day I was working in my frontline hospital role, and the spiritual care office received a phone call from a nurse on one of the hospital's medicine units. There was a Caucasian female patient in her sixties

DOI: 10.4324/9781003466147-5

on this unit who was requesting contact with the spiritual care team. Since I was the team member who usually covered this unit, I made my way there and introduced myself to the patient. The patient told me her name was Bonnie and we began to talk about what had brought her to hospital. From what Bonnie told me, she had a complicated medical condition that caused her to experience recurring infections. Because her condition had compromised her immune system, it was not uncommon for the physicians to struggle to get these infections under control.

While Bonnie described herself as a person of faith who belonged to an evangelical Christian church, her ongoing experiences with the healthcare system were causing her to question many of the teachings of her tradition. In particular, she was beginning to wonder whether God was punishing her for what she perceived as "sinful" behaviors and actions she had observed in her family during her childhood. Even though her tradition taught that God is pure love and that there is no sin that cannot be forgiven, the only explanation Bonnie could find for her recurring ill health was to wonder whether her family's "sinfulness" had somehow caused God to take out God's wrath on her.

Now, those familiar with the spirituality and mental health literature will know there is a growing body of research that documents and studies these kinds of spiritual struggles. American clinical psychologists Kenneth I. Pargament and Julie J. Exline (2022) have, in fact, recently published a book exploring how psychotherapists can address such struggles within their clinical practices. While there are several similarities between my approach and Pargament and Exline's, their understanding of spiritual struggles is somewhat different from mine. Within my approach, a person drawing the conclusion that their illness is punishment from God is an interpretative decision that is intricately bound up with how they engage and understand their realities (Lasair, 2019). In other words, such a person's theological conclusion is their way of bringing language and concepts to themes they are perceiving within their life's narrative. To recall the language I introduced in Chapter Two, such an individual's recollection of their life occurs in such a way that they remember their life's events in accordance with a specific coherence that they ascribe to their life's story (see also Lasair, 2020). For Bonnie to conclude that her illness was a punishment from God, then, was to render a particular coherence in her narrative, which she remembered as being specific-ally characterized by illness and its negative effects. Whether or not all the events in such a person's life actually conform to such an ascribed coherence is something that Spiritual Care Practitioners can explore in conversation with such clients. I described one way to approach such dynamics in Chapter Two, when I discussed Jeff and his case.

With Bonnie, however, the situation was quite different. While Bonnie's tradition was explicit in describing God as a being of love, there was also the possibility in Bonnie's faith that God could be vengeful. Given my own history growing up in evangelical Christian commu-nities, I recognized the theological themes Bonnie was drawing upon to reach the conclusion that God was punishing her. Also, knowing that religious language, concepts, and beliefs are inextricable parts of a religious person's daily experiences (recall my summary of Downes' [2011] perspective in Chapter Two), I furthermore knew I needed to tread carefully. Because Bonnie took her faith very seriously, she had made significant emotional, existential, and intellectual investments in seeing her tradition's teachings confirmed in and through her daily experiences. It was therefore possible that Bonnie's belief about being punished by God might also be affecting her overall health and well-being (Pargament & Exline, 2022; Maté & Maté, 2022; Wright & Bell, 2009). In fact, psychiatric services had been consulted to determine whether Bonnie might be experiencing a depression or some other diagnosable mental health condition. In the end, psychiatry felt that Bonnie's emotional distress was mostly circumstantial and would probably best be treated therapeutically rather than pharmacologically. Given all this, I couldn't help but wonder the extent to which Bonnie's internal narrative regarding divine punishment was also affecting her mental, emotional, spiritual, and physical health as a whole.

While it is true I shared several interactions with Bonnie during her hospital stay, it is also true that this was one of the more difficult patient cases I engaged at this stage of my career. Because Bonnie's experiences of the healthcare system had been quite frequent, and because her overall quality of life had suffered significantly due to her recurring infections, her belief that she was being punished by God had taken deep root within her frame for reality. The fact that she did not feel safe talking about her belief concerning divine punishment with members of her family, or even with her faith community and clergy, seemed to make it that much more insidious. I was therefore glad that Bonnie felt free to talk about her struggle with me, but it was also evident there would be much work ahead if Bonnie was going to find some resolution in her relationship with God and the rest of reality.

SPIRITUAL STRUGGLE AS *SPIRITUAL* STRUGGLE

At this point it is helpful to recall a number of distinctions I made earlier in this book. First, recalling my citation of Pargament and Exline (2022) earlier in this chapter, much of the psychotherapeutic litera-ture on these kinds of struggles rightly describes them as spiritual, but this literature also uses the term "spiritual" in a slightly different way than I do in these pages. According to much of the literature, reli-gion and spirituality are almost the same phenomenon, to the point that many authors in this field conflate the terms to talk about R/S struggles without teasing out the specific dynamics of either religious or spiritual phenomena (e.g., Pargament & Exline, 2022; Abu-Raiya, Pargament, Krause, & Ironson, 2015; Abu-Raiya, Pargament, & Krause, 2016; Pargament, 2007). In contrast, my approach, as I described it in the introduction and in Chapter One, understands the term "spiritu-ality," on the one hand, as describing all the processes that produce a person's unique understandings of and engagements with reality. This is why the concept of a person's frame for reality is so central to my approach, as described in Chapters Two and Three. A person's religion, on the other hand, provides the conceptual, linguistic, behavioral, and ritual content that informs their spirituality. Moreover, because reli-gion in this approach is a macro-cultural phenomenon, secular, cul-tural, scientific, philosophical, and psychological traditions, among others, can also fulfill "religious" functions in a person's life (e.g., Lynch, 2012; Taylor, 2007; Milbank, 2006). To describe struggles like Bonnie's as spiritual in my approach, then, draws attention to the processes through which a person like Bonnie arrives at conclusions about the nature of reality and their position in it. What made Bonnie's case challenging, however, was how closely she held her religious beliefs and experienced them as deeply rooted parts of her identity (see Chapter Two and Lasair, 2020). If Bonnie was going to find some resolution to her spiritual struggle, then, she would need to gain some emotional and existential distance from her religious beliefs so she could reflect upon and engage with them more objectively. To explain the theoretical underpinnings of this task, it is again helpful to draw upon Karen Barad's (2007) ideas.

SPIRITUALITY, FRAMES FOR REALITY, AND APPARATUSES

In their discussion of Niels Bohr's philosophy-physics, Barad (2007, pp. 97–131) offers a deeper account of intra-action within their philosophy. As I discussed in Chapter Two, Barad's term *intra-action* describes the entangled relationships that all discernable entities share within the context of an overall phenomenon. The way I made this idea concrete in Chapter Two was to describe how the strained relationship between my patient Jeff and his wife was the product of Jeff's illness, Jeff's increasing needs for physical and emotional support, and his wife's resentment toward him regarding his increasing disabilities and resulting unemployability. In this setting, the relationship Jeff and his wife shared was the overall phenomenon, whereas all the factors I just named, and many more that could not be named, were the discernable contributors to the overall phenomenon. Barad (2007) builds on this notion in their exploration of Bohr's understanding of apparatuses' roles within scientific experimentation.

In Barad's (2007) philosophy, Niels Bohr's thought experiments regarding physics experiments play a crucial role. According to Barad, in quantum physics' early stages as a scientific field it was common for physicists to perform thought experiments concerning how they might design experimental apparatuses to explore the sub-atomic world. These thought experiments would enable physicists to think through the possible effects specific experimental setups might have on the phenomena being studied. In particular, these thought experiments helped physicists to determine how their experimental apparatuses would reveal the specific entities they desired to study.

Bohr, however, according to Barad (2007), pushed this practice to its limits philosophically to demonstrate that sub-atomic entities could not be stated to exist in any verifiable way prior to being revealed by the apparatuses used to study them. In other words, the apparatuses used to study specific sub-atomic particles were what made these particles identifiable, but only under the conditions created by the apparatuses themselves (Barad, 2007; see also Chapter Two). It was therefore impossible to state with any empirical certainty what kind of existence these particles might or might not have apart from what the experimental apparatuses revealed about them under the conditions of particular experimental designs. As a result, Barad concludes that in physics experiments, not only do experimental apparatuses govern how reality is revealed, but the studied realities also emerge in response to the scientists' education, class, gender, and physical abilities (Barad, 2007). All these factors, and more, impact how apparatuses are built and maintained. Sub-atomic realities in quantum physics experiments thus appear through the nexus of physical, social, cultural, economic, gendered, technological, and theoretical realities that all inform the design of experimental apparatuses.

In light of these realities, Barad (2007) concludes that all of reality is co-constructed; one part of reality informs how other parts of reality come into being, regardless of whether these different parts of reality exhibit traits of consciousness or not. In Barad's (2007) approach, sub-atomic particles become identifiable in response to numerous theoretical and technological advances. All these advances then enable physicists and other scientists to construct apparatuses that make such particles visible. Bringing this idea into human domains, Barad (2007) argues that the co-constructed and entangled nature of reality necessitates that human agents embody significant ethical awareness. Ethical awareness, in Barad's approach, means attempting to pursue the good in relation to all discernable entities with whom a person shares relationships. From Barad's perspective, such ethical awareness is crucial for effective intra-action because intra-action is the use of agency within an overall phenomenon (Barad, 2007). Specifically, *intra-action* refers to how all the relationships between the various entities within a particular overall phenomenon contribute to the phenomenon's specific nature and qualities (Barad, 2007). By mobilizing and restructuring the relationships between the various entities that contribute to an overall phenomenon's existence, then, the overall phenomenon can be transformed in numerous signifi- cant ways. This last sentence describes the essence of intra-action within Barad's (2007) approach. It was this idea that informed my interventions with Jeff as I described his relationship with his wife in Chapter Two. It was also this idea that I thought might prove helpful in my work with Bonnie as described in this chapter. The crucial thing in all this, however, was to help Bonnie see her belief system as part of the apparatus she brought to her understandings of and engagements with reality. To draw attention to the therapeutic path that I chose in relation to Bonnie, it is worth recapping some of the theoretical themes I have been developing to this point.

PROJECTION: ANTICIPATING THE FUTURE THROUGH CONSISTENCY AND CHANGE

In previous chapters I spent extensive space describing the intricate dynamics of a person's frame for reality. Not only does a person's frame integrate all their life's experiences, but it also uses language, concepts, rituals, and practices to assist in establishing the meaning(s) of this person's life-narrative. In Barad's (2007) language, a person's frame for reality is the apparatus through which they engage the various realities in their life. Furthermore, in my discussion in Chapter Two, I indicated that when it comes to a person's use of religious language and concepts, this is just as much an everyday phenomenon as is that same person's description of their preferred dish detergent (see also Downes, 2011). As people experience them, religious language, concepts, rituals, and practices are but one set of resources they can use to make cognitive sense of their realities (Lasair, 2020; Downes, 2011; de Cruz & de Smedt, 2015). It is therefore impossible to cleanly separate a person's identity from their use of these religious resources—often people predicate their identities on seeing the cognitive dimensions of their frames confirmed in and through their daily experiences (Watts, 2017; McAdams, 1993; Downes, 2011; Williams, 2014; Corbett, 2012; Culliford, 2012). For those who have strongly held religious beliefs, then, these beliefs tend to be accompanied by significant emotional investment in seeing their beliefs' truth-claims borne out in external realities. Even in cases like Ernest's, as described in Chapter Three, where people closely associate their identities with their perceptions of reality (regardless of whether these perceptions are framed in traditional religious terms or not), people typically desire to see the stories they tell themselves about their realities confirmed by the events through which they live. This desire is the essence of projection, and it can be either healthy or unhealthy depending on the circumstances.

Now, at this point readers will likely be reminded of the descriptions I articulated regarding consistency and change in Chapter Two (see also Ricoeur, 1991, 1992, 1984). To recap briefly, consistency and change are the competing dynamics through which any person lives; these dynamics are bound up with humans' experiences of time. As I stated in Chapter Two, we all need to find the right balance of consistency and change in our lives so we can feel healthy and fulfilled. If a person experiences too much consistency, life can seem boring or stagnant; if a person experiences too much change, it can seem like little in life is stable, and a person can experience varying degrees of stress and/or trauma as a result. Each person must therefore find the right balance of consistency and change for themself.

When considering projection, then, it becomes evident that this phenomenon is a specific dimension of how a person anticipates and experiences their movement into the future. Recalling Figure 2.1, all humans are bound by their movement through time. We can only experience ourselves in the present, but we remember the past in specific ways, often ascribing particular coherences to different parts of our life's narrative (see also Lasair, 2020; Ricoeur, 1992). A person then determines whether the coherences they ascribe to the past have remained consistent or have changed over time. I alluded to this concept above when I discussed how Bonnie arrived at the conclusion she was being punished by God. From Bonnie's perspective, her consistent experiences of illness made her wonder whether divine punishment was informing why she did not seem to experience any significant changes in her medical status. When anticipating the future, however, we typically have our desires, but these desires are also informed by how we understand "the good" in our lives (see Chapter Two and Lasair, 2020). As a result, when I was describing Ernest's experience of receiving care in Chapter Three, his sense of the good was intimately bound up with his desire and capacity to help people. Because Ernest could no longer help people when I met him due to his medical crisis, his sense of the good felt extremely distant. Ernest's circumstances had changed, but his expectations concerning how he might pursue the good remained consistent with the realities he had experienced before his illness. Ernest therefore began blaming his caregivers for not properly doing their jobs because he had to remain in hospital longer than he expected. In other words, Ernest was projecting his notion of the good onto his current experience and encountering significant frustration because his caregivers did not seem to acknowledge or engage this value that was such a central part of his identity.

One significant complicating factor in Bonnie's case, however, was her belief that her illness and the recurring infections it caused were punishments from God. Recalling my discussion of religious language in Chapter Two, according to Downes, religious language at least partially originates in humans' capacities to ascribe a theory of mind to all sorts of objects, animate and inanimate alike. In Chapter Two I demonstrated how this insight reveals the everydayness of religious language, in that any object a person encounters in their daily life can potentially be perceived as having properties of consciousness to varying degrees. McGilchrist substantiates this idea in his assessment of Indigenous cultures, which was cited in Chapter One (McGilchrist, 2021). Specifically, McGilchrist (2021) notes that Indigenous cultures often ascribe life and consciousness to all manner of seemingly inanimate objects. From McGilchrist's perspective, this is because Indigenous cultures likely prioritize traits that he associates with the brain's right hemisphere when they experience and engage their lived realities. When Bonnie ascribed consciousness to Ultimate Reality, naming it God, then, she was behaving consistently with many human cognitive, emotional, and intuitive norms (McGilchrist, 2021; Downes, 2011; Williams, 2014; de Cruz & de Smedt, 2015). Moreover, for her to wonder whether God was punishing her was to draw upon the language of her faith tradition in an attempt to find some plausible meaning for the difficult medical experiences through which she was living. However, Bonnie's cognitive conclusion that her recurring infections were punishments from God proved difficult to engage from typical healthcare perspectives. These difficulties emerged because such a belief is impossible to verify using standard Western scientific methods (see Chapter One and Habermas, 2003, 2008).

PROJECTED COGNITIONS, EMOTIONS, AND INTUITIONS

Now, if my clinical approach was informed by cognitive behavioral therapy (e.g., Sokol, 2019), it would have been easy to challenge Bonnie's belief. I could have asked Bonnie what evidence she had to support her belief that she was being punished by God. She might have responded that her recurring infections suggested that God was punishing her. I could then have pushed her further by asking what evidence she had that *God* was causing her recurring infections. At that point Bonnie's belief might have begun breaking down because it is very difficult to provide incontrovertible cognitive or empirical evidence to substantiate claims of divine action (see Habermas, 2008, 2003). However, because spirituality within these pages is understood primarily as a relational phenomenon that often prioritizes a person's emotional and intuitive concerns (see Chapter One and Williams, 2014; Downes, 2011; Puchalski, Vitillo, Hull, & Reller, 2014; McGilchrist, 2021), I knew it would be important to take a different approach with Bonnie.

While it is true that Bonnie's belief was expressed in cognitive terms, the most important aspect of it from my perspective was the emotional subtext it communicated. When placed in the context of Bonnie's overall narrative, it was clear that trust between herself and God had been broken (see Pargament & Exline, 2022; Abu-Raiya, Pargament, & Krause, 2016). Bonnie felt she did not deserve her long-term illness and the recurring infections it caused. Because she felt she did not deserve these experiences, and because she also believed there needed to be a reason for her ongoing ill health, Bonnie concluded that God must be punishing her for the "sinful" behaviors manifested by her family members during her childhood. From Bonnie's perspective, it was impossible to find any other explanation for her emotional, physical, and spiritual suffering. In other words, Bonnie was ascribing a meaning to her experience that she expressed in the language that made the most sense to her—the language of her faith and theology, which were intimately bound up with her frame for reality (see Downes, 2011; de Cruz & de Smedt, 2015; Williams, 2014). Put in Barad's (2007) terms, Bonnie's faith and theology were key components of the apparatus through which she discovered the meanings of her realities. If Bonnie could draw different conclusions about her illness, then, or at least provisionally set her belief about divine punishment aside, I felt she might find some meaningful ways to engage her ongoing experience of illness. As in the last chapter, insights from neuroscience can again shed some light on these dynamics.

NEUROSCIENCE, CHANGE, AND PROJECTION

There is a growing consensus among neuroscientists that human perception occurs because, over their lifetimes, people build mental models of their physical, emotional, relational, political, social, cultural, religious, and spiritual environments (Cozolino, 2017; Graziano, 2019; Seth, 2021). Using my terminology, these models are the cognitive and emotional components of a person's frame for reality. Typically, these models reside beneath the surface of a person's conscious awareness. Or, using Barad's (2007) terminology, these mental models are the implied apparatuses people use to discover what reality means for them. According to neuroscientists, mental models not only shape and form how people experience their everyday realities; they also inform how people encounter unfamiliar realities (Graziano, 2019; Seth, 2021; Cozolino, 2017). A person's mental models serve as filters for whatever they experience in life: they reveal when something has changed in a person's everyday physical or social environments (Graziano, 2019; Seth, 2021). These changes are revealed because something within those environments no longer conforms to what a person's mental model indicates is typical for these environments. However, because mental models seem to be oriented toward maintaining consistency, people will often try to fit realities they have not previously encountered into whatever mental models they might have built for themselves. Such forced fittings often occur because a person typically encounters new realities before their mental models have adjusted to account for whatever the new realities entail in themselves; people typically impose their existing mental models onto new realities, even though the new realities might completely undermine the validity of the models themselves (Graziano, 2019; Seth, 2021). This last sentence is yet another way of describing the dynamics specific to projection.

In many respects, then, this neurological approach offers a different account of why people find significant changes in their lives difficult to navigate. Often a person's mental models remain consistent with their previous realities, insofar as mental models rarely adjust themselves spontaneously to the changes through which a person is living (Cozolino, 2017). In my experience, it is often necessary to assist people to adjust their mental models in spiritual care clinical situations, simply because they are experiencing realities for which their mental model is inadequate (see Chapter Two). Therefore, when I was working with Bonnie, a significant task for us was to explore together how her mental model, or in my terminology, her frame for reality, had responded to the dynamics of consistency and change produced by her illness.

For comparison, recalling the discussion above, Ernest's circumstances had changed suddenly, so initially in my work with him, he struggled with the reality that he could no longer live his vision of the good because of his admission to hospital. In contrast, Bonnie's change in medical status had been protracted over a number of years, and this long-term experience was causing her to question whether God, her Ultimate Reality, could really be trusted. Bonnie's consistent experiences of frustration, disappointment, anger, and grief were causing her to wonder whether God was indeed as loving as her tradition presented. As Bonnie and I explored her theology together, then, she described how previously her tradition had taught her that faith in God would enable things to go well in her life. Yes, she may have some short-term experiences of illness or misfortune, but things would turn out alright in the end. Bonnie shared that in her illness's early stages she had held tightly to this belief. But when the infections kept coming and she began spending more time in hospital than in her home, Bonnie's beliefs began to shift. Bonnie started to see parts of the Bible referring to divine punishment and retribution as potentially applying to her. She wondered, had she or her family done something that required her to endure these ongoing experiences of ill physical health, anger, disappointment, frustration, and grief?

To bring Bonnie's experiences into dialogue with Barad's concepts, a particular experimental apparatus is only able to reveal the portions of reality it is specifically designed to reveal (Barad, 2007). Or, drawing upon my own concepts, unless a person is open to the reality that multiple interpretative options are available to them regarding the potential the meaning(s) of their experiences, they will usually experience their automatic perceptions as providing the only real option (Lasair, 2020, 2019). As I discussed in the last chapter, an initial step in nurturing clients' openness to multiple interpretative options is to help them become more aware that their perceptions are occurring automatically, without much intentional reflection. Often this can be accomplished by asking such clients where their perceptions are coming from or what in their life caused them to draw their conclusions about their current circumstances. A second step can then address how clients are projecting their perceptions onto the realities through which they are currently living.

UNHEALTHY PROJECTIONS: FORECLOSURE

In Bonnie's case, however, the work we did was further complicated not only because she was projecting her belief about divine punishment onto God, her Ultimate Reality, but in doing so she was also restricting the possible meanings she could ascribe to her experience. This is a phenomenon I call "foreclosure," and it typically occurs when clients have significant emotional and existential investments in maintaining their projected perceptions of reality. There were traces of foreclosure in Ernest's case, particularly when he was blaming his caregivers for not doing their jobs properly. Yet in Ernest's case, it was relatively easy to shift his foreclosures, largely because he already had some emotional connection to the healthcare system due to his work as a first responder. In contrast, Bonnie needed to revisit much of her faith and theology. Because Bonnie's tradition had been so convincing in how it presented its teachings, and because she had seen many of these teachings confirmed in her experiences prior to her illness, Bonnie held her projected and foreclosed perceptions more tightly than Ernest held his. For Bonnie to reconfigure her faith and theology would thus require changing much of her relationship with almost all of reality. For Bonnie, and many others in her position, such a reconfiguration would entail change of such magnitude that it could have upset irrevocably the right balance of consistency and change in her life.

In many ways, it would therefore have been easier for Bonnie to maintain her belief that she was being punished by God than it was for her to revise and overhaul it. Yet with some work, Bonnie came to see how her belief about divine punishment was beginning to affect her relationship with her husband, her experiences of herself, and how she engaged her friends and faith community as she moved through her illness. With all these people, Bonnie was trying to embody an almost impossible vision of goodness in the hope that somehow gentle, kind, and gracious attitudes on her part might convince God she was worthy of receiving a miraculous cure. Yet as she was putting significant time and energy into embodying this vision of goodness, Bonnie was also becoming increasingly convinced she was being punished because her miraculous cure was not forthcoming. Bonnie was therefore mentally, emotionally, spiritually, and physically exhausted, and none of this was helping her body fight the infections that were coursing through its systems. By projecting her belief that she needed to convince God to cure her, Bonnie was causing herself distress in most parts of her life. From a medical perspective, Bonnie's distress in non-physical domains was also causing distress in her body, and all this combined was making her body's fight against its infections that much more difficult. Judith Butler's thought sheds some additional light on Bonnie's predicament. Many know Butler as the pioneer of queer theory through her famous books *Gender Trouble* (1990) and *Bodies that Matter* (2011). However, Butler has also done significant work exploring how people can use words, concepts, and practices to injure one another. In her book *Excitable Speech*, Butler (1997) examines a phenomenon she sources in the thought of French political philosopher Louis Althusser (see Althusser, 2005; Žižek, 1999). The phenomenon is called "interpolation."

UNHEALTHY PROJECTIONS: INTERPOLATION

According to Butler (1997), when Althusser (2005) was exploring how political states mobilize their power, he used an example from the Christian New Testament. For Althusser (2005), the fact that Jesus named his disciple Simon "Peter" in the gospels shows how an act of naming can draw a person into an overall frame of reference that pre-exists them; in his act of naming, Jesus assigned his disciple a divinely ordained role that the disciple himself had not previously occupied (i.e., the foundation of the Christian church), at least not to his knowledge (the name *Peter* in Greek means "rock," and Jesus states that he will build his church upon this rock [Matthew 16:18]). Similarly, then, agents of the state, like police officers, can accuse individuals of criminal activity, regardless of whether such individuals have actually engaged this kind of activity or not (Butler, 1997; Althusser, 2005; Žižek, 1999). From the perspective of both the state and the individual, these accusations result in the relationship between both parties being completely restructured. Where accused individuals would previously have functioned as free citizens, the state now requires such individuals to move through extensive judicial processes to establish whether they are guilty or not guilty of the crimes of which they have been accused. Through a simple act of naming, then, an entire state apparatus is invoked, and that apparatus has the power to decide how a person's life will proceed from the time they are accused into their foreseeable future (Butler, 1997; Althusser, 2005; Žižek, 1999). Specifically, once a person is named a potential criminal, that person's life is interpolated into a state apparatus, and that apparatus plays a significant role in constructing that person's life from that moment onward.

Now, while Bonnie was likely unaware of the concept of interpolation, it was evident that this phenomenon was operating in her life. Even though she had not been accused of criminality by human authorities, Bonnie's reading of the Bible suggested to her that her family's "sinfulness" had prompted divine judgment and punishment to become active in her life. These apparatuses were constituent parts of her faith and theology, even though her church did not emphasize them that much. From Bonnie's perspective, her recurring infections, lengthy hospital admissions, and persistent feelings of frustration and disappointment all indicated she had become a target of God's wrath. Furthermore, even though she tried in numerous ways to convince God that her punishment ought to end, she did not experience the miraculous cure she so deeply desired. If Bonnie was going to experience her illness differently, she needed to become open to the reality that her belief about God's punishment was only one way to interpret her situation. I therefore wondered if working with Bonnie's self-imposed designation as an object of God's wrath would shift her foreclosed perception that God was punishing her. Here is a portion of an interaction Bonnie and I shared about midway through our work together:

SpC: You told me that you and God used to share quite a loving relationship. Can you tell me more about that?

B: When I was younger my relationship with God was wonderful. I felt very close to him; he and I would talk all the time, and I felt that whatever prayers I prayed were answered quickly.

SpC: That does sound beautiful. But you also said that at some point something changed in this relationship?

B: That's right. When I started getting sick God all of a sudden felt distant. I prayed and I prayed, but I couldn't get that sense of closeness back and I just kept getting sicker and sicker. I felt betrayed. I felt like God didn't care about me anymore. I wondered what I had done to deserve being sick like this.

Then it dawned on me: when I was growing up my family wasn't Christian, and they did some very bad things. Maybe my sickness was punishment for the things my family did when I was younger!

SpC: Do you still feel like your sickness is punishment?

B: I don't see how it can be any other way—no one deserves to be as sick as I am.

SpC: Wow ... (*long pause*) ... That's a really difficult place to be in ...

B: (*tears up*) ... I know ... And the most frustrating thing is, I've tried so hard to be a good person ... I help my family, I help my friends, I try to be involved with my church as much as I can, but I just don't get better. Why won't God stop punishing me?!

SpC: (*pause*) ... If you're right that God is punishing you, do you have a sense as to why your punishment isn't ending?

B: I have no idea. I just don't know what I can do to convince God that I can't handle much more of this.

SpC: I'm just wondering what your sense is of what Jesus did on the cross.

B: He took our sins away?

SpC: I mean, what do you believe that means for you that Jesus took your sins away?

B: I'm not sure ...

SpC: I know that some Christians believe that Jesus took the punishment all of us were deserving onto himself. Is that what you believe?

B: I don't know ... I guess so ... I mean, that's what I was always taught at church ...

SpC: If that's what your church taught, what do you make of that now, in your current situation?

B: I don't know ... (*tears up*) ... these past number of years have just been so hard ... I haven't been able to be the person I know I am ... It's like I don't know myself anymore, and I can't understand why God would let this happen to me.

SpC: Is that why you believe God might be punishing you?

B: Yes ...

SpC: But if your church teaches that Jesus took the punishment you were deserving, how does that fit with everything you've experienced?

B: I just don't get it! Nothing seems to make sense anymore! I feel I used to know God, I used to know myself, but now nothing makes any sense anymore!

SpC: You seem quite angry about this …

B: Yes, I guess I really am angry—I didn't do anything to deserve this, but now I'm living it, so now what do I do?!

Our conversation continued for some time after this point. Bonnie and I explored her senses of loss and grief in response to the changes brought about in her life by her illness. We also discussed what kind of relationship she wanted to have with God, even though she felt God had betrayed her. Over several subsequent interactions, Bonnie and I also explored questions of trust and what trust looks like, particularly how she might rebuild her trust and connection with God, even if she might not receive the miraculous cure for which she had been hoping and praying.

Analysis

At the beginning of this extract, I asked Bonnie to walk me through how her relationship with God had changed. This was a crucial way for me to get some sense of how the dynamics of consistency and change had been active in Bonnie's life, particularly in her relationship with God. As the extent of change in Bonnie's relationship with God became evident, much of what Bonnie stated also showed how deeply rooted religious language and concepts were within her frame for reality. I write this because there is increasing medical and psychiatric evidence suggesting that changes in medical health can have significant effects on a person's mental health for biological as well as psychological reasons (e.g., Bullmore, 2018). It is therefore possible that the close emotional and intuitive connection Bonnie experienced with God prior to her illness had diminished in response to her body's attempts to fight the diseases within it. Yet exploring this possibility would not have worked with Bonnie, at least not initially, precisely because her religious language and concepts were her primary resources for framing and engaging her lived realities. Moreover, Bonnie had already stated on several occasions that she felt God was punishing her. I therefore knew I would need to engage Bonnie's religious language within her frame for reality so she could gain some independence from this belief that was oppressing her. In doing so, I would need to demonstrate that the meaning she had assigned her experiences was only one of several available options—this is why I cited the common evangelical Christian teaching that when Jesus was crucified, he took the punishment all humanity deserved upon himself. In introducing this idea, I was careful not to assume it was what Bonnie herself believed, hence I phrased my intervention "I know that some Christians believe …" Nevertheless, as the extract above demonstrates, Bonnie's response to this intervention was both pronounced and immediate.

BIRTHING OPENNESS

When Bonnie's cognitive assessment of her situation began to break down, it was possible to witness a significant upsurge of emotion within her. I named this emotion "anger" in my response, but in some ways this name only seemed to capture part of what Bonnie was expressing. In theoretical terms, the upsurge of emotion that Bonnie experienced demonstrated that her foreclosed belief in divine punishment had worked to contain the myriad emotions that were causing her mental, emotional, and spiritual distress. Yet, as noted above, it was also clear Bonnie's foreclosed conclusion was also perpetuating her feelings of distress, specifically because she was not receiving the answer to prayer that she so deeply desired. By providing a cognitive alternative to Bonnie's internal assessment of her experiences, then, I sought to open a space in Bonnie's awareness where she could receive the depth and complexity of what was going on within her. Through the intensity of Bonnie's response, it was evident my intervention accomplished what it set out to achieve. Yet it was also evident my intervention created a vacuum of cognitive meaning within Bonnie that would somehow need to be addressed if she was going to regain her mental, emotional, spiritual, and religious equilibrium. In many clinical situations, simply opening up the possibility that there might be multiple options for how a client might interpret their experiences is sufficient for them to have lasting clinical benefits.

Nevertheless, part of what made Bonnie's situation so challenging was the extent to which she had interpolated herself into her perceived apparatus of divine punishment. Yes, it was impossible to verify empirically whether she was actually being punished by God or not, but the high levels of emotional distress Bonnie manifested prior to my intervention indicated the extent to which this apparatus had become embedded within her frame for reality. To undermine that apparatus' functioning, then, demanded that Bonnie almost comprehensively reconstruct her ways of engaging her current lived realities. Yet it was also clear that Bonnie already had some resources that could assist in that reconstruction. My citation of the evangelical teaching concerning what Jesus did on the cross was one such tool. In fact, my citation of this idea would not have been effective had Bonnie not already partially believed it, at least at a cognitive level. But Bonnie's cognitive beliefs were not my primary concern. What concerned me more was that Bonnie's trust in her Ultimate Reality (i.e., God) had been broken and, somehow, she needed to rebuild that trust. Bonnie's belief in divine punishment was one way she had tried to make cognitive sense of how her trust in God had been broken. Yet now that Bonnie's self-imposed belief in this regard had been shown to be inconsistent with her broader belief system, she needed to re-evaluate how her trust had been broken, how she might rebuild it, and find another way to explain her experience in the process. In other words, my work with Bonnie, as recorded in the brief verbatim account above, opened Bonnie up to numerous possibilities concerning what her experiences of ill health might mean, undermining the efficacy of her projected and foreclosed perceptions in the process. At this point a number of clinical considerations need to be articulated.

CLINICAL CONSIDERATIONS

My intervention producing this openness in Bonnie occurred at a time in our relationship when we had already shared several interactions and had built sufficient trust and rapport that we could be open and honest with one another. In acute care settings this is not always possible, given how many patients are short-stay and also given how many patients are not medically stable enough to engage numerous follow up interactions. Practitioners thus need to judge in the moment whether utilizing an intervention like the one I recorded above is warranted and safe for any given patient. In Bonnie's case I knew she had been stable enough for some time that I would likely be able to follow up with her within the next few days. Furthermore, toward the end of the interaction recorded above, I was also careful to provide an emotional and spiritual container for Bonnie. I did this by guiding her back to a place of emotional safety by the end of our interaction, in that we ended our conversation by exploring how she experienced trust in her relationships with her friends and family. I also offered a prayer for Bonnie—with her consent—that God would hold her and help her feel safe, even while she was in an emotional and spiritual place of not knowing and uncertainty. In therapeutic terms, both these interventions helped to reinforce the trust Bonnie had in me as her Spiritual Care Practitioner (see Chapter Three on therapeutic alliance). Even more so, my hope was that Bonnie could begin to feel her way into trusting God again as I prayed for her, even if her prayers for a miraculous cure did not produce the specific result she was hoping for.

THEORETICAL IMPLICATIONS

In terms of the theory being developed in these pages, my hope was that the openness Bonnie experienced in response to our interaction would ultimately become a more fulsome openness to her relationship with her Ultimate Reality, whom she named "God." Early in my work with her, it was evident Bonnie's belief in divine punishment was preventing her from having this full openness in her relationship with the divine. Because of her belief, Bonnie could not allow herself to experience the full spectrum of feelings she might need to express in her relationship with God: the griefs, the angers, the joys, the sorrows, the frustrations, etc. Instead, she placed a huge amount of pressure on herself to embody a vision of goodness that she felt might convince God to take her illness away. Yet instead of her illness going away, Bonnie's admissions to hospital increased, as did her inner turmoil; Bonnie felt her declining health was further evidence that God was punishing her. The entirety of Bonnie's relationship with all reality therefore became constructed around her belief that God was punishing her, and this belief was preventing her from finding emotional healing and greater spiritual health.

As discussed in earlier chapters, however, spiritual health entails finding the right balance between the different elements of Raimon Panikkar's *cosmotheandric* principle (Panikkar, 2010). In Bonnie's situation, her ill physical health was causing distress in her body, or the parts of her being that can be identified with the *cosmos*. Similarly, her mental and emotional turmoil were causing Bonnie very human, or *andric*, distress.

The result was Bonnie could not find her inner connection with *theos*, or the infinite or divine realms. In my assessment of Bonnie, I felt her self-imposed understanding regarding divine punishment was a significant contributor to her felt lack of connection to the infinite or divine realms. My interventions in the extract above were therefore directed toward addressing these belief structures, which were limiting Bonnie's sense of connection with God (see also Pargament & Exline, 2022; Wright & Bell, 2009). My interventions in subsequent interactions continued this work of building Bonnie's sense of connection by engaging her feelings of trust for God and working directly with them to enhance and fortify them. In taking this approach I was consistent with the definition of professional spiritual care I articulated in Chapter One, in that I worked with Bonnie to build, maintain, and enhance her relationship with all reality, prioritizing her felt senses of emotional and intuitive connection in the process.

None of this would have been possible, however, had Bonnie and I not built good trust and rapport. Some helping professions call trust and rapport between a therapist and client a "secure therapeutic alliance"; in Chapter Three I described this dynamic using Schore's idea regarding the synchronization between the right hemispheres of the client's and therapist's brains. Regardless of the language used, this felt sense of emotional resonance and connection is the main tool Spiritual Care Practitioners use to help build, maintain, and enhance clients' relationships with all reality. There will be more to state in this regard in Chapter Five, when I will discuss the freedom and wisdom that emerge when clients experience growing inner neutrality. With Bonnie, however, the trust that she and I built helped her to overcome her projected and foreclosed perception that God was punishing her, opening her to the possibility that perhaps the Ultimate could be trusted, even if her prayers might not be answered in the ways she felt they ought to be. Engaging this reality thus required Bonnie and me to reflect extensively on her theology and how it had helped or not helped her to be in a fully open and honest relationship with God. While this work was not entirely completed by the time Bonnie was discharged from hospital, I did feel she had enough religious and spiritual resources that she could maintain her better spiritual health in the community, even if she might require support from a qualified Psychospiritual Therapist (Pastoral Counselor) to do so. I therefore provided Bonnie with a referral to someone outside the hospital to ensure she had access to adequate and qualified support in case she felt she needed to pursue this work further. To date, I have not encountered Bonnie again.

CONCLUSION

In this chapter I explored my work with my patient Bonnie in depth. Through this exploration, the following theoretical conclusions emerged:

- When a person perceives reality, they often impose their perceptions on the situations through which they are living. I have called these impositions "projection," and through my exploration of Bonnie's case I demonstrated how projection can take on unhelpful dynamics in people's lives.
- While projection can be unhelpful in many situations, I also demonstrated how it can be a benign expression of a person's frame for reality due to its connection with a person's mental model for their life as embodied in their specific neurobiology. This neurobiological perspective revealed how important it is for both Practitioners and clients to address the dynamics of foreclosure in clients' lives.
- Foreclosure, as I have described it, limits the possibilities for how individuals might make cognitive, emotional, and intuitive sense of their life's narrative. Foreclosure therefore limits a person's openness to and sense of connection with all reality.
- Drawing upon Butler's engagement with the phenomenon called "interpolation," I showed how acts of naming or self-designation can invoke large conceptual, social, and/or cultural apparatuses that can reinforce and perpetuate various gestures of foreclosure.
- Through my analysis of an interaction I shared with Bonnie, I demonstrated how working to facilitate enhanced openness in a client's life seeks to address the unhelpful dynamics that can occur when that person projects and forecloses their perceptions of their life and its meaning(s).
- I demonstrated how openness is a key component of spiritual health because it mediates between the three domains identified in Panikkar's *cosmotheandric* principle. In Bonnie's case, openness was needed in her relationship with the divine or infinite domains, so those specific areas were the main focus of my interventions.

All these conclusions are consistent with the definition of spiritual care I articulated in Chapter One. In that definition I indicated that spiritual care seeks to build, maintain, and enhance a person's relationship with all reality by focusing on their emotional and intuitive connections with all that is. Through this chapter and the previous one I therefore demonstrated how awareness and openness are key components in these felt connections. In the next chapter I will begin to describe how freedom and wisdom build upon the dynamics of awareness and openness to produce yet further dimensions of spiritual health in clients' lives.

Reflection Questions

- When have you seen projection and foreclosure in your clients' lives? How did these dynamics manifest themselves?
- When you have seen projection or foreclosure in your clients' lives, how have you engaged these dynamics? What factors did you consider when choosing whether to engage them or not?
- What factors might inform how you engage such dynamics in the future?

Clinical Assessment and Intervention Questions

- What perceptions might the client be projecting into their current situation?
- To what extent might the client's perceptions be foreclosed?
- To what extent is interpolation a factor within the client's frame for reality?
- What resources are available within the client's frame for reality that can help to counterbalance the dynamics of unhelpful projections, foreclosures, and/or interpolations?
- Are there any other areas in the client's frame for reality that might benefit from enhanced openness?
- What safety concerns must be considered when working to facilitate enhanced openness in this client's life?
- How can you address these safety concerns if enhancing the client's openness is still clinically warranted?

REFERENCE LIST

Abu-Raiya, H., Pargament, K., & Krause, N. (2016). Religion as problem, religion as solution: religious buffers as the links between religious/spiritual struggles and well-being/mental health. *Quality of Life Research*, 25, 1265–1274.

Abu-Raiya, H., Pargament, K., Krause, N., & Ironson, G. (2015). Robust links between religious/spiritual struggles, psychological distress, and well-being in a national sample of American adults. *American Journal of Orthopsychiatry*, 85(6), 565–575.

Althusser, L. (2005). *For Marx* (B. Brewster, Trans.). London, UK: Verso.

Barad, K. (2007). *Meeting the universe halfway: quantum physics and the entanglement of matter and meaning.* Durham, NC: Duke University Press.

Bullmore, E. (2018). *The inflamed mind: a radical new approach to depression.* New York, NY: Picador.

Butler, J. (1990). *Gender trouble: feminism and the subversion of identity.* New York, NY: Routledge.

Butler, J. (1997). *Excitable speech: a politics of the performative.* New York, NY: Routledge.

Butler, J. (2011). *Bodies that matter: on the discursive limts of sex.* New York, NY: Routledge.

Corbett, L. (2012). *Psyche and the sacred: spirituality beyond religion.* New Orleans, LA: Spring Journal Books.

Cozolino, L. (2017). *The neuroscience of psychotherapy: healing the social brain* (3rd ed.). New York, NY: Norton.

Culliford, L. (2012). *The psychology of spirituality: an introduction.* London, UK: Jessica Kingsley.

de Cruz, H., & de Smedt, J. (2015). *A natural history of natural theology: the cognitive science of theology and philosophy of religion.* Cambridge, MA: MIT Press.

Downes, W. (2011). *Language and religion: a journey into the human mind.* Cambridge, UK: Cambridge University Press.

Graziano, M. S. (2019). *Rethinking consciousness: a scientific theory of subjective experience* (Kindle ebook ed.). New York, NY: Norton.

Habermas, J. (2003). *Truth and justification* (B. Fultner, Ed., & B. Fultner, Trans.). Cambridge, MA: MIT Press.

Habermas, J. (2008). *Between naturalism and religion: philosophical essays* (C. Cronin, Trans.). Cambridge, UK: Polity Press.

Lasair, S. (2019). What's the point of spiritual care? A narrative response. *Journal of Pastoral Care & Counseling*, 73(2), 115–123. doi:10.1177/1542305019846846

Lasair, S. (2020). A narrative approach to spirituality and spiritual care in health care. *Journal of Religion and Health*, 59, 1524–1540. doi:10.1007/s10943-019-00912-9

Lynch, G. (2012). *The sacred and the modern world: a cultural sociological approach.* Oxford, UK: Oxford University Press.

Maté, G., & Maté, D. (2022). *The myth of normal: trauma, illness & healing in a toxic culture.* Toronto, ON: Knopf Canada.

McAdams, D. (1993). *The stories we live by: personal myths and the making of the self.* New York, NY: Guilford Press.

McGilchrist, I. (2021). *The matter with things: our brains, our delusions and the unmaking of the world.* London, UK: Perspectiva Press.

Milbank, J. (2006). *Theology and social theory: beyond secular reason* (2nd ed.). Malden, MA: Blackwell.

Panikkar, R. (2010). *The rhythm of being: the unbroken trinity: the Gifford lectures.* Maryknoll, NY: Orbis.

Pargament, K. (2007). *Spiritually Integrated psychotherapy: understanding and addressing the sacred.* New York, NY: Guilford Press.

Pargament, K. I., & Exline, J. J. (2022). *Working with spiritual struggles in psychotherapy: from research to practice.* New York, NY: Guilford Press.

Puchalski, C., Vitillo, R., Hull, S., & Reller, N. (2014). Improving the spiritual dimension of whole person care: reaching national and international consensus. *Journal of Palliative Medicine, 17*(6), 642–56.

Ricoeur, P. (1984). *Time and narrative* (Vol. 1) (K. M. Laughlin, & D. Pellauer, Trans.). Chicago, IL: University of Chicago Press.

Ricoeur, P. (1991). Life: a story in search of a narrator. In M. J. Valdes (Ed.), *Paul Ricoeur: reflection and imagination* (pp. 425–437). Toronto, ON: University of Toronto Press.

Ricoeur, P. (1992). *Onself as another* (K. Blamey, Trans.). Chicago, IL: University of Chicago Press.

Seth, A. (2021). *Being you: a new science of consciousness* (Kindle ebook ed.). New York, NY: Dutton.

Sokol, L. (2019). *The comprehensive clinician's guide to cognitive behavioral therapy.* Eau Claire, WI: PESI Publishing.

Taylor, M. C. (2007). *After God.* Chicago, IL: University of Chicago Press.

Watts, F. (2017). *Psychology, religion, and spirituality: concepts and applications.* Cambridge, UK: Cambridge University Press.

Williams, R. (2014). *The edge of words: god and the habits of language.* London, UK: Bloomsbury.

Wright, L. M., & Bell, J. M. (2009). *Beliefs and illness: a model for healing.* Calgary, AB: 4th Floor Press.

Žižek, S. (1999). *The ticklish subject: the absent centre of political ontology.* London, UK: Verso.

Working toward Neutrality

Facilitating Growth in Freedom and Wisdom

Five

INTRODUCTION

To lay the ground for this chapter's discussion, it is helpful to draw attention to the connections between many of the concepts explored so far. Over the past three chapters I have developed the concept of a person's frame for reality. I have done this mainly by drawing upon the tools of hermeneutic philosophy (Chapter Two), science studies (Chapters Two and Four), neuroscience (Chapters Three and Four), and psychology (Chapters Three and Four). All these fields, in their own distinct ways, describe how any person's frame for reality is generated over their lifetime, integrating their numerous experiences into an overall relationship with and understanding of reality. This integration occurs according to the various dynamics specific to a person's individual neurobiology. The result is that every person's relationship with and understanding of reality is particular to them because it relies upon the person's lifelong cognitive, emotional, and intuitive tendencies. Religious ideas, concepts, teachings, practices, and rituals all play various roles in these relationships with and understandings of reality. They play these roles because religion is part of the macro-cultural heritage individuals inherit from their families of origin, faith communities, educational systems, preferred expressions of popular culture, and any other entities that contribute to their socialization and enculturation over time. Various secular, social, scientific, and/or cultural systems of thought can play roles similar to those of religion in a person's frame for reality, as well.

When a person's frame for reality is understood, therefore, as it is in these pages, to be the fundamental expression of their spirituality, it then becomes possible to identify specific traits that enable them to be spiritually healthy. As described in the previous chapters, spiritual health is evident when a person can build, maintain, and enhance their felt emotional and intuitive connections with all reality.

DOI: 10.4324/9781003466147-6

Raimon Panikkar's (2010) *cosmotheandric* principle has been instructive in this regard because it shows how spirituality connects all people to the physical universe (*cosmos*), to the depths of their humanity (*aner/andros*), and to the infinite, divine, and transcendent realms (*theos*). Again, a person does not need to be a religious adherent, nor even a theist or polytheist, to experience the kind of transcendence to which Panikkar refers. Nevertheless, this book has argued that people experience and understand the three *cosmotheandric* domains through their frames for reality. For this reason, it becomes evident that specific dynamics within a person's frame for reality can either help or hinder the building, maintaining, and enhancing of the relationships that are bound up with their *cosmotheandric* identity. In the previous two chapters, awareness and openness were two such dynamics that were demonstrated as foundational for spiritual health in any individual because they structure that person's inner realities in ways that help them consciously engage the three domains in Panikkar's principle. How might these structuring dynamics be illustrated?

THE RELATIONSHIP BETWEEN AWARENESS AND OPENNESS

I introduced the dynamics of awareness and openness in the previous two chapters through my discussions of Ernest's and Bonnie's cases. In Ernest's case I demonstrated how the scope of this patient's inner awareness needed to expand to include more of his emotional realities in the human domain because his automatic perceptions of his situation did not reflect what was actually occurring for him. Concretely, Ernest's awareness only encompassed the realities in his life of which he possessed explicit conscious awareness. When I met him, Ernest was not explicitly aware of the fact that his admission to hospital was producing significant fear in him. Before my work with him he may have had a vague intuition that his medical crisis was causing him to experience fear. It was also likely that when Ernest blamed his caregivers for not properly doing their jobs, he was subconsciously protecting himself from experiencing his fear's full magnitude. When I first met him, then, Ernest likely experienced his fear only at the fringes of his awareness. It was therefore necessary for Ernest to increase his openness to the reality that fear was part of his experience before he could allow himself a fuller awareness of how significant that fear actually was.

A similar dynamic was operating in Bonnie. By holding tightly to her foreclosed perception that she was being punished by God, Bonnie prevented herself from feeling the myriad emotions that were swirling within her because of her long-term illness's effect on her overall quality of life. Specifically, Bonnie's belief was affecting her experiences in human domains and in the divine/infinite/transcendent realms. That belief was also causing distress in the physical domain inhabited by her body, in that her emotional distress was creating difficulties in her body's fight against the organisms infecting it. As a result, Bonnie needed to be open to the awareness that there were, in fact, numerous cognitive and emotional options for how she might make sense of her illness and its potential religious and/or spiritual meanings. Bonnie needed this openness so she could begin to build different understandings of what her illness and emotions meant and so she could rebuild her relationship with her Ultimate Reality, whom she named God. As discussed in the last chapter, once Bonnie let go of her belief that God was punishing her, she experienced a significant upsurge of emotion that she then needed to make sense of. As a result, Bonnie and I spent substantial time reconstructing her theology. Yet, as in my work with Ernest, Bonnie's growth in openness increased her awareness, and this increase in awareness also required her to continue working on remaining open to the richness of what her awareness might render within her.

AWARENESS AND OPENNESS IN CLINICAL ASSESSMENTS AND STRATEGIES

Now, the previous paragraphs may have given the impression that Spiritual Care Practitioners need to engage a client's relative openness clinically before that client's awareness can increase. In the context of the Practitioner's intervention strategy, this might be true. However, before a Practitioner introduces specific interventions, their baseline assessment of a client often works to establish the scope of the client's awareness. Practitioners assess this so they can determine how best to engage the client's awareness of both their internal and external dynamics. If aspects of the client's awareness are limited, or if some of the client's projected perceptions are foreclosed—or even interpolated into unhelpful emotional and conceptual apparatuses—then the client's awareness can only be increased by first establishing the extent to which the client is open to perspectives other than their own. If the client is open to other perspectives, then their limited awareness is often relatively straightforward to address. If, however, foreclosure or interpolation are significant factors in the client's perceptions of their situation, addressing the client's lack of openness often takes greater clinical priority. Ultimately, all this indicates that there is a reciprocal relationship between awareness and openness in all people's lives, and this reciprocity needs to be accounted for when working clinically to improve or enhance a client's overall spiritual health.

Considering the relationship between awareness and openness, then, it becomes evident that a person must manifest both these traits to consciously engage all three domains of their *cosmotheandric* identity (see Lasair, 2021; Panikkar, 2004, 2010). Without awareness, a person will be able to describe neither their inner dynamic nor how they relate to external realities. It will therefore be impossible for such a person to get in touch with their human (*aner/andros*) emotions and intuitions and with how these emotions and intuitions connect them to physical (*cosmos*) or human realities outside themselves, or to the divine/infinite/transcendent realms (*theos*). A person must consequently be open to becoming aware of what is occurring in all three domains. Sometimes such awareness can be limited because of a person's conceptual understanding of what constitutes reality (McGilchrist, 2021; Corbett, 2012; Downes, 2011; de Cruz & de Smedt, 2015). Other times awareness can be limited by internal emotional or intuitive barriers that a person sets up to protect themself from parts of reality they might not understand or that produce fear in them (e.g., Schore, 2019). The result is that a Practitioner's initial assessment of a client needs to determine what might be limiting the client's awareness and how best to engage these limitations. As part of this assessment Practitioners also need to determine how the client uses concepts, emotions, and intuitions to construct their relationship with all reality (see e.g., Lasair, 2018). Each of these human phenomena can either limit or enhance a client's openness to physical, human, or divine/infinite/transcendent domains. Practitioners therefore need to understand any client's particular use of conceptual, emotional, or intuitive approaches to realities both within and outside themself. Such an assessment reveals how the Practitioner might engage the dynamics of their client's frame to assist the client to build, maintain, and enhance their relationship with all reality as manifest in their specific *cosmotheandric* identity.

PRACTITIONERS' AWARENESS AND OPENNESS IN THEIR DIFFRACTION PATTERNS

Now, as implied in previous chapters, the dynamics of clients' frames surface in clinical encounters mainly because of the interpersonal dynamics that Practitioners generate in response to their clients' behaviors, attitudes, actions, interpersonal dynamics, body language, and so on. In Chapter Two I discussed the idea of diffraction patterns (see also Barad, 2007); in Chapter Three I engaged Schore's (2019) notion that in therapeutic situations therapists synchronize their own brains' right hemispheres to the right hemispheres of their clients' brains. Both ideas (synchronization and diffraction patterns) communicate a reality of which counselors, psychotherapists, and social workers have long been aware: in all human interactions there exists an emotional field of which many are unaware but which, regardless, influences actions, behaviors, attitudes, thoughts, and decisions. What makes a therapist's involvement in human interactions unique is the therapist's conscious awareness of such fields (see Chapters Two and Three). Skilled therapists are also able to intentionally engage such fields' dynamics for the purpose of improving clients' mental, emotional, or spiritual wellbeing (Schore, 2019). All this means that, when providing spiritual care, Practitioners deliberately create specific kinds of emotional and spiritual diffraction patterns between themselves and their clients. The Practitioner's intent in doing so is to help clients build their capacities for awareness and openness within the context of their overall spiritual health. Practitioners' diffraction patterns also help clients build their capacities for other aspects of spiritual health, which will be described in further detail below. As previous chapters demonstrated, a Practitioner's diffraction pattern in relation to their client is often constructed through the intricate relationship between the Practitioner's body language, affect, use of language, and capacity to bring the emotional and intuitive dimensions of the client's story to the surface of clinical interactions. There are several theoretical perspectives that help to explain this dynamic.

Diffraction's Contextual Dimensions

Recalling my discussion of Jürgen Habermas' political philosophy in Chapter One, part of what enables Practitioners to create specific kinds of diffraction patterns in clinical contexts is their capacities to co-construct emotional and cognitive meaning with their clients (Habermas, 1984). When it comes to co-constructing meaning, as discussed in Chapter One, Habermas (1984) believes that in organizational and political contexts participants in conversation need to agree on the processes that will govern the making of decisions before any decisions can be made. From Habermas' perspective, there are certain agreed-upon principles that ought to inform Western democratic decision-making processes. In Chapter One I noted that commitments to secular, empirical, and scientific ways of knowing are hallmarks of Habermas' approach (Habermas, 2003, 1992). In Chapter One, however, I also noted Charles Taylor's critique of Habermas' position. From Taylor's perspective, Habermas' approach is exclusionary because it is not likely that most people in the West make decisions according to Habermas' perceived secular norms (Taylor, 2011). Taylor argues instead that people make decisions for numerous kinds of reasons, including religious ones. Therefore, Western decision-making contexts ought not to be too restrictive about the kinds of reasons that are understood as admissible in public contexts when people consider how to proceed regarding any specific issue (Taylor, 2011).

When it comes to healthcare settings, medical personnel understand the anatomical, physiological, and pharmacological factors that need to be accounted for when making decisions about a patient's care. These factors align medical personnel with the secular decision-making norms that Habermas (1992, 2003) describes. However, there are also increasing numbers of medical personnel who understand that emotional, intuitive, and spiritual and/or religious concerns can play important roles in patients' and families' medical decision-making processes (see e.g., Balboni et al., 2017; Wirpsa et al., 2019; Steinhauser, Fitchett, et al., 2017; Puchalski, Vitillo, Hull, & Reller, 2014). These perspectives can be seen to align more fully with Taylor's approach. Nevertheless, most medical personnel lack the training to assess the true nature of patients' and families' religious and/or spiritual concerns. Medical personnel typically also lack the training to engage such concerns clinically. Spiritual Care Practitioners are thus uniquely situated in healthcare to assess and engage these kinds of patient and family perspectives (Wirpsa et al., 2019). Not surprisingly there is a growing body of literature that demonstrates as much through rigorous clinical research. Regardless, this clinical situatedness is only part of what enables Practitioners to create specific kinds of diffraction patterns in relation to their clients.

Through their CPE training specifically, Practitioners are invited to build their own capacities for awareness and openness (Lasair, 2020; Vanderstelt, van Dijk, & Lasair, 2022). This is true not only regarding their own personal narratives, but it is also true regarding their awareness of and openness to the dynamics of client narratives. Part of Practitioners' training thus involves building competence with one or more psychotherapeutic modalities and marrying these modalities with various religious/theological/spiritual perspectives (e.g., CASC/ACSS, 2019). The purpose of all this is to assist Practitioners to build language and concepts that describe, assess, and engage the almost-infinite client presentations they encounter in their clinical work. This training also provides vocabularies and concepts that assist Practitioners in engaging the secular clinical languages, procedures, and policies that can be pervasive in their workplaces, especially in healthcare. The result is that Practitioners have several conceptual, emotional, religious, and spiritual tools available to them for engaging clients and their narratives. Yet, as indicated above, among the most important of these are the Practitioner's own capacities for awareness and openness, which were built during their CPE training (Lasair, 2020; Vanderstelt, van Dijk, & Lasair, 2022). Maximizing these traits' capacities helps Practitioners monitor and modify their own inner dynamics in relation to their clients. Practitioners' awareness and openness also help them receive and consciously assess and address clients' ways of relating in clinical situations.

Drawing upon psychoanalytic perspectives, Practitioners' awareness and openness thus help them perceive and mitigate whatever dynamics of transference and countertransference they might experience in relation to their clients (Schore, 2019; Pedhu, 2019). In Chapter Three I introduced the concepts of transference and countertransference, drawing upon Schore's (2019) understanding of these phenomena. Space does not permit a full discussion of how Practitioners understand transference and countertransference, but in terms of spiritual health, awareness and openness help Practitioners see when and how aspects of their own histories are being invoked by something a client is describing—this is an effect of awareness. These traits also help Practitioners to understand how prior events affect them in the present behaviorally, emotionally, physically, and spiritually—this is an effect of Practitioners' openness to whatever learning their awareness might produce in them.

Diffraction Patterns' Foundations: Neutrality and Freedom

Ultimately, what a Practitioner's CPE training renders in them is a kind of neutrality in relation to their automatic perceptions and their tendencies to project their perceptions onto reality in specific ways (Lasair, 2021). This neutrality is one of the significant aims of Practitioners' awareness and openness. Moreover, Practitioners' neutrality enables them to experience growing measures of freedom from their automatic tendencies in perception and projection (Lasair, 2021). In other words, Practitioners can modify their inner responses to clients because they have gained freedom from their automatic perceptive and projective tendencies. This freedom enables Practitioners to maintain their inwardly and outwardly neutral stance in relation to whatever their clients might disclose to them. Whatever reactivity Practitioners might have exhibited in clinical situations prior to their CPE is therefore largely resolved through their training (Vanderstelt, van Dijk, & Lasair, 2022; see also Jankowski et al., 2008). The specific clinical result is that clients typically feel both safe and comfortable when interacting with Practitioners who have been well-formed in their personhood and professional identities (see Lasair, 2020; Vanderstelt, van Dijk, & Lasair, 2022). The previous sentences offer the most concrete description of Practitioners' clinical diffraction patterns to this point in these pages. As previously, Schore's (2019) perspectives on the role of the brain's right hemisphere in psychotherapy are helpful at this point.

Neutrality and Freedom's Neurobiological Dimensions

From Schore's (2019, Chapters Three and Four) perspective, one phenomenon that makes his approach to psychotherapy effective is therapists' capacities to enter what he calls a "mutual regression process" with their clients. According to Schore, regression occurs when a secondary cognitive process is set aside so both therapist and client can attend to primary cognitive processes. Throughout his book *Right Brain*

Psychotherapy (and this approach is confirmed by McGilchrist's [2009, 2021] engagements with the neuroscience), Schore (2019) describes explicit cognition as a secondary process that is typically associated with the left hemisphere of the human brain. The right hemisphere, in contrast, is more focused on the primary processes of world perception and construction, using emotions and intuition as its main tools. From a neuroscientific perspective, the brain's right hemisphere typically processes information faster than the left hemisphere (McGilchrist, 2009); therefore the right hemisphere's engagements with reality are correctly understood as primary, and the explicit cognition associated with the left hemisphere is best understood as secondary because it occurs later (Schore, 2019). From this standpoint, then, distorted or disrupted cognition is a symptom of an underlying disturbance in a person's capacity to construct and embrace healthy emotional and intuitive relationships with themself and the world around them. Schore (2019) therefore indicates that to address these disturbances it is necessary for therapists to "synchronize" their brain's right hemisphere with their client's right hemisphere. Through this synchronization, therapists can vicariously experience (through transference and countertransference) the dynamics specific to their clients' emotional and intuitive lives. Because therapists schooled in Schore's approach know when and how transference and countertransference are operating for them, they can help their clients skillfully navigate often-fraught emotional territory. The goal of such navigation is to assist clients to reconstruct their emotional and intuitive relationships with the rest of reality (Schore, 2019). Such reconstruction is accomplished by therapists helping clients to resolve whatever emotional or intuitive dynamics might be creating disturbances in their relationships with the world around them, assuming they are not due to any neurological difference. All this is what Schore means by "mutual regression." Based on this discussion, and similar discussions in previous chapters, it should now be possible to detect how Schore's approach connects with spiritual care.

Neutrality and Freedom's Contemplative Dimensions

While Spiritual Care Practitioners are sensitive to the dynamics of transference and countertransference that are so central to Schore's approach (see e.g., Pedhu, 2019), Practitioners often go further in their engagements with clients' emotions and intuitions. Because spiritual care typically integrates practices and perspectives from several religious and/or spiritual traditions, contemplative approaches to human existence usually play at least some role in Practitioners' frontline work. In many such traditions (I am most familiar with Christian and Buddhist approaches to contemplation) there is much attention paid to allowing thoughts (i.e. explicit cognitions), bodily sensations, emotions, feelings, and intuitions to rise within oneself (see e.g., Frenette, 2012; Bourgeault, 2016). The goal is not to suppress, ignore, or eliminate these inner phenomena. Rather, the goal of contemplation is to attend to these phenomena from a position of detachment (i.e., not getting "hooked" by them), and then let them go (Bourgeault, 2016; Frenette, 2012). It is this capacity for detached attention or mindfulness that is evident in many Practitioners' approaches to care. Even traditionally trained psychotherapists are increasingly integrating such contemplative or mindful approaches into their delivery of care, as attested by the growing number of publications on the topic (e.g., Loizzo, Brandon, Wolf, & Neale, 2023).

What distinguishes spiritual care from these more psychotherapeutic approaches is in part the context of care (in many cases healthcare, corrections, military, or faith-community settings). Spiritual care is also distinguished by the formation of the caregiving relationship. Where psychotherapeutic or counseling clients often seek their caregivers out to address specific issues, Spiritual Care Practitioners often view their care as being client-driven—whatever the client wants to discuss is up to them (Doehring, 2015; Gerkin, 1986; Lasair, 2019; Scheib, 2016). For Spiritual Care Practitioners, building, maintaining, and enhancing their relationships with clients is the main orientation of their care (see Chapter One and Rogers, 1965). Building, maintaining, and enhancing of relationships are the principal tools that Practitioners have to assist their clients in building, maintaining, and enhancing their own relationships with the rest of reality (Rogers, 1965; Schore, 2019). What Practitioners bring to their caregiving relationships, then, is, at least initially, a specific quality of embodied relationship. In previous generations of spiritual care or chaplaincy scholarship, this relationship was specifically referred to as a "ministry of presence," largely because of its embodied quality (e.g., Gerkin, 1986).

Considering the discussion in this chapter, however, it might be more accurate, in fact, to refer to this relational quality of spiritual care-giving as the Practitioner's own deep and broad embodiment of the *cosmotheandric* principle (Panikkar, 2010). Practitioners are trained to engage their own bodies so they might attend to what is occurring in their connection to the physical world. Practitioners are also trained to attend to the human domains of thoughts, feelings, emotions, and intuitions, understanding these phenomena as important indicators of their own—and others'—relationships with the rest of reality (Parameshwaran, 2015). Finally, Practitioners are trained to build, maintain, and enhance their own relationships with the Ultimate, no matter how that is understood. These three domains, as experienced in Practitioners' own specific embodiments, and through their own frames for reality, provide the context and container for whatever a client might bring to them in a caregiving relationship. What do I mean by *context* and *container*?

As discussed above, for a Practitioner to function in the three *cosmotheandric* domains, they themself need to manifest high levels of awareness and openness (Lasair, 2021, 2020). I also alluded above to the growing neutrality Practitioners experience within themselves and in relation to others. This neutrality is like the detachment described in many contemplative or mindfulness teachings (e.g., Bourgeault, 2016; Frenette, 2012). It can also be expressed using the language of "unconditional positive regard" made famous by American psychologist Carl Rogers (1965). A Practitioner's neutrality is therefore the anchor that enables them to manifest the so-called "non-anxious presence" that is often discussed in the chaplaincy and spiritual care literature.

However, when described in terms of a Practitioner's embodied depth and breadth of the *cosmotheandric* principle, this non-anxious presence takes on a significantly different nuance. Specifically, when described this way, a Practitioner's neutrality is a concrete manifest-ation of their deeply felt senses of physical, emotional, intuitive, *and cognitive* connection with all three *cosmotheandric* domains (Panikkar, 2010; McGilchrist, 2009; Parameshwaran, 2015). For Practitioners to remain aware of and open to the physical universe, human domains, and the divine/transcendent/ultimate realms, they cannot allow their perceptions and projections to limit any encounter with any entity connected to their *cosmotheandric* identity. As a result, Practitioners understand—viscerally, if not cognitively—that neutrality and freedom are central features of their own relationships with reality. Practitioners also understand that part of their role is to guide their clients into similar manifestations of these traits. Neutrality and freedom provide the container of inner spaciousness needed to engage any portion of reality (or any entity) in awareness's and openness's fullness. The *cosmotheandric* principle is the context for any person's individual neutral container (Panikkar, 2010, 2014). For clients to experience increased spiritual health, then, they need to discover similar neutral spaciousness within themselves. By implication, clients also need increasing freedom from automatic perceptions and projections for their neutrality to grow (Lasair, 2021). Clients' growth in neutrality thus renders greater freedom within them; growth in freedom also renders greater neutrality in clients' inner lives—another reciprocal relationship! So, what does this look like clinically?

A CLINICAL EXAMPLE: JUDY

Judy was a middle-aged female patient who had been admitted to one of my hospital's medicine units. Shortly after she was admitted, Judy's nurse paged me, indicating that Judy was having a tough time and was asking to speak with someone from spiritual care. Because I live and work in the largest city in my Canadian province (Saskatchewan), many people come to my hospital from remote rural communities to receive specialized care. Judy was in my hospital because the acute-care site in her home community did not have the capacity to care for her complex medical needs. Judy's distance from her family, the complexity of her medical situation, and being in an unfamiliar environment were all weighing heavily on her.

As Judy and I talked, however, it became evident that in many ways Judy was different from many other patients I had encountered in my work. As she described the intricacies of her life, her joys and her sorrows, the strains in her relationships, and her almost-uncanny ability to experience good luck, Judy was able to enter the emotions connected with whatever she said, and then simply let them go when she moved on to the next part of her story. There were several times when she teared up telling me about her life, but there were also as many times she broke into a wide grin that made her eyes sparkle.

In many respects, Judy's life had been hard: she came from a background with many broken relationships, and addiction had been a persistent feature in her family. Yet Judy had also done a lot of work on herself by drawing upon the teachings of her faith and engaging her past, all for the purpose of finding significant measures of healing. I therefore experienced Judy as very frank about the brokenness in her past and the ongoing struggles experienced by many members of her extended family. This frankness, however, also enabled Judy to be similarly honest about what brought her joy in life. Judy had worked hard to help others in her community, and she was devoted to her family, even while they continued to struggle and engage in patterns of unhealthy and dangerous behavior. Unlike many other patients I had encountered in my frontline hospital role, Judy was able to hold all aspects of her life in tension, embrace the emotions she experienced in relation to each, and still embody wholeness throughout it all.

I could state a lot about the work I needed to do with Judy, largely because her baseline spiritual health was already quite high. I will, in fact, revisit some of the themes manifest in her story in Chapter Seven. What stands out for this discussion, however, is how her story connects to the notions of frames for reality and mental models, as discussed in Chapters Two and Four. As discussed in Chapter Four, a person's mental model is embodied in the neurological structures that enable them to perceive and navigate their way through the emotional, social, physical, spiritual, religious, and interpersonal dynamics manifest in their everyday lives. While such mental models are very sensitive to small changes in any dimension of a person's everyday life, if there are more significant changes it can often take a person more time to adjust their model (e.g., Cozolino, 2017; Graziano, 2019; Seth, 2021). This additional time is required because in many cases the changes are of such a magnitude that large portions of the person's model need to be reconstructed. If the person's model does need reconstruction, they must also often renegotiate how they relate to both their inner and outer worlds. To engage such work can feel very threatening. Moreover, if such work is required of a person suddenly, like when some life-altering event occurs, emotional and/or spiritual trauma can be the result. All this information reinforces the need for Practitioners to pay close attention to the competing dynamics of consistency and change in their clients' lives, as discussed in Chapters Two and Four.

While trauma was not a feature of Judy's experience when I met her, it was evident that being at a distance from her family and having to stay in an unfamiliar environment were causing Judy some distress. She was worried for several of her family members, who, due to difficult relationships and ongoing experiences of trauma, were living at significant risk. When Judy was nearer to her family, she felt she could help and support them within the limits of what she could offer. However, now that she was in hospital in the city, she could not act to help her family members in the same ways she would when she was nearer to them. Yes, Judy could phone her family and connect with them that way but given how at-risk some of her family members were, brief phone calls did little to allay Judy's fears, at least when she was alone in her hospital room.

From the outset of our conversation, however, it was clear that prayer was a significant feature of Judy's life. She talked extensively about how she prayed that God would keep her family members safe. She also talked about how she expressed her anger to God when she felt her prayers were not being answered in the ways she needed. It was, in fact, this feeling that God wasn't answering her prayers that was causing Judy's feelings of distress to increase. When I first encountered her, then, Judy had been alone with her uncomfortable feelings for most of the day, and this had resulted in her becoming more and more agitated. When I arrived in her room, she therefore welcomed me warmly and invited me to sit opposite her in a chair by her bedside. Here is what the first portion of our conversation looked like:

SpC: So, Judy, what's been happening?

J: It's just been really tough. I live with my family and most of them are having a tough time, and I'm here and I can't help them.

SpC: That does sound really difficult. Is there anything in particular that seems to be bothering you?

J: Yeah, my daughter's living with me right now, and she's just getting off drugs, but her boyfriend is right into that stuff and she doesn't want to break it off with him. I see how he goes out every day and does that stuff, and I see how my daughter is trying hard to get off it herself, but she says she loves him and she wants to help him, but I know things don't work that way.

I was in a relationship like that years ago, and it took me leaving him and cleaning up my life for me to finally get things on track. I see my daughter hurting herself exactly the same way I did, and I wish she wouldn't do it to herself.

SpC: Wow, all that feels really heavy.

J: It is, and I pray that God would help her, and there have been some things that have happened that make me feel like God is helping her, but with me being here and my daughter being back home I can't check in on her the way I usually do, so all that's been worrying me.

SpC: I can understand why you feel worried.

J: I know, I just feel like a whole bunch of bad stuff has happened to me recently, and I don't want more bad stuff to happen.

SpC: Bad stuff?

J: Yeah, last week my car got broken into and my purse was stolen so I had to take care of all of that, and then I got really sick and had to come into the hospital, and the hospital back home thought I was so sick that I needed to come here, and then my son, who's on disability, had another accident and I couldn't be around to help him. I dunno, it just feels like there's a lot going on.

SpC: That does feel like a lot.

J: Yeah, but then a couple weeks ago they were having a draw at the co-op and I had a bit of extra money so I bought a ticket and I won five hundred dollars' worth of gift cards!

SpC: Wow! What do you make of that?

J: I dunno. I just seem to get lucky. There was another draw about a month ago, and I won that too!

SpC: Wow! So even though you say you've had some bad stuff happen recently, you've also had some really good stuff happen.

J: Yeah, I guess that's true.

SpC: What do you make of that?

J: I guess things aren't as bad as I thought they were … I dunno, I also feel like I was just having a rough day today, being far away from my daughter and not being able to see her. When I think of it, my daughter does have some good people around her. She's got a friend who lives down the street who's been through some of the same stuff, and she'll help my daughter if she needs it. I trust her; she's a good person. I'm glad my daughter has a friend like that.

SpC: Seems like there are some good things to be thankful for.

J: There are, and I thank God for them.

Our conversation continued for some time after this point. Together Judy and I explored her relationship with God and how that relationship had helped her through some experiences of significant difficulty in her life. At the end of our conversation, Judy thanked me for what I did, saying she felt much better because of our interaction.

Analysis

While this interaction has been condensed for the sake of its presentation in this chapter, what I offered above captures the somewhat stream-of-consciousness dynamic that was present in Judy's contributions to our conversation. I was not concerned about this dynamic during our interaction, because it did not seem to reflect anything particularly unusual or diagnosable from a psychiatric perspective (see American Psychiatric Association, 2013). Rather, I viewed Judy's dynamic as one I have often experienced with people who have done a lot of work to come to places of emotional and/or spiritual healing. I have seen many such people move freely from topic to topic in conversation, not shying away from experiences of difficulty while being able to recognize good things in their lives at the same time. Prior to our interaction, however, Judy had been "hooked" by her feelings of distress concerning how her daughter was home alone while Judy herself was receiving medical care. Judy had also prayed for her daughter, but this had not allayed her feelings of distress, even though she admitted she had seen some things that indicated to her that perhaps her prayers were being answered. For whatever reason, Judy was not able to resolve these distressing feelings on her own, and, as it turned out, my presence was the catalyst Judy needed to help shift her back into the relatively neutral emotional and spiritual space that seemed more her norm. As demonstrated above, Judy's return to neutrality required minimal interventions on my part. What interventions I did use were therefore more like standard active listening, and those seemed more than enough to help Judy return to her usual stance of inner neutrality. The interaction's dynamics themselves, however, are worth noting.

In each of my reflective statements above I was careful to acknowledge and name the emotions behind Judy's story while also not stating too much. This somewhat minimalist approach prompted Judy to open up more about what she had been living through while I maintained my stance of free neutrality (see Lasair, 2021; Parameshwaran, 2015). My maintaining of this stance enabled me to receive whatever Judy felt she needed to tell me. During my CPE training, especially in its early stages, I might have reacted more negatively to some aspects of Judy's story, particularly those portions of it concerning her family members' ongoing struggles with various kinds of addictions (Jankowski et al., 2008; Vanderstelt, van Dijk, & Lasair, 2022). Yet because I had heard many such stories by the time Judy and I shared this interaction, I was able to acknowledge within myself how I was perceiving Judy and not allow those perceptions to intrude into our interaction through unchecked projections on my part (see Pedhu, 2019). This freedom and neutrality within me therefore freed Judy to do whatever emotional processing she needed to do without any disruption or interference from me (Parameshwaran, 2015). As demonstrated above, within a short time, Judy was able to regain her emotional and spiritual equilibrium. Had I manifested a different interpersonal dynamic, or had some of my perceptions intruded into our interaction through projection, Judy might have experienced a different outcome.

There was one telling moment in the interaction Judy and I shared, however. It occurred when Judy said, "I guess things aren't as bad as I thought they were ... I dunno, I also feel like I was just having a rough day today, being far away from my daughter and not being able to see her." This sentence was telling because it indicated Judy had enough inner distance from her thoughts and emotions that she was able to name and reflect upon them explicitly (see Parameshwaran, 2015). This inner distance is different from what I experienced in Ernest and Bonnie. Ernest was initially so bound to his perceptions that he blamed his caregivers for not properly doing their jobs (see Chapter Three). Similarly, Bonnie was so convinced she was being punished by God that she struggled to accept other perspectives, and when she did accept other perspectives, her new awareness and openness required that she undertake significant work to reconstruct her theology (see Chapter Four). Judy's emotions, in contrast, were simply emotions—she did not attempt to project them onto other people; neither did Judy construct elaborate conceptual apparatuses into which she interpolated her experiences. In this sense, then, Judy's capacity to name and reflect upon her experiences prevented her from becoming distressed in ways that were too difficult to remedy easily. In contrast, Ernest's distress was connected to how he experienced his long-term and deeply rooted identity as a first responder. Similarly, Bonnie's distress was the result of her attempts to make religious and spiritual sense of her experiences of ill physical health over a long period of time. Judy, however, had previously undertaken extensive work to understand herself and navigate her life by embodying emotional and spiritual health. It was therefore easier for her than it was for Ernest or Bonnie not to get "hooked" by feelings and experiences that might cause distress or pain. Her acknowledgment that she was probably just having a bad day before I saw her was thus an indication of how easily she was able to reframe her experiences simply by adjusting her inner dynamic in relation to them. All this indicates that Judy was able to embody yet another trait of spiritual health: wisdom.

WISDOM

As discussed in previous chapters, wisdom is a trait that features prominently in several religious traditions, to the extent that specific portions of their sacred writings bear the name "wisdom." There are portions of the Jewish and Christian scriptures, for example, that contain so-called "wisdom literature." In those corpora, wisdom is treated as a metaphysical entity that can inform human behaviors and interactions (see e.g., Proverbs). Likewise, in some Christian traditions Jesus is understood as the embodiment of God's wisdom (see e.g., Williams, 2018; Bourgeault, 2008). In other Christian traditions, wisdom is treated one name for the Holy Spirit and is considered a gift of God to which all Christians ought to aspire (see, e.g., Seely, 2024). As further examples, contemplative thought in Buddhism, Christianity, Muslim Sufism, and Hindu yoga are often stated to contain wisdom teachings. In short, all these understandings of wisdom denote teachings and practices—and even metaphysical entities—that help humans to navigate their lives in ways that enable them to better pursue and embody the good. In many such contexts, wisdom is a trait that emerges once a person has grappled with some of the superficial dynamics of their frame for reality (e.g., their tendencies in perception and projection) and begun to move into deeper dynamics that many traditions identify as capacities for self-mastery (e.g., Bourgeault, 2008; Aurobindo & Mother, 1998; Barnhart, 2018).

Therefore, in the system articulated in these pages, wisdom is a trait that depends on the inner neutrality I described above (Lasair, 2019, 2020, 2021; Parameshwaran, 2015). Wisdom depends on neutrality because it assumes good awareness of and openness to learning from one's own tendencies in perception and projection. Based on this awareness and openness (and a resulting growth in neutrality), wisdom enables a person to make choices about how they move into the future based on what they have experienced as helpful or unhelpful in the past, with particular reference to their perceptive and projective tendencies (Lasair, 2019, 2021). As such, wisdom enables a person to understand and engage their inner dynamic, similar to what I described in relation to Judy above. Wisdom also helps a person monitor and change their behaviors, actions, attitudes, and interpersonal dynamics in the spaces they share with others. In these pages, behaviors, actions, attitudes, and interpersonal dynamics are outward extensions of a person's tendencies in perception and projection (see Chapters Two, Three, and Four); these in turn are deeply entangled with the dynamics of a person's frame for reality. As a result, neutrality and freedom form the basis for a person's wise engagements with themself and others. Wisdom also enables a person to continue to build their capacities for awareness, openness, neutrality, and freedom over time because wise people often see how embodying these traits makes it possible for them to build, maintain, and enhance their overall emotional and spiritual health in relation to the rest of reality.

Put in terms of the themes developed in this chapter, wisdom is a trait that enables an individual to intentionally engage the three domains of their *cosmotheandric* identity. Such engagement is possible because wisdom depends on a person's awareness, openness, neutrality, and freedom. By being aware that their identity participates in the three *cosmotheandric* domains, regardless of whether the domains are named using the terminology employed in these pages or not, a wise person can work to remain open to whatever their awareness reveals in the physical world, human domains, or divine/infinite/transcendent realms. A wise person's neutrality toward and freedom from their automatic perceptive and projective tendencies helps them to discern the truth of their situation, along with the roles they played in constructing it due to their participation in the domains bound up with their cosmotheandric identity. This concern for truth will be the explicit topic of Chapter Six.

At this point, however, it is simply worth noting that when neutrality, freedom, and wisdom emerge in a person's life, concerns for truth become more important for them because wise people have worked with sometimes-uncomfortable truths about their perceptive and projective tendencies. By working with these truths, wise people have gained the knowledge that, had they not worked with these truths, their pursuit of the good would have been greatly limited. Such limitations occur when a person's automatic perceptive and projective tendencies create difficulties for them when they are building, maintaining, and enhancing their relationships with all reality. Wisdom thus necessitates that a person face and engage their own shortcomings and limitations. All this is done so such a person can use their awareness of and openness to these shortcomings and limitations as catalysts for growing into greater spiritual health.

With Judy it was therefore evident she had engaged her own shortcomings and limitations to such an extent that she was able to make deliberate choices around how best to build, maintain, and enhance her relationships with all her daily realities. Her capacity for such choices was particularly manifest in how she expressed her trust that her daughter would likely be supported by a friend while Judy herself was away in hospital. Judy's wisdom was thus a natural outgrowth of her capacities for neutrality and freedom. It was for this reason that I assessed her baseline spiritual health as already being quite high. It was therefore a great privilege for me to share my one interaction with Judy. I have no doubt that Judy was consequently able to navigate her experience in hospital with the same grace and fortitude that was so evident in her one interaction with me. After that one interaction, I did not encounter Judy again.

CONCLUSION

This chapter began by reviewing the reciprocal dynamics between awareness and openness. It ended by describing how wisdom emerges as a direct result of individuals' growing capacities for neutrality and freedom. In sum, this discussion produced the following conclusions:

- When a client works on building their awareness of both their internal and external dynamics, they must also manifest an openness to receiving the perspectives of others. This openness facilitates growth in their awareness, but for this openness to be present, the client must also have a baseline (at times intuitive) awareness that their specific perspective does not capture the sum total of their realities. This reciprocal and sometimes paradoxical relationship between an individual's awareness and openness is the foundation for whatever growth they might experience into greater spiritual health.

- When individuals work on building awareness and openness, they also begin to experience greater inner neutrality in relation to their automatic perceptive and projective tendencies. This neutrality then renders freedom within such individuals because they are no longer "hooked" by their automatic perceptions and projections, at least not in the same ways as previously.

- Spiritual Care Practitioners can guide their clients into increasing measures of neutrality and freedom by embodying a specific kind of diffraction pattern. Schore's (2019) account of the neuro-biology of mutual regression provided one perspective on how such diffraction patterns operate in clinical contexts; contemplative approaches offered another perspective.

- Pannikar's *cosmotheandric* principle emerged as a significant factor in Practitioners' diffraction patterns due to its foundational role in informing Practitioners' own manifestations of spiritual health.

- Wisdom emerged as a trait that allows individuals to consciously engage the three domains bound up with their *cosmotheandric* iden-tities. Wisdom allows this conscious engagement because of how it works with the dynamics of awareness, openness, neutrality, and freedom in individuals' lives. The discussion of my interaction with my patient Judy illustrated how wisdom can become manifest in clients' lives.

- The discussion ended by showing how growth into neutrality, freedom, and wisdom necessitates increasing concern for truth in clients' and Practitioners' lives alike. This concern for truth will receive more comprehensive treatment in Chapter Six.

Reflection Questions

- How did you experience your own growth in awareness, openness, neutrality, and freedom in your clinical training? In your own view, how did your growth prepare you to engage your clients?
- In what clinical situations have you seen neutrality and freedom in your clients' lives? How would you describe the specific dynamics that suggested these clients possessed high measures of inner neutrality and freedom?
- Clinically, if you assess a client as needing to grow into neutrality, freedom, and wisdom, what strategies might you use to facilitate such growth? How would you mobilize the client's relative awareness and openness to do so?

Clinical Assessment and Intervention Questions

- To what extent is this client able to view their perceptions and projections with relative neutrality?
- What observations can be neutrally shared about the client's perceptive and projective tendencies?
- How does the client respond to the sharing of these observation?
- To what extent does the client move into a more neutral stance with regard to themself and their circumstances over the duration of the clinical interaction(s)?
- What are the potential barriers preventing the client from moving into a more neutral space? How can these barriers be addressed intuitively, emotionally, cognitively, and interpersonally?
- What reflective questions can be posed to the client about their experiences to prompt their growth into wisdom?

REFERENCE LIST

American Psychiatric Association (2013). *Diagnostic and statistical manual of mental disorders: DSM-5* (5th ed.). Washington, DC: American Psychiatric Publishing.

Aurobindo, S., & the Mother. (1998). *Powers within* (A. S. Dalal, Ed.). Ojai, CA: Institute of Integral Psychology.

Balboni, T., Fitchett, G., et al. (2017, September). State of the science of spirituality and palliative care research part II: screening, assessment, and interventions. *Journal of Pain and Symptom Management, 54*(3), 441–453.

Barad, K. (2007). *Meeting the universe halfway: quantum physics and the entanglement of matter and meaning.* Durham, NC: Duke University Press.

Barnhart, B. (2018). *The future of wisdom: toward a rebirth of sapiential Christianity.* Rhinebeck, NY: Monkfish.

Bourgeault, C. (2008). *The wisdom Jesus: transforming heart and mind: a new perspective on Christ and his message.* Denver, CO: Shambhala.

Bourgeault, C. (2016). *The heart of centering prayer: nondual Christianity in theory and practice.* Boulder, CO: Shambhala.

Canadian Association for Spiritual Care/Association canadienne de soins spirituelle (CASC/ACSS) (2019, May 2). *Competencies.* Retrieved July 30, 2024, from Canadian Association for Spiritual Care/Association canadienne de soins spirituelle: https://spiritualcare.ca/cascacss_competencies/

Corbett, L. (2012). *Psyche and the sacred: spirituality beyond religion.* New Orleans, LA: Spring Journal Books.

Cozolino, L. (2017). *The neuroscience of psychotherapy: healing the social brain* (3rd ed.). New York, NY: Norton.

de Cruz, H., & de Smedt, J. (2015). *A natural history of natural theology: the cognitive science of theology and philosophy of religion.* Cambridge, MA: MIT Press.

Doehring, C. (2015). *The practice of pastoral care: a postmodern approach* (Revised and expanded ed.). Louisville, KY: Westminster John Knox.

Downes, W. (2011). *Language and religion: a journey into the human mind.* Cambridge, UK: Cambridge University Press.

Frenette, D. (2012). *The path of centering prayer: deepening your experience of God.* Boulder, CO: Sounds True.

Gerkin, C. V. (1986). *Widening the horizons: pastoral responses to a fragmented society.* Philadelphia, PA: Westminster.

Graziano, M. S. (2019). *Rethinking consciousness: a scientific theory of subjective experience* (Kindle ebook ed.). New York, NY: Norton.

Habermas, J. (1984). *The theory of communicative action* (Vol. 1: Reason and the rationalization of society) (T. McCarthy, Trans.). Cambridge, UK: Polity Press.

Habermas, J. (1992). *Postmetaphysical thinking: philosophical essays* (W. M. Hohengarten, Trans.). Cambridge, MA: MIT Press.

Habermas, J. (2003). *Truth and justification* (B. Fultner, Ed., & B. Fultner, Trans.). Cambridge, MA: MIT Press.

Jankowski, K. R., Vanderwerker, L. C., Murphy, K. M., Montonye, M., & Ross, A. M. (2008). Change in pastoral skills, emotional intelligence, self-reflection, and social desirability across a unit of CPE. *Journal of Health Care Chaplaincy, 15*(2), 132–148. doi:10.1080/08854720903163304

Lasair, S. (2018). Understanding, assessing, and intervening in the spiritual nature of medical events: theological and theoretical perspectives. *Practical Theology, 11*(5), 374–386. doi:10.1080/1756073X.2018.1528749

Lasair, S. (2019). What's the point of spiritual care? A narrative response. *Journal of Pastoral Care & Counseling, 73*(2), 115–123. doi:10.1177/1542305019846846

Lasair, S. (2020). What's the point of clinical pastoral education and pastoral counselling education? Political, developmental, and professional considerations. *Journal of Pastoral Care & Counseling, 74*(1), 22–32. doi:10.1177/1542305019897563

Lasair, S. (2021). HAVE-H: five attitudes for a narratively grounded and embodied spirituality. *Journal of Pastoral Care & Counseling, 75*(1), 13–22. doi:10.1177/1542305020965546

Loizzo, J., Brandon, F., Wolf, E. J., & Neale, M. (Eds.) (2023). *Advances in contemplative psychotherapy: accelerating personal and social transformation* (2nd ed.). New York, NY: Routledge.

McGilchrist, I. (2009). *The master and his emissary: the divided brain and the making of the Western world.* New Haven, CT: Yale University Press.

McGilchrist, I. (2021). *The matter with things: our brains, our delusions and the unmaking of the world.* London, UK: Perspectiva Press.

Panikkar, R. (2004). *Christophany: the fullness of man* (A. DiLascia, Trans.). Maryknoll, NY: Orbis.

Panikkar, R. (2010). *The rhythm of being: the unbroken trinity: the Gifford lectures.* Maryknoll, NY: Orbis.

Panikkar, R. (2014). *Mysticism and spirituality* (Vol. 1). Maryknoll, NY: Orbis.

Parameshwaran, R. (2015, Jan–Mar). Theory and practice of chaplain's spiritual care process: a psychiatrist's experiences of chaplaincy and conceptualizing trans-personal model of mindfulness. *Indian Journal of Psychiatry, 57*(1), 21–29. doi:10.4103/0019-5545.148511

Pedhu, Y. (2019). Efforts to overcome countertransference in pastoral counseling relationships. *Journal of Pastoral Care & Counseling, 73*(2), 74–81. doi:10.1177/1542305019852587

Puchalski, C., Vitillo, R., Hull, S., & Reller, N. (2014). Improving the spiritual dimension of whole person care: reaching national and international consensus. *Journal of Palliative Medicine, 17*(6), 642–656. doi:10.1089/jpm.2014.9427

Rogers, C. R. (1965). *Client-centered therapy* (Paperback ed.). Boston, MA: Houghton Mifflin.

Scheib, K. (2016). *Pastoral care: telling the stories of our lives.* Nashville, TN: Abingdon Press.

Schore, A. N. (2019). *Right brain psychotherapy.* New York, NY: Norton.

Seely, A. (2024). *What is wisdom?* Retrieved December 2024, from Thomas Aquinas College: www.thomasaquinas.edu/about/what-wisdom

Seth, A. (2021). *Being you: a new science of consciousness* (Kindle ebook ed.). New York, NY: Dutton.

Steinhauser, K., Fitchett, G., et al. (2017, September). State of the science of spirituality and palliative care research part 1: definitions, measurement, and outcomes. *Journal of Pain and Symptom Management, 54*(3), 428–440. doi:10.1016/j.jpainsymman.2017.07.028

Taylor, C. (2011). Why we need a radical redefinition of secularism. In E. Mendieta, & J. van Antwerpen (Eds.), *The power of religion in the public sphere: Judith Butler, Jurgen*

Habermas, Charles Taylor, Cornel West (pp. 34–59). New York, NY: Columbia University Press.

Vanderstelt, H., van Dijk, A., & Lasair, S. (2022). Transformational education: exploring the lasting impact of students clinical pastoral education experiences. *Journal of Health Care Chaplaincy*, 29(1), 89–104. doi:10.1080/08854726.2022.2040892

Williams, R. (2018). *Christ: the heart of creation*. London, UK: Bloomsbury Continuum.

Wirpsa, M., Johnson, R., Bieler, J., Boyken, L., Pugliese, K., Rosencrans, E., & Murphy, P. (2019). Interprofessional models for shared decision making: the role of the health care chaplain. *Journal of Health Care Chaplaincy*, 25, 20–44. doi:10.1080/08854726.2018.1501131

Six

INTRODUCTION

At the end of the last chapter, it became evident that truth is a significant concern for people who have started to manifest the trait of wisdom. In that chapter I began to articulate an understanding of wisdom that featured a person's growing neutrality toward and increasing freedom from their automatic tendencies to perceive reality in specific ways and to project these perceptions into the spaces they share with others. This chapter will therefore work to develop an understanding of truth that relates directly to the conception of spiritual health that is being discussed in these pages. This definition will avoid the numerous philosophical, political, and forensic challenges bound up with defining and delimiting truth by arguing that truth is established and assessed in a person's spiritual health to the extent that it enables such a person to deepen their connection with and embodiment of the silence behind the *cosmotheandric* principle. Therefore, truth works directly to lay bare and address whatever emotional and intuitive barriers a person might have that limit their capacity to build, maintain, and enhance their connections with all that is as bound up with this silence. To begin this discussion, it is helpful to summarize and further develop many of the themes that have been explored to this point.

SPIRITUAL HEALTH: MOVING TOWARD PERSONAL INTEGRATION

I present Figure 6.1 at the beginning of this discussion because it concretizes and expresses the relationships between many of the phenomena that have been discussed to this point in these pages. At the top of the figure are phenomena of which a person possesses explicit awareness, whereas at the bottom are phenomena of which they are unaware. Using the language of psychoanalysis there is a rough correspondence between the top of the diagram and the so-called "ego" and

DOI: 10.4324/9781003466147-7

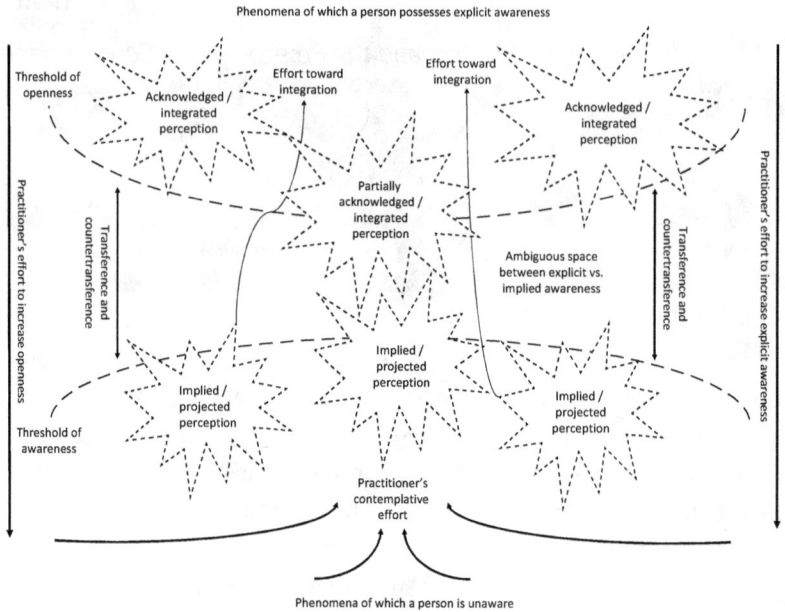

Figure 6.1 Dynamic Movements That Integrate Perceptions into Explicit Conscious Awareness

the bottom of the diagram and the unconscious (Butler, 2005; Jung, 2011; Schore, 2019a, 2019b). I have chosen to avoid this psychoanalytic terminology in the diagram, however, because the conceptual and cultural baggage associated with both the Freudian and Jungian uses of these terms is unhelpful for the purposes of this discussion. Nevertheless, I do want to draw attention to this rough correspondence as one potential reference point regarding how I understand these various phenomena.[1]

Working toward the middle of the diagram, I have called the dashed arc toward the bottom the "threshold of awareness." I placed this arc here because often a person might possess a vague or underdeveloped awareness of something going on inside them before they are completely open to integrating this perception or phenomenon into their fully explicit awareness. This was particularly true with Ernest and his fear, as discussed in Chapter Three. I have therefore called the upper dashed arc the "threshold of openness." This threshold is where a person works directly with their inner dynamic, namely their emotional and intuitive resistances, to enable specific perceptions, and the narrative elements connected to them, to become fully integrated into their explicit awareness. This threshold was specifically addressed in my work with Bonnie, as described in Chapter Four. In this case, Bonnie's belief in divine punishment was limiting her capacity to be fully open to all the emotions she was experiencing in response to her long-term chronic illness.

Between these two thresholds, however, there is an ambiguous space where perceptions and other phenomena can intrude, but they haven't been fully integrated into a person's explicit awareness. These phenomena have not been integrated into explicit awareness because they have yet to pass the threshold of openness, even though an individual might have a vague awareness that something is happening within them. In this space the dynamics of transference and countertransference are often manifest because whatever awareness a person might have of what is happening inside them has not yet been fully integrated (Schore, 2019b; Pedhu, 2019). A person may thus continue to project their perceptions from this ambiguous space into the external physical and social spaces they share with others. In Chapter Five, Judy's agitation in response to being at a distance from her daughter was an example of a perception that was located in this ambiguous space without being fully integrated. The dotted stars in the diagram, and their various labels, therefore express the extent to which specific perceptions have been integrated into a person's explicit awareness based on the perception's location in relation to the two thresholds.

Through this description it is evident that not only is cognitive content bound up with perception (i.e., the facts of whatever a person is experiencing in their external circumstances), but emotional and intuitive is, as well (Lasair, 2021; Panksepp, 2013; Parameshwaran, 2015). In Judy's case the cognitive content of her perception was correct: Judy was at a distance from her daughter, and that meant she would not be able to help her daughter in the ways she would normally when she was closer to home. This factual reality was not in dispute. Yet Judy was running into problems in her engagements with the emotional implications of this factual reality. Judy was agitated because she knew her daughter needed support, and, when I first met her, Judy wasn't aware of anyone who could look in on her daughter during her time in hospital. This lack of external awareness caused Judy to experience significant anxiety. Furthermore, when Judy prayed, she was not certain that God was answering her prayers because she did not receive any internal emotional reassurance that everything would be okay.

In my intervention with Judy, however, my own neutral and free stance enabled Judy to release many of the anxious feelings she was experiencing (Parameshwaran, 2015; Lasair, 2020b; Vanderstelt, van Dijk, & Lasair, 2022; Schore, 2019b). This release then enabled Judy to deepen her awareness of her lived realities to the extent that she realized there was another person her daughter's age in her home community who could look in on her daughter while Judy was in the city receiving medical care. This realization helped Judy to receive the reassurance she needed so she could return to the internal neutrality and freedom that was more her norm.

In the terms expressed in Figure 6.1, the work I did with Judy, as minimalist as it was, drew her thresholds of openness and awareness further into the territory of phenomena of which Judy, at least when I first saw her, was unaware. The efforts to move these thresholds are symbolized by the arrows on the left and right sides of Figure 6.1. As a result, the movements of these thresholds enabled Judy to have a fuller appreciation of her and her daughter's situation, and this fuller appreciation was the main tipping point that allowed Judy to return to her more customary neutral and free stance.

The downward movement of these thresholds was further reinforced by the contemplative stance I embodied during the inter- action Judy and I shared (Lasair, 2021; Parameshwaran, 2015; Loizzo, Brandon, Wolf, & Neale, 2023). The movement of this stance is symbolized by the curved arrows at the bottom of Figure 6.1, labeled "Practitioner's contemplative effort." Yes, the right hemispheres of my and Judy's brains were synchronized much in the way Schore's per- spective expressed (Schore, 2019b), as discussed in Chapter Five. I demonstrated as much when I named Judy's feelings and articulated how I understood Judy's feelings within the context of her overall narrative (Parameshwaran, 2015). However, the neutral and free con- templative dimension of simply allowing Judy's emotions to be what they were without any reactivity on my part probably did greater good in terms of bringing Judy back to her own neutral and free stance than anything else in our interaction. In the terms discussed in Chapters Three and Five, this was a fine example of my diffraction pattern having a direct and measurable effect on Judy's overall state of wellbeing (see also Barad, 2007; Schore, 2019a; Pedhu, 2019). In psychotherapeutic circles this dynamic is often called "co-regulation." This dynamic helped Judy to exercise her own efforts in integrating the parts of her perceptions that had previously been below the thresholds of her own awareness and openness. These internal efforts are symbolized in the arrows connected to the perceptions in the middle of Figure 6.1, labeled "Effort toward integration."

LANGUAGE IN A PRACTITIONER'S WORK

All this indicates that in clinical interactions Practitioners engage the inner dynamics of a client's frame for reality to help facilitate the client's work of integrating everything that is going on for them internally into their explicit conscious awareness (Parameshwaran, 2015; Schore, 2019b; Lasair, 2021). Practitioners' engagements with clients' frames therefore operate on multiple levels simultaneously. First, there is the verbal level wherein a Practitioner uses words and language to describe and name what they are sensing through the dynamics of transference and countertransference (Schore, 2019b; Parameshwaran, 2015; Lasair, 2021). By synchronizing their brain's right hemisphere with the client's brain's right hemisphere, Practitioners attend to the discrete emotions and intuitions that the client might be experiencing. Individuals often express these intuitions and emotions through their body language, mood, affect, tone of voice, facial expressions, etc. (see Chapters Two and Three). All these elements contribute to a client's overall clinical presentation— Practitioners assess their clients' relative spiritual health on the basis of such presentations (see e.g., Lasair, 2018).

Yet, as discussed in previous chapters, part of a person's spiritual health also concerns how they navigate the dynamics of consistency and change in their life (see Chapter Two; Lasair, 2020a; Ricoeur, 1992, 1991). Specifically, people construct different elements in their frame for reality in response to these dynamics. Practitioners therefore use language not only to name what they are sensing within their clients, but also to invite their clients into deeper engagements with whatever they are living through (Parameshwaran, 2015; Lasair, 2019). These deeper engagements are intended to invite clients to consider how they might have constructed their frames in response to their prior experiences (Lasair, 2019). In this sense, then, Practitioners use language in its capacity to describe and name as well as its capacity to invite and inquire. Practitioners often use questions to ask about a client's past experiences, but behind such inquiries is an invitation for clients to revisit emotions connected to these past experiences. Practitioners invite such consideration so both Practitioner *and client* can assess the extent to which such emotions inform the client's experiences in the present (Parameshwaran, 2015; Lasair, 2020b).

At a deeper level, Practitioners are also acutely attuned to the dynamics of their clients' diffraction patterns (see Chapters Two, Three, and Four). As already discussed, this attunement begins initially with the synchronization of the Practitioner's and client's brains' right hemispheres (Schore, 2019b). However, as a Practitioner's perception of diffraction patterns becomes increasingly subtle, such a Practitioner can also perceive how the client's current experiences rest upon a silence that can only be detected through sustained contemplative practice (Parameshwaran, 2015; Loizzo, Brandon, Wolf, & Neale, 2023). Such silence is a staple of contemplative writing, and Panikkar explores it extensively in his *Omnia Opera, Vol. 1: Mysticism and Spirituality, Part 1: Mysticism, Fullness of Life* (2014). In this first volume of his collected works, Panikkar lays out his understanding of spirituality and how it relates to several of the mystical traditions within various world religions, Christianity, Hinduism, and Buddhism being the most prominent in his discussion.

WORD, SPEECH, AND SILENCE

From Panikkar's (2014) perspective, silence is the foundation of speech, in that the truth of a statement can be measured by the extent to which it integrates silence into its specific formulation (see also Valle, 2019; Picard, 1948; Ross, 2014; Sardello, 2008). Panikkar (2014, Chapter Six) identifies four kinds of silence at the beginning of his discussion: the suffocation of words; the bewilderment of words; the inadequacy of words; and the absence of words. It is this last kind of silence that mainly concerns Panikkar, and he treats it as largely synonymous with the infinite depths of God as described in Christian perspectives (see also Ross, 2014; Valle, 2019; Sardello, 2008). Nevertheless, Panikkar also draws upon other faith perspectives in his discussion. From Hindu perspectives, this infinite ocean of silence is often called *brahman*; from

Jewish Kabbalistic perspectives, *ein sof* (see Matt, 1997; Scholem, 1954, 1991); in atheist or humanist perspectives such silence can be expressed in terms of the feelings of awe and wonder that often fill a person in response to perceiving the infinite vastness of the physical universe (see M. C. Taylor, 2007; Blankholm, 2022).

As Panikkar (2014) describes this silence, he indicates that its resounding vastness in fact embodies a kind of speech; this silence communicates something that can never properly be put into words. Words fail this kind of silence, so whatever language is used to engage it always points beyond itself. The object of this language is the meaning-filled absence of words that founds any kind of speech. Accordingly, this infinite silence does communicate, but it does so through the primordial, non-linguistic Word, the *Logos*, that spoke creation into being, at least according to Panikkar's (2014, 2010, 2004) understanding of Jewish and Christian creation narratives (see also Genesis 1 and John 1). This primordial Word, the *Logos*, is what allows any communication to be meaning-filled, hence its capacity to speak worlds into being or, conversely, to speak worlds out of being, as some Kabbalistic Jewish thinkers might put it (e.g., Scholem, 1954, 1991; Matt, 1997).

Regardless of how this poetic and mythological expression may or may not capture the universe's origins, Panikkar's affinity for Christian perspectives is most evident at this point. Specifically, Panikkar indicates that the relationship between the primordial word and infinite silence cannot be understood outside a trinitarian framework (Panikkar, 2014, 2010).

From Panikkar's (2014) perspective the relationship between word and silence is not analogous to the relationship between being and non-being. Rather, the relationship between these two seeming opposites is one of dynamic interaction: the Word resounds with silence's power because it integrates silence's unspeakability into each and every utterance (see also Picard, 1948). Likewise, silence renews the Word's efficacy by always drawing the Word back into itself (Panikkar, 2014). In traditional Christian terms, silence corresponds to God the Father and the Word to God the Son because Jesus is described by the Bible as the Word (*Logos*) become flesh; God the Holy Spirit is the force that animates the interplay between the first two persons of the Christian Godhead. Panikkar (2014) even uses the ancient Greek word *perichoresis* to describe the dynamics that govern the interplay of words and silence more generically. Many prominent early Christian thinkers also used this word to describe the dynamic relationship between the three divine persons of the Christian Holy Trinity (see Williams, 2018). It is not my intent to delve too deeply into Panikkar's interpretation of trinitarian thought.[2] Nevertheless, Panikkar's (2014) understanding of the relationship between word, silence, and the so-called "third eye" is important for this discussion.

The notion of the third eye is often associated with either Hindu or Buddhist teachings. Yet Christianity also possesses teachings about the third eye. In Christian contexts the third eye is often called the "eye of the Spirit" or the "eye of contemplation" (Panikkar, 2014, 2010). In all these traditions the third eye is typically associated with intuition or spiritual perception. In Panikkar's (2014) understanding, spiritual perception is necessary in relation to silence because the dynamic interplay between silence and speech goes beyond the dualism that most people experience between physical and non-physical realities. From Panikkar's perspective, the third eye perceives—in a non-dualistic sense—where and how silence is present in various modes of expression (Panikkar, 2014). Through such perception the third eye illumines where and how speakers can shape their expressions so those expressions might embody greater or lesser degrees of silence. From this perspective, then, speech, or expression, is a fundamentally creative act, and the truth and power of specific communicative acts can be measured precisely by the extent to which they embody silence through the particularities of their formulations (Panikkar, 2014; see also Valle, 2019; Picard, 1948).

SILENCE, APPARATUS, AND THE *COSMOTHEANDRIC* IN CLINICAL PRACTICE

At this point some readers might wonder how this somewhat lengthy engagement with Panikkar's thought helps to describe Spiritual Care Practitioners' clinical practices. The connection between Panikkar's thought and spiritual care work becomes evident when recalling Barad's (2007) notion of the apparatus. Barad's concept, as discussed in Chapter Four, is similar to my own idea of a person's frame for reality.

It is not worth reviewing all the intricacies of Barad's (2007) concept at this point. However, it is worth recalling that, in Barad's view, an apparatus is constructed for physics experiments in response to many factors. From Barad's (2007) perspective, many of these factors are beyond the awareness or control of physicists themselves. The apparatuses that individuals use to perceive and understand their lived realities likewise include factors that are well beyond the individual's comprehension and control. Such factors include individuals' genetic inheritances, their specific temperament, their attachment patterns in early childhood and throughout their life, the interpersonal and emotional dynamics in their family of origin, the places where they attended school, their religious, social, and cultural upbringing, their specific experiences of gender and sexuality, their specific abilities and aptitudes, and so on (see Chapters Three and Four; Barad, 2007). In these pages I have indicated that all these factors contribute to a person's frame for reality; I have also drawn upon the neuroscientific concept of mental models as yet another way to express how these factors inform a person's ways of relating to the world around them (Graziano, 2019; Seth, 2021).

Nevertheless, Barad's (2007) understanding of an apparatus reveals that a person's frame for reality connects them to all reality through relationships that are often beyond their explicit conscious awareness. Some of these relationships can easily be brought into explicit conscious awareness, especially if a person has undertaken significant psychotherapeutic work (Schore, 2019b; Jung, 2011). However, as Judith Butler discusses in *Giving an Account of Oneself* (2005), it is often impossible for individuals to fully comprehend all the different factors that have contributed to their distinct experiences of selfhood and identity. The result is that Spiritual Care Practitioners typically tread the fringes of what clients can name (and what they cannot) so that the truth of who clients are in relation to themselves and all reality can be revealed within the context of clinical encounters (Lasair, 2021; Parameshwaran, 2015). While aspects of this practice clearly overlap with techniques and theories found in numerous psychotherapeutic modalities (e.g., Siegel, 2013; Schore, 2019b; Madigan, 2019; Béres & Crawley, 2023), a key distinguishing feature in spiritual care is the relationship between silence and speech so crucially expressed in Panikkar's notion of third-eye seeing, explored above.

What needs to be highlighted at this point is how an individual's relationships with both silence and speech encompass their relationship with reality *as a whole*. I write this because a person's relationship with silence calls them back to their origin while also pointing them toward their ultimate destiny (Panikkar, 2014; Ross, 2014). What do I mean by this? Prior to a person's birth, all that is known about them is silence. Similarly, silence is typically all that responds when grief is completed, and the remains of a person's physical life have been returned to the infinite. Silence is therefore the realm of both endings and beginnings (Sardello, 2008; Ross, 2014; Picard, 1948; Valle, 2019). When individuals relate to silence, then, that relationship calls them back to who they have been and who they will be, except during this short time when they relate with speeches and actions that can be heard and received by others. Here, in this temporary domain, lives can be built, relationships enjoyed, wealth accumulated, and loves shared. Yet endings and beginnings are persistent parts of whatever existences we inhabit with others. Silence thus surrounds and permeates all our shared lives, if only we have eyes and ears to perceive, encounter, and respond to it.

From this perspective, silence is a crucial aspect of how a person embodies the *cosmotheandric* principle. As discussed in Chapter Five, a Practitioner's free, open, and aware neutrality depends on their embodiment of the *cosmotheandric*. Silence, as a gateway into felt emotional and intuitive awareness of relationship with all reality, thus enables Practitioners to deepen their embodiment of this principle (Panikkar, 2014). Engaging silence deepens such embodiment because silence encompasses any person's relationship with their body and, by extension, the physical universe (*cosmos*). Silence also permeates a person's relationship to their distinctly human inner consciousness (*aner/andros*), as well as their relationship to the infinite/divine/transcendent domains (*theos*). The beginnings and endings that invoke a person's contact with silence are consequently experienced through all three *cosmotheandric* domains (Panikkar, 2014; Ross, 2014; Valle, 2019). When a Practitioner cultivates their own spiritual health, and especially their wisdom, they begin to return again and again to silence, learn from it, and bring this learning into the interactions they share with others (Panikkar, 2014; Ross, 2014; Picard, 1948; Valle, 2019). Those who cultivate a sustained relationship with silence therefore embody a different quality in life; such people's uses of speech and action often resound with depths that can be noticeably absent in others (see e.g., Ross, 2014; Sardello, 2008; Valle, 2019).

When Practitioners interact with clients, then, not only does silence inhabit their speech, but Practitioners' presence and use of language also invites clients into their own interactions with silence. There can thus, at times, be a poetic quality to the words and phrases Practitioners use in relation to their clients (e.g., Parameshwaran, 2015). Because any individual's frame for reality is founded on silence (regardless of whether they are consciously aware of it or not) a Practitioner's sometimes-poetic approach works to draw clients' awareness back to the foundations of their frames (Lasair, 2019; Parameshwaran, 2015). The goal of such engagement is to help clients encounter silence's creative capacities so the contours of their frames can be actively reshaped in the process (see Valle, 2019). Because silence has a close, if not symbiotic relationship with the primordial Word (the *Logos*), contact with silence has the potential to release a creative energy within a client that might not have been accessible to them previously (Panikkar, 2014; Ross, 2014; Valle, 2019). A Practitioner's role in this process is thus to assess and engage whatever resistances their clients might display in relation to silence. Practitioners' intervention strategies are therefore based in the understanding that their embodiment of silence in presence and speech is one of their most potent therapeutic tools (Valle, 2019; Parameshwaran, 2015). A Practitioner's engagements with their clients consequently tend to be invitational rather than confrontational, with some exceptions depending on the circumstances. Now, there are a number of qualifications that need to be made in light of these realities.

METAPHOR AND EXPERIENCE

In this chapter, much of the language I have used to this point could be described as highly symbolic or metaphorical. This was especially true when I was discussing Panikkar's notion of third-eye seeing, as well as the theological ideas he associated with experiences of silence. While these ideas are familiar in several religious traditions, especially contemplative Christianity, I also recognize that in clinical environments these ideas may be less intelligible. Such ideas are very difficult to assess within the frame of empirical scientific thought. Yet I believe this question of intelligibility can be addressed through a brief discussion regarding the nature of linguistic metaphors.

In a now-classic study of metaphorical language, George Lakoff and Mark Johnson discuss how many metaphors originate in a person's bodily relationship with the rest of reality (Lakoff & Johnson, 1980; see also Ricoeur, 1981). For example, when a person says they will visit a friend who lives "over the bridge," the phrase "over the bridge" does not necessarily mean that the friend's residence is somehow suspended over a bridge that spans a valley or body of water. Rather, "over the bridge" means that the individual must cross over the bridge to travel to the friend's house. The individual's use of this metaphor therefore locates them in space and shows something of how they physically relate to a specific part of the world. All this contributes to Lakoff's and Johnson's (1980) overall thesis that metaphor is a central feature of language, in that metaphors often play crucial roles in revealing and structuring our relationships with all of reality (see also Ricoeur, 1981).

Charles Taylor (C. Taylor, 2016) built on this idea when discussing how metaphors disclose portions of reality that are not accessible otherwise. According to Taylor (2016), since the late 19th century many prominent Western philosophers have argued that language use is philosophically valid only when it refers to phenomena that are empirically verifiable. This theme connects with what I explored briefly in Chapter One regarding Taylor's understanding of Western secularity (C. Taylor, 2007): Western secular perspectives typically restrict reality to that which can be understood within a purely immanent frame. As indicated in Chapter One, Taylor is critical of these perspectives in that he argues such philosophical stances narrow the cultural and philosophical scope of what can be granted legitimacy in the West (C. Taylor, 2007, 2011). When Western philosophers argue that language can properly be used only to refer to empirically verifiable objects, therefore, Taylor believes these philosophers also undermine the common experience that metaphors and symbols disclose parts of reality that are incapable of being detected by exclusively literal uses of language (Taylor, 2016). Panikkar's (2014) notion of third-eye seeing is a case in point. For Panikkar, this complex metaphor denotes a person's capacity to hold seemingly contradictory experiences together to render a unified, albeit apparently paradoxical, vision of reality (see also Bourgeault, 2016). From the perspective of formal logic, such visions of reality are simply not possible.

However, within many faith-traditions, seeming paradox is a normal part of discourse; paradoxical uses of language are often necessary to express the great mystery at the core of many religions (Downes, 2011; Williams, 2014). Now, Taylor does not spend much space addressing the unusual status of much theological language. Yet he does argue that metaphors can play roles similar to those of literal language in terms of disclosing reality (Taylor, 2016). In doing so, Taylor leaves open the possibility that figurative, symbolic, and metaphorical language can contribute legitimately and meaningfully to scientific and other Western public discourses. This approach contrasts starkly to typical Western approaches to symbol, figure, and metaphor, where these linguistic forms are often stigmatized by being overtly restricted to rhetorical, metaphysical, and/or theological uses (Ricoeur, 1981; Taylor, 2016).

To refer to an individual's relationship with silence, then, invites consideration of an experiential domain that has been discussed and engaged for millennia within numerous spiritual and/or religious traditions. The discussion of silence above can therefore not be seen as only metaphorical. Rather, in many ways this discussion is strikingly literal: it is common for people to become overwhelmed by silence when words are no longer adequate to express something they have encountered within their experience (Valle, 2019). In spiritual care it is common for Practitioners to invite their clients into such experiential domains (Lasair, 2021; Parameshwaran, 2015). However, because silence can, at times, be elusive, such territory is often best entered through in-depth explorations of clients' concrete experiences. Here is a clinical example of what an emergence of silence can look like.

LIAM

When I met Liam, he was in his early 40s and had been admitted to hospital due to acute weakness and emergent cardiac issues. According to the physicians, these conditions were likely caused by some longstanding lifestyle choices Liam had made. When I introduced myself as a spiritual care team member, Liam was very open to interacting with me. I learned he had been a regular church-attender growing up and that he still professed belief in the faith of his upbringing. Life had, however, taken him in several unusual directions. As Liam told it, he had a lifelong passion for extreme motor sports. While several injuries prevented him from driving a vehicle in these sports much past his teen years, he had traveled extensively as a member of the support crews for several professional competitors. Liam loved this life. He loved being on the road, he loved living the thrills of competition from the frontlines, and he loved the party culture that accompanied his times away from home. While drug and alcohol addictions had been parts of Liam's life in the past, he said that once he met his wife, he put all that behind him. It was not surprising, then, that Liam described his spouse as the love of his life. When I asked him what attracted him to his wife, he responded that she was always happy to do the things he wanted, and that for him it was a joy to take care of her.

As Liam and I explored his relationship with his wife a bit further, however, it became evident that while substance addiction was no longer part of Liam's life, he still continued to manifest a fiercely independent approach to his life and relationships. Specifically, Liam's independence was limiting his awareness of how his lifestyle was taking a significant toll on both his medical health and the health of his relationships with his wife and family. Liam's medical health had, in fact, been declining for some time, largely in response to several lifestyle choices he was continually making. His wife and children had been urging him to take better care of himself, but Liam refused. He loved his food, he loved his vehicles, and no one was going to tell him what to do. Yet now all Liam's choices had brought him to hospital, and it was questionable as to whether he would be able to live independently again—his medical needs were becoming too great. All this had produced significant frustration for Liam's wife, mainly because she had been urging Liam for years to pay more attention to what his lifestyle was doing to his body. Liam, however, had often brushed off his wife's concerns, not because he didn't think his lifestyle was harmful, but because Liam believed he had only one life to live, therefore he ought not waste it doing things that didn't make him happy.

From a clinical perspective, Liam's case thus presented several challenges. On the one hand, Liam was bright and articulate, but on the other hand he did not seem open to receiving the emotional information behind what his wife and children were communicating to him. Even though I never met Liam's wife and children, from my perspective it was obvious they were deeply worried about where Liam's lifestyle was taking him. It was for that reason that they repeatedly expressed their concern and frustration about the choices he made. In fact, from a medical perspective Liam's health was reaching a turning point, in that his physicians wondered whether Liam's body was capable of regaining many of the physical functions he had previously enjoyed. Yet I could also understand why Liam perceived his family's and physicians' warnings as limiting his sense of enjoyment and fun. For Liam to regain some physical health he would need to significantly reduce his intake of junk food and work to include more physical activity as part of his daily routine. Nevertheless, at least initially in our conversations, none of this seemed to sink in; Liam simply wanted his life to return to the way it was prior to his hospital admission. There was, however, a crucial turning point during our first interaction. Here is what it looked like:

SpC: Could you tell me again what your doctors are saying about where all this is going?

L: Yeah, well it seems they're not sure. My heart's not working the way it needs to, and they say I've got Type 2 diabetes now, and that's why I needed to come to hospital, not to mention that I can barely stand on my own anymore … I guess they're just waiting to see if I can get my blood sugar under control and also regain some strength for standing and walking.

SpC: That sounds like it could be a lot of work …

L: It could be, I guess. I'm not worried, though. In my life I've often found myself in tough jams and it all seems to work out in the end.

SpC: Could you tell me about one of those situations?

L: Yeah, well, I was on the road this one time and my buddy and me were at a bar after a race—my buddy and I worked on the same crew … Anyway, we were at the bar and this guy walked up and started talking at us … I don't even remember what he was talking about, but pretty soon he was shouting at us, accusing us of all sorts of stuff that we had no part of. We were trying to calm him down, but he just got louder and louder. By this time people were starting to gather to see what was going on. We didn't want to cause any fuss because we were hitting the road again the next morning, so we got up and tried to leave, but this guy wouldn't let us go. Finally, the owner came and tried to calm the guy down and all that gave my buddy and me a chance to leave. We laughed about it afterward because we knew we could have easily needed to fight our way out of that bar. Crazy!

SpC: Wow, all that seems really scary!

L: Kinda yes and kinda no. I've been in those kinds of situations half a dozen times. It comes with being on the road and with being part of events at some rougher places. Maybe the first time that kind of thing happened I was a little scared, but pretty soon you know what's what and you figure out how to handle yourself.

SpC: So, would you say you're taking the same kind of approach to your situation here in hospital?

L: I don't know ... I guess so.

SpC: From what you told me before, the doctors are saying you're going to have to make some pretty big changes. How do you feel about that?

L: Yeah, well, that's what the doctors say. I've done things pretty well my own way my whole life. I don't see that changing much, to be honest. I'll be alright.

SpC: But it sounds like your wife and kids are scared too. How does that fit into everything?

L: My sense? I think they're a bit too touchy about all this. I've been through this kind of thing lots of times before and it's always turned out alright.

SpC: You're like the cat that's got nine lives ...

L: You got it—I'm a lucky guy who knows his way around life ...

SpC: So how will you know when your luck is running out and you're getting down to life eight or nine?

L: I dunno, I guess I just trust that God's got my back, you know?

SpC: That may be true, but from what the doctors are saying and from what your family is telling you, it seems they're all worried that your luck might be running out.

(Long pause.)

L: I don't know what to do with that ... I'm going to have to think about that for a bit.

The conversation didn't last much longer after this point. I told Liam I'd be happy to let him think about what we talked about for a day or so and that I'd follow up with him the next time I was on his unit. In the end, Liam and I did have one or two follow-up interactions. In those interactions Liam was beginning to take a much more serious look at what was going on for him medically, yet by the time he was discharged, I still wasn't sure he had either the will or the inclination to make the kinds of changes that were needed so he could experience improvements in his physical, relational, and/or spiritual health. After he was discharged, I never saw Liam again.

Analysis

As is obvious from my presentation, confrontation was necessary in my interaction with Liam. Liam's approach to life, his pursuit of enjoyment no matter the cost, and his dismissal of his family's and physicians' concerns all created a dilemma for me. On the one hand, I could read his approach to his medical condition as optimistic, but such an interpretation would not support what I was observing in terms of Liam's denial of the gravity of his medical situation. On the other hand, to be very blunt with Liam would probably have disrupted the therapeutic alliance we were still navigating and negotiating. This is why I reflected back to him that I understood he saw himself as something like "a cat with nine lives." My use of this simile proved important strategically because it helped Liam articulate this perception in his own words, namely, "You got it—I'm a lucky guy who knows his way around life …" In response to this statement, I was then able to name that both Liam's family and physicians were likely worried that his luck was beginning to run out. It was at this point that a greater awareness of the gravity of his situation seemed to open up within Liam, prompting him to pause from his bluster and bravado and acknowledge that this was something that had not occurred to him until that moment. From my perspective this pause was a potential opening into silence. What remained to be seen was whether Liam would begin intentionally working with this silence or not.

THEORETICAL IMPLICATIONS

I was keenly aware that Liam was facing a potentially significant ending in his life. Given the changes in Liam's physical functioning and that his physicians wondered whether Liam could continue to live independently, I knew an encounter with silence would likely emerge in this conversation. Put in terms discussed previously, the magnitude of change through which Liam was living would probably disrupt many of the things he had experienced as consistent up to that point (see Chapter Two; Lasair, 2020a; Ricoeur, 1992). Concretely this meant the mental, emotional, physical, and spiritual frame Liam used to configure his lived realities would likely no longer be adequate to engage the new realities in which he was living. For his own wellbeing I therefore felt somewhat responsible for helping Liam begin his shift into this new experiential domain that was going to require a passage through silence.

However, even in our subsequent interactions Liam was reluctant to consider how significantly his life would need to change because of his medical crisis. By the time Liam was discharged, I knew I had done due diligence by at least offering him opportunities to explore the potential directions his life might take from that time onward. Yet the fact that Liam was reluctant to engage this territory was his own responsibility, as was the overall direction for his life. In many ways I just needed to sit with the reality that once Liam was discharged, he would likely continue living his life in whatever way he chose; how he might engage the consequences of doing this was ultimately Liam's choice, not mine. Nevertheless, I was able to consider Liam's brief encounter with silence, as indicated by the long pause in the verbatim report above, a success insofar as it required him to at least partially confront the depth of his situation.

Let's draw the theoretical threads together: Liam was reluctant to fully engage the silence that only began to partially emerge for him in our interaction; it is likely he did not completely grasp the truth of his situation. To use the terminology built in these pages, Liam had a partial awareness, or at least a cognitive awareness, of the changes his medical condition was going to require from him. However, he did not permit himself to be fully open to the magnitude of these changes, either cognitively, emotionally, or spiritually. As indicated above, I was attempting contemplatively to hold the silence that needed to emerge in my interactions with Liam. Yet it was also evident that Liam's identity was so bound to his unhealthy lifestyle that his experiences of inner freedom and neutrality were not that significant; Liam's capacity to manifest wisdom was thus also significantly reduced.

CONTENTMENT

While this case clearly did not result in the kind of therapeutic outcomes many would consider ideal, it did provide a clear counterexample illustrating the potential consequences of ill spiritual health. Because Liam refused—either consciously or unconsciously—to fully engage the truth of his situation, he was not able to mobilize silence's creative potentials to envision a different way of moving through life (see Panikkar, 2014; Valle, 2019; Ross, 2014). A fulsome encounter with silence could have enabled Liam to grapple with the gravity of his physical health's ending. Such an encounter could also have helped him consider how he might have responded holistically to everything his family and physicians were telling him. I could hypothesize that Liam experienced some measure of fear when considering a fulsome encounter with silence; to encounter silence requires significant vulnerability. This hypothesis does seem superficially warranted because, from my perspective, Liam's life appeared predicated on avoiding any feelings of vulnerability. Yet it would also be speculative to push the hypothesis further, and to do so would not have helped me engage Liam clinically given the constraints on my time, the nature of my role, and the demands of my workplace.

Now, within the approach to spiritual health being explored herein, contentment emerges when a person becomes more fully aware of and open to the true depth and breadth of their lived realities (see also Lasair, 2021). Specifically, contentment emerges along the following trajectory: first, depth and breadth in awareness and openness require a person to assume a neutral and free relationship with their tendencies in perception and projection; second, wisdom emerges when a person gains the insight that it is necessary for them to maintain and grow their awareness and openness, as well as their neutrality and freedom, when building, maintaining, and enhancing their relationship with all reality; third, wisdom enables a person to begin making deliberate choices around how to engage their automatic tendencies in perception and projection, as illustrated by Figure 6.1 (this figure specifically captures the concrete dynamics associated with wisdom); fourth, contentment starts to emerge when a person recognizes all these inner dynamics as inherent parts of their identity (i.e., they see these dynamics as parts of the truth of who they are); fifth, with this conscious recognition, such a person begins to actively discern—using both wisdom and contentment—what will be most helpful for building, maintaining, and enhancing their relationships with all that is. Such wise discernment requires contentment, because this last trait helps a spiritually healthy person engage the depth and breadth of their life as fully as possible. Such depth of engagement is a manifestation of a person's relationship with silence as the main foundation of the truth of their identity. Without contentment, therefore, and all the other traits discussed in these pages, a person's spiritual health is significantly limited, both in its manifestation and in its efficacy.

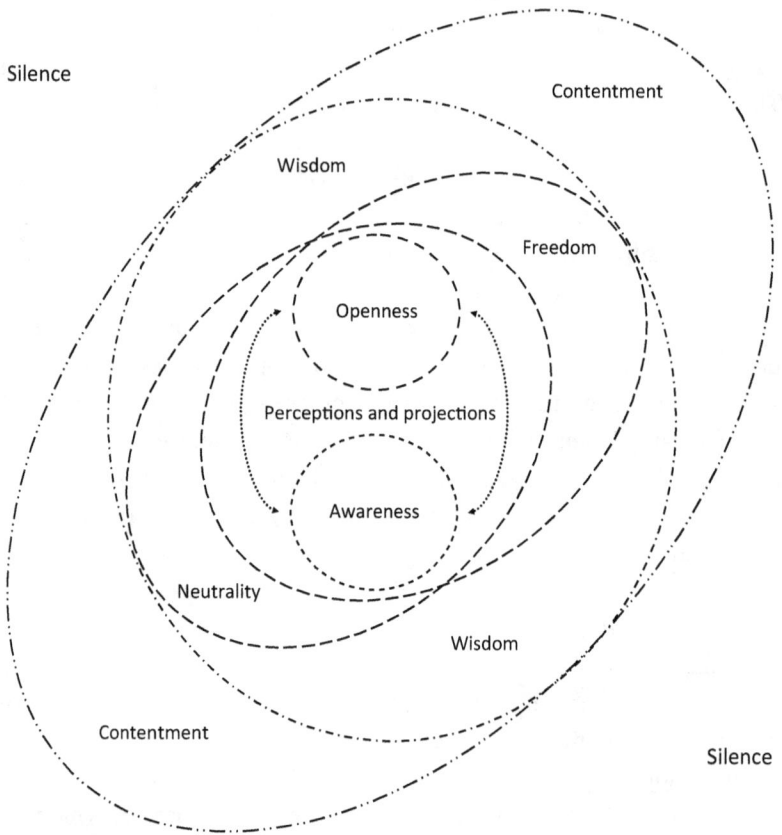

Figure 6.2 A Graphic Representation of the Relationships between All the Traits of Spiritual Health Discussed So Far and Silence

All this reveals that, in many respects, Liam was likely not content with his life. To a certain extent Liam was happy to maintain his patterns of unhealthy behavior. However, considering the overall understanding of spiritual health that has been articulated in these pages, Liam's patterns of behavior seem oriented toward affecting relationships negatively rather than building, maintaining, and enhancing them. That statement might, admittedly, appear overly judgmental. Yet when considering the strains in Liam's relationships with his wife and children, it was questionable how much longer his family could tolerate his behavior. Liam's physicians were also becoming similarly frustrated with his refusals to take their warnings and recommendations seriously. It was therefore becoming clear to almost everyone who encountered him that Liam was keen to avoid the realities of his life, regardless of the costs this approach demanded from his relationships and medical wellbeing.

When viewed from this perspective, the truth that silence embodies becomes especially poignant. Because silence is the domain of endings and beginnings, it also communicates how very little in life is permanent. Readers will no doubt see the connection between this silence and Buddhist teachings about the impermanence of all relative realities (see e.g., Trungpa, 2018; Wilber, 2017). Since many Buddhist teachers understand relative realities like our physical bodies and our various inner states to be mutable, such teachers encourage their followers to engage with absolute reality using various meditation techniques. Christianity similarly teaches that when individuals embrace the fullness of their humanity, they become deeply aware of their own personal finitude (Williams, 2018). By imitating the inner life of Jesus the Christ through contemplation and prayer, Christians believe they can encounter the infinite, absolute reality they name God (e.g., Williams, 2018; Panikkar, 2004). For atheists and humanists, the ending of material existence marks the body's return to the cosmic matter that makes up all that is. When a life falls silent, then, a person returns to the elements from which they were made. At that point many atheists and humanists understand that consciousness ends because consciousness is yet another manifestation of humanity's ultimately physical nature (Blankholm, 2022).

In all its various manifestations and in all the ways it's named, then, silence underpins all of existence, illuminating how much of what we as humans take for granted is bound up in cycles of life, death, and then life again. Within the framework articulated in these pages, part of contentment is coming to an explicitly conscious awareness of how any life is connected to these ultimate human and cosmic realities. For Liam to spend a lot of energy avoiding such truths, was consequently to display a lack of engagement with the nature of human existence generally and with the distinct changes he was experiencing in his own physical, mental, emotional, and spiritual existence in particular. As will be demonstrated in the next chapter, truthful contentment is a person's gateway into flourishing. It is therefore impossible for a person to be spiritually healthy when they are not truthfully content with many, if not most, dimensions of their silence-framed life and existence.

CONCLUSION

The following theoretical conclusions can be drawn from this chapter's discussion:

- All the specific phenomena explored in previous chapters point Practitioners and clients toward the work of personal integration. This work was represented graphically in Figure 6.1. Later on, the chapter indicated that the dynamics illustrated in this figure captured the specific inner movements associated with wisdom.
- A Practitioner's use of language was shown to be a crucial component of their provision of care. Because a Practitioner's contemplative approach to their work sees language as founded on silence, this means there is often a poetic quality to a Practitioner's use of language in relation to their clients. Such uses of language invite clients to engage meaningfully with the silence that exists beneath each aspect of their cosmotheandric identity.
- Silence was viewed as a phenomenon that frames all existence. While noting that several traditions understand this silence as divine and use various names to describe it, this chapter also indicated that atheists and humanists can nurture meaningful relationships with silence as well. As such, silence was demonstrated to be a distinct experiential domain that enables all people to encounter the truth of their existence, the nature of which is both impermanent and deeply meaningful.

- A clinical example exploring the case of patient Liam helped to illustrate what can happen when individuals do not take the reality of silence seriously.
- Contentment emerged as another trait of spiritual health. Specifically, contentment was shown to depend on silence because contentment requires that individuals be truthful with themselves and others about the nature of their identities. Content truthfulness was thus demonstrated as revealing the cosmic horizon within which all humans exist, opening the way for Chapter Seven's discussion of flourishing.

Reflection Questions

- When and how have you experienced the silence described in this chapter? What was that like for you? How might you describe those experiences to others?
- When and how have you seen silence emerge in clinical settings? How have you engaged it when it has emerged in your work with clients? What worked and what didn't?
- How do you see the connection between silence and the *cosmotheandric* in your own life?
- How would you describe the relationships between silence, truth, and contentment when you have seen it in your own life and in the lives of clients?

Clinical Assessment and Intervention Questions

- What beginnings and/or endings is this client living through?
- To what extent has this client engaged the work of personal integration in the past?
- To what extent does this client appear sensitive to the dynamics of silence in their own life either in manifesting a reflective attitude toward their life or in how their presence manifests itself?

- To what extent is the client capable of responding to silence either verbally or non-verbally?
- If silence emerges in an interaction with this client, how does the client respond? How might you name some potential meanings of the silence to help the client engage it more fully?
- If silence does not emerge in your interaction with this client, how would you explain this based on what you know of the client and their experience? How might you invite this client into an encounter with silence in a follow-up interaction, if this is clinically warranted?

NOTES

1 It is worth noting the similarity between this diagram and the contemplative psychology articulated in Keating (2005, Chapter Thirteen).

2 It is worth stating that as far as Christian contemplatives are concerned, Panikkar's trinitarian interpretation of silence and the Word is somewhat unique. For a more traditional Roman Catholic treatment of the Holy Trinity in contemplation see Merton (2007). For a treatment of silence and the Word that is closer to Panikkar's treatment of the topic, Anglican theologian George Pattison (2024) offers a very insightful approach drawing upon philosopher Martin Heidegger's understanding of language and being. From Pattison's perspective, Christian prayer invites those praying into a palpable encounter with silence, from which only three primordial words can be the proper response: "help," "amen," and "alleluia." "Help" signals a person's need for divine assistance in the midst of their circumstances. "Amen" signals a person's acceptance of their circumstances and whatever aid might come to them—hence "amen" is prayed in the sense of "so be it." Finally, "alleluia" is a person's expression of praise and thanksgiving for the divine presence that helps and sustains them through all of life's ups and downs (Pattison, 2024, Chapter Four). Both Merton's and Pattison's approaches to prayer are somewhat different from Panikkar's as presented herein. Panikkar's approach is indebted to Heidegger's discussion of being and language (see Pattison, 2024) and hence takes a phenomenological approach to this topic. However, Keating's (2005) techniques for centering prayer demonstrate the concrete overlap between all these approaches within Christian contemplative practice. From Keating's perspective, a person may use a one- or two-syllable word to invite them into a concrete encounter with the silent presence of God, and this is the basis for his approach to contemplative prayer (Keating, 2005; see also Pattison, 2024).

REFERENCE LIST

Barad, K. (2007). *Meeting the universe halfway: quantum physics and the entanglement of matter and meaning.* Durham, NC: Duke University Press.

Béres, L., & Crawley, D. (2023). *The language of the soul in narrative therapy: spirituality in clinical theory and practice.* New York, NY: Routledge.

Blankholm, J. (2022). *The secular paradox: on the religiosity of the not religious.* New York, NY: New York University Press.

Bourgeault, C. (2016). *The heart of centering prayer: nondual Christianity in theory and practice.* Boulder, CO: Shambhala.

Butler, J. (2005). *Giving an account of oneself.* New York, NY: Fordham University Press.

Downes, W. (2011). *Language and religion: a journey into the human mind.* Cambridge, UK: Cambridge University Press.

Graziano, M. S. (2019). *Rethinking consciousness: a scientific theory of subjective experience* (Kindle ebook ed.). New York, NY: Norton.

Jung, C. G. (2011). *The undiscovered self: with symbols and the interpretation of dreams.* Princeton, NJ: Princeton University Press.

Keating, T. (2005). *Manifesting God* (Kindle ebook ed.). New York, NY: Lantern Books.

Lakoff, G., & Johnson, M. (1980). *Metaphors we live by.* Chicago, IL: University of Chicago Press.

Lasair, S. (2018). Understanding, assessing, and intervening in the spiritual nature of medical events: theological and theoretical perspectives. *Practical Theology, 11*(5), 374–386.

Lasair, S. (2019). What's the point of spiritual care? A narrative response. *Journal of Pastoral Care & Counseling, 73*(2), 115–123. doi:10.1177/1542305019846846

Lasair, S. (2020a). A narrative approach to spirituality and spiritual care in health care. *Journal of Religion and Health, 59,* 1524–1540. doi:10.1007/s10943-019-00912-9

Lasair, S. (2020b). What's the point of clinical pastoral education and pastoral counselling education? Political, developmental, and professional considerations. *Journal of Pastoral Care & Counseling, 74*(1), 22–32.

Lasair, S. (2021). HAVE-H: five attitudes for a narratively grounded and embodied spirituality. *Journal of Pastoral Care & Counseling, 75*(1), 13–22. doi:10.1177/1542305020965546

Loizzo, J., Brandon, F., Wolf, E. J., & Neale, M. (Eds.) (2023). *Advances in contemplative psychotherapy: accelerating personal and social transformation* (2nd ed.). New York, NY: Routledge.

Madigan, S. (2019). *Narrative therapy* (2nd ed.). Washington, DC: American Psychological Association.

Matt, D. C. (1997). *The essential Kabbalah: the heart of Jewish mysticism.* Edison, NJ: Castle Books.

Merton, T. (2007). *New seeds of contemplation* (Kindle ebook ed.). New York, NY: New Directions.

Panikkar, R. (2004). *Christophany: the fullness of man* (A. DiLascia, Trans.). Maryknoll, NY: Orbis.

Panikkar, R. (2010). *The rhythm of being: the unbroken trinity: the Gifford lectures*. Maryknoll, NY: Orbis.

Panikkar, R. (2014). *Mysticism and spirituality* (Vol. 1). Maryknoll, NY: Orbis.

Panksepp, J. (2013). Affective neuroscience: implications for understanding emotional feelings and development of new therapeutics. In D. Siegel, & M. Solomon, *Healing moments in psychotherapy* (pp. 169–193). New York: Norton.

Parameshwaran, R. (2015, Jan-Mar). Theory and practice of chaplain's spiritual care process: a psychiatrist's experiences of chaplaincy and conceptualizing transpersonal model of mindfulness. *Indian Journal of Psychiatry*, 57(1), 21–29.

Pattison, G. (2024). *A philosophy of prayer: nothingness, language, and hope* (Kindle ebook ed.). New York, NY: Fordham University Press.

Pedhu, Y. (2019). Efforts to overcome countertransference in pastoral counseling relationships. *Journal of Pastoral Care & Counseling*, 73(2), 74–81.

Picard, M. (1948). *The world of silence* (S. Godman, Trans.). Merseyside, UK: The Lost Lit Library.

Ricoeur, P. (1981). *The rule of metaphor: multi-disciplinary studies of the creation of meaning in language* (R. Czerny, Trans.). Toronto, ON: University of Toronto Press.

Ricoeur, P. (1991). Life: a story in search of a narrator. In M. J. Valdes (Ed.), *Paul Ricoeur: reflection and imagination* (pp. 425–437). Toronto, ON: University of Toronto Press.

Ricoeur, P. (1992). *Oneself as another* (K. Blamey, Trans.). Chicago, IL: University of Chicago Press.

Ross, M. (2014). *Silence: a user's guide* (Vol. 1: Process). London, UK: Darton, Longman, and Todd.

Sardello, R. (2008). *Silence: the mystery of wholeness*. Berkeley, CA: Goldenstone Press.

Scholem, G. (1954). *Major trends in Jewish mysticism*. New York, NY: Schocken.

Scholem, G. (1991). *On the mystical shape of the godhead: basic concepts in the Kabbalah* (J. Chipman, Ed., & J. Neugroschel, Trans.). New York, NY: Schocken.

Schore, A. N. (2019a). *Right brain psychotherapy*. New York, NY: Norton.

Schore, A. N. (2019b). *The development of the unconscious mind*. New York, NY: Norton.

Seth, A. (2021). *Being you: a new science of consciousness* (Kindle ebook ed.). New York, NY: Dutton.

Siegel, D. (2013). Therapeutic presence: mindful awareness and the person of the therapist. In D. Siegel, & M. Solomon, *Healing moments in psychotherapy* (pp. 243–269). New York: Norton.

Taylor, C. (2007). *A secular age*. Cambridge, MA: Belknap Harvard University Press.

Taylor, C. (2011). Why we need a radical redefinition of secularism. In E. Mendieta, & J. van Antwerpen (Eds.), *The power of religion in the public sphere: Judith Butler, Jurgen Habermas, Charles Taylor, Cornel West* (pp. 34–59). New York, NY: Columbia University Press.

Taylor, C. (2016). *The language animal: the full shape of the human linguistic capacity*. Cambridge, MA: Belknap/Harvard University Press.

Taylor, M. C. (2007). *After God*. Chicago, IL: University of Chicago Press.

Trungpa, C. (2018). *The future is open: good karma, bad karma, and beyond karma* (C. R. Gimian, Ed.). Boulder, CO: Shambhala.

Valle, R. (2019). Toward a psychology of silence. *The Humanist Psychologist*, 47(3), 219–261.

Vanderstelt, H., van Dijk, A., & Lasair, S. (2022). Transformational education: exploring the lasting impact of students clinical pastoral education experiences. *Journal of Health Care Chaplaincy*, 29(1), 89–104.

Wilber, K. (2017). *The religion of tomorrow: a vision for the future of the great traditions: more inclusive, more comprehensive, more complete* (Audiobook ed.). Denver, CO: Shambhala.

Williams, R. (2014). *The edge of words: God and the habits of language*. London, UK: Bloomsbury.

Williams, R. (2018). *Christ: the heart of creation*. London, UK: Bloomsbury Continuum.

Seven

INTRODUCTION

This chapter argues that all the traits of spiritual health discussed in these pages are the foundation upon which individuals can build experiences of flourishing in their lives. Some space is used to discuss recent contributions to understandings of flourishing in the research literature. Then, by revisiting a clinical case from an earlier chapter, the chapter explores how flourishing can be detectable clinically in the lives of clients. Spiritual practice is demonstrated to be a crucial component in this case, but this is so because such practices are deemed crucial for building, maintaining, and enhancing individuals' felt emotional and intuitive connections with all of interconnected reality. The chapter will conclude the book's argument by addressing the question of what makes spiritual care a unique caregiving profession, especially in relation to psychology and social work. This final section will conclude this book's overall argument.

REVIEW OF KEY CONCEPTS

To outline how flourishing emerges in a person's life it is worth recalling the general contours of Figure 2.1. In that figure it was evident that all people integrate notions of the good into their lives. These notions of the good come from individuals' cultures and families of origin, various religious and social institutions, and other cultural and social realities (Chapter Two; Lasair, 2020). These notions do not pertain only to how people act and behave, as in some approaches to morality. Rather, these understandings of the good embody the deepest values a person might pursue in life (Chapter Two; Lasair, 2020). In some cases, this means individuals pursue certain material or social goods; in other cases, such goods are expressed in terms of religious, spiritual, or self-development aspirations.

DOI: 10.4324/9781003466147-8

As people pursue their understandings of the good, however, they may find it either easy or difficult to achieve them. The relative ease or difficulty a person encounters in this pursuit then invites them to consider whether they assess themself as good or not-so-good in relation to the rest of reality. These self-assessments form the basis for an individual's internal identity narrative, and this narrative becomes furthermore embodied in their frame for reality as expressed in their attitudes, actions, behaviors, affect, body language, and so on (Chapter Two; Lasair, 2020). It is when such self-assessments occur that individuals begin to reflect on their lives and can thus start to work with and modify the dynamics in their frame for reality.

All the traits of spiritual health that have been described in these pages therefore require a certain amount of conscious effort, both to begin cultivating them, as well as to maintain them over a person's lifespan. The relationships between the different traits were represented visually in Figure 6.2 (see Chapter Six). This figure demonstrated how each successive trait of spiritual health requires a greater scope of engagement than the previous ones. This is because the traits located more centrally in the figure provide the inner foundations for traits that often develop later. This does not mean that all these traits will develop in a linear way; it is common for individuals to experience several partial manifestations of all these traits at different times in their overall personal and spiritual development. However, for someone to be spiritually healthy, each of the traits described in these pages needs to manifest consistently in their life; otherwise such a person may only experience temporary moments of flourishing, and this last trait will not characterize their life as a whole.

FLOURISHING IN CURRENT RESEARCH

Human flourishing has, in fact, received significant attention in the research literature in recent years. Positive psychologists have given this topic extensive attention (e.g., Seligman, 2011; Keyes & Haidt, 2003), as have some Christian theologians (e.g., Volf, 2015; Volf & Croasmun, 2019). In many cases these scholarly engagements with flourishing also align with the teachings of several traditional religions. For example, the wisdom literature found in Jewish and Christian Bibles could easily be described as offering clear pathways toward flourishing (e.g., Proverbs). Similarly, Christian, Hindu, and Buddhist contemplative traditions often describe union with the divine as characterized by experiences of bliss, nirvana, and non-duality (e.g., Aurobindo, 2001; Bourgeault, 2016; Trungpa, 2018). Humanists and atheists also often use the language of flourishing to describe what it is like for humans to live vibrant and fulfilling lives (e.g., Blankholm, 2022; C. Taylor, 2007; M. C. Taylor, 2007). Now, while the experiences described by these various religious, secular, and scholarly traditions may not be precisely identical, there is enough similarity between them to suggest a phenomenon that can be experienced by many human populations, regardless of their cultures, nationalities, religions, genders, or any other distinguishing traits.

Accordingly, Tyler J. VanderWeele of the Harvard Human Flourishing program has published extensively on flourishing and has identified six domains connected to this phenomenon that have now received cross-cultural validation. VanderWeele's work is important because he has consolidated many of the findings of positive psychology. He has also been explicit in connecting his understanding of flourishing to the teachings of several traditional religions. To review, VanderWeele's six domains of flourishing, as introduced in Chapter One, are happiness and life satisfaction; mental and physical health; meaning and purpose; character and virtue; close social relationships; and financial and material security (see Höltge et al., 2023).

Now, in a recent cross-cultural study of flourishing, an international team of researchers that included VanderWeele discovered that for flourishing to occur, people need to experience most, if not all, of these six domains in their life as "good" (Höltge et al., 2023). However, the research team also discovered that people did not need to experience "good" financial and material security to flourish in the other five domains. All this indicates that while flourishing is a complex phenomenon from an empirical perspective, it is not necessary for a person to experience all six domains as good to flourish in other parts of their life (Höltge et al., 2023).

VanderWeele's work is furthermore relevant to the present discussion because of his description of religion and spirituality as one pathway toward flourishing (see e.g., VanderWeele, 2020, 2017; VanderWeele, Long, & Balboni, 2021). For VanderWeele, religion and spirituality connect to a person's sense of meaning and purpose as well as to their senses of character and virtue. Because questions of meaning, purpose, character, and virtue are deeply embedded in the teachings of many, if not most, traditional religions, VanderWeele shows how participation in a religious tradition can help individuals and communities embody flourishing in ways that are different from those who have no religion of their own.

In this way, VanderWeele's work adds further perspective to Duke University psychiatry professor Harold Koenig's work (e.g., Koenig, 2008; Koenig, VanderWeele, & Peteet, 2023). Koenig has repeatedly demonstrated numerous positive correlations between religious participation and overall good medical health. Among the correlated positive health outcomes in religious adherents identified by Koenig and colleagues are increased longevity and lower rates of cardiovascular disease (Koenig, 2008; Koenig, VanderWeele, & Peteet, 2023). Koenig and colleagues speculate these positive health benefits might be related to reduced rates of alcohol and tobacco use in religiously engaged populations. Yet Koenig and colleagues maintain that the precise mechanisms contributing to these correlations remain unknown. Nevertheless, from their perspective, the correlations are compelling enough to demonstrate that participation in faith communities can have positive benefits on a person's overall medical health. However, it is worth stating that Koenig and colleagues acknowledge that their measures of religiosity are contested (Koenig, 2008). Likewise, in the current discussion, religion is understood differently from Koenig and colleagues; from their perspective *religion* is a term that describes involvement in established faith communities.

Regardless, VanderWeele's work contributes to this discussion by demonstrating why people might experience positive health benefits due to religious involvement, as described in the human flourishing research (VanderWeele, 2020). From VanderWeele's perspective, meaning, purpose, character, and virtue all enable individuals who manifest goodness in these domains to feel engaged in life and to avoid making choices that might lead to stressful or harmful consequences (VanderWeele, 2017). Such meaningful engagement with life and wise decision making thus enable individuals to move through their lives in ways that support good mental and physical health as direct benefits of their experiences of goodness in these former two domains.

However, while VanderWeele's work provides an empirical account of what flourishing can look like, his approach does not significantly grapple with some of the ontological conditions that can contribute to flourishing. Ontology typically addresses questions of reality's dynamics and structures, particularly how various objects and/or people fit within these dynamics and structures (see e.g., Badiou, 2006; Przywara, 2014). This ontological dimension of flourishing points toward the specific contributions religious and spiritual traditions can make to discussions of flourishing. Positive psychology and VanderWeele's work, an offshoot of this secular discipline, are not equipped to explore questions regarding the nature of reality and how individuals' and groups' relationships with all reality might or might not contribute to their overall health and wellbeing.

It could therefore be argued that what I have presented in these pages aligns with much of the emerging research in positive psychology. There might be some truth to such perspectives. However, the approach taken in these pages also goes beyond many of the discussions in the positive psychology literature by inviting consideration of the silence that surrounds all that is, as discussed in the last chapter. In this sense, there is a distinctly ontological dimension to the picture of spiritual health I have been constructing. When the foundational dynamic of spiritual health is understood as a person's capacity to build, maintain, and enhance their relationships with all that is, this idea also assumes that all people are embedded in their numerous daily realities in ways they can only ever partially name. Furthermore, and as argued in Chapter Six, all of reality is held by a silence that can barely be named, but which connects everything that is experienced as material reality. This sense of connection, often experienced through a person's emotions and intuitions, is central to the approach to spirituality, spiritual care, and spiritual health articulated in these pages.

JUDY'S MANIFESTATION OF FLOURISHING

Of the patient cases explored in this book, Judy's presented the most compelling picture of spiritual health. This was not because Judy was exceptionally healthy in a physical sense; had Judy possessed good physical health, she would not have needed to come to hospital. In some ways Judy did not even experience good financial and material stability—many of the social challenges encountered by members of her extended family made it difficult for her to maintain a standard of living that many other people would take for granted. Yet, as

VanderWeele's empirical research reveals, it is not necessary for individuals to experience all the domains he identifies as good for them to flourish in other areas of life (see Höltge et al., 2023). Indeed, Judy had many close social relationships. She also had a strong sense of character and virtue that helped her make difficult choices about where she would invest her limited time and personal and financial resources, particularly when helping her extended family. Moreover, Judy was also able to describe herself as a person who had significant happiness and life satisfaction, even when accounting for all the challenges she encountered previously and continued to live through. In fact, overcoming all the challenges she had experienced contributed to Judy's sense of meaning and purpose, particularly when considering how she understood caring for her family as one of her primary roles. During my one interaction with her, it was furthermore evident that Judy's faith supported and sustained her through her life, again confirming several aspects of VanderWeele's understanding of flourishing.

When approached purely from the perspective of VanderWeele's work, then, Judy seemed to manifest one kind of human flourishing. This does not mean she did not experience challenges or difficulties in her life—the distress that caused her to request spiritual care was enough to indicate that she would probably not describe her life as "perfect." Nevertheless, according to what Judy reported to me, she would likely have scored herself as experiencing life as "good" in at least four of VanderWeele's six domains. Yet none of this reveals why Judy might be assessed as flourishing according to the perspective I have been articulating in these pages.

Among the crucial components of spiritual health explored in this book are a person's capacities for awareness and openness, particularly when it comes to understanding the origins and dynamics of their automatic tendencies in perception and projection. Perception and projection in these pages are narratively grounded, in that they cannot be divorced from a person's neurobiology, temperament, prior experiences, and cognitive ability to make sense of their life and its meaning (Chapters Two and Three). As awareness and openness grow in a person, they become increasingly neutral in their inner life (Chapters Four and Five). This neutrality frees them from their automatic tendencies in perception and projection. This growth in neutrality and freedom similarly helps individuals to make concrete choices regarding how they might respond to their perceptions and projections, both in the context of their inner dynamic and in their outer behaviors, attitudes, and actions (Chapter Five). When a person invests more in the inner deliberation required to make these kinds of choices, they also become increasingly able to assess whether their prior responses to their perceptions and projections either helped or hindered them in their pursuit of the good in life. When a person assesses the quality of their choices in these regards, this signals the beginning of wisdom for them. Wisdom, when pursued further, produces even greater insight within an individual regarding their own inner dynamic. As it takes deeper root, wisdom furthermore reveals the truth of how every life is framed by the silent absence of words that holds and permeates all reality, as discussed in Chapter Six. Contentment is the natural outgrowth of such deep wisdom, mainly because engaging with silence reveals the impermanence of all relative realities, guiding individuals repeatedly to contemplate the ultimate nature of reality, however they might name and understand it. Again, Figure 6.2 illustrates these relationships in visual form (see Chapter Six).

ONTOLOGICAL DIMENSIONS OF FLOURISHING IN JUDY'S CASE

At this point it is not worth recounting how Judy embodied the traits of spiritual health identified in these pages—much of that analysis was already accomplished in Chapter Five. However, it is worth discussing how Judy's relationship with silence enabled her to navigate the various ups and downs she experienced in life.

As mentioned in Chapter Five, Judy had an active spiritual life that included several practices, prayer being one of them. While Judy and I did not explore her various practices to any great extent, it was evident all of them helped Judy to deepen her connection with all that is, especially by enabling her to release troubling perceptions or projections into silence. In fact, it is likely that Judy's relationship with silence mobilized a process within her similar to what was described in the paragraph that concluded the previous section—from enhancing awareness and openness, moving through growth in neutrality, freedom, wisdom, and contentment. This dynamic was so well-established in Judy's life that I believe it even manifested itself in her self-presentation. In Chapter Five I drew attention to the seeming stream-of-consciousness way Judy had of expressing herself. I also noted how sometimes tears would appear in her eyes as she was telling me about something troubling in her life, only for her to break into a wide grin a few minutes later as she was telling me about some of her joys. In some cases, such a wide range of emotions in quick succession (i.e., from one moment to the next) is called *emotional lability* and can be a potential indication of an underlying psychiatric condition, psychoneurological disorder, or acquired brain injury (American Psychiatric Association, 2013). Yet Judy did not present as particularly labile. Rather, her experiences in life were so diverse and so emotionally engaging that her visible displays of emotion came across as entirely consistent with the events and experiences she was narrating.

What I found remarkable in all this, however, was how Judy was able to maintain her underlying stance of neutrality and freedom in light of her more superficial expressions of emotion. Silence therefore did emerge significantly in the conversation that Judy and I shared. Specifically, silence made itself known after Judy and I had discussed how grateful she was for all the goodness in her life, even amidst all the challenges and difficulties in her extended family. Perhaps most notably, the silence emerged after I had spent well over an hour with Judy. I therefore felt I had a good grasp of the many factors in Judy's life that were causing her concern. In the emergence of this silence, both Judy and I experienced a deep sense of connection with Judy's story, not only due to the emotional intensity of working together, but also due to a powerful sense of the transcendent that seemed to emerge between us (Valle, 2019). In some of the literature, such silence can be labeled as "the sacred," "the transcendent," or "God," depending on the authors' orientations (e.g., Valle, 2019; Pargament, 2007; Lynch, 2012).

When this silence emerged between Judy and me, she and I sat in it for a short time. I then offered to say a prayer on Judy's behalf. Both Judy and I could sense the silence, and prayer seemed the most appropriate response. Judy consented, so in my prayer I referred to much of what Judy had communicated to me. I also asked that Judy might be aware of God's presence surrounding and holding her. I used this language to name the silence because it was appropriate for Judy's frame—with patients from other traditions I usually use different language; with patients from no religious tradition, I typically offer a poetically phrased insight or hope for wellness rather than a prayer. By addressing the silence this way in prayer, I felt I might help Judy release her cares and worries into the infinite. In this sense, the prayer could serve as an emotional and spiritual conduit that might enable Judy to deepen her manifestations of neutrality and freedom (see also Pattison, 2024).

By allowing me to help her renew her sense of connection to the silence she named God, then, my hope was Judy would use her awareness, openness, and wisdom to help her release her feelings of emotional distress while I prayed. I also hoped this process of letting go might help Judy rebuild some contentment in relation to her time in hospital. I therefore approached Judy's consent to and affirmation of the prayer I offered as expressing her desire to reconnect to the silence that would be so crucial in shifting her perceptions of her own spiritual wellbeing. Through all this, my hunch was that the relationality that so characterized Judy's life was a key to enabling her to deepen her manifestation of flourishing, even while she still experienced physical, emotional, and interpersonal challenges.

FLOURISHING, RELATIONALITY, AND ONTOLOGY

When approached from this perspective, the picture of spiritual health I have been outlining describes the inner dynamic a person needs to build, maintain, and enhance their relationships with all reality. I have described this capacity for relationship as characterizing overall spiritual health, and, to a certain extent, it also describes the dynamics of flourishing. To bring further definition to flourishing as described herein it is important to recall the ontological dimensions of contentment that were discussed in Chapter Six, specifically a person's relationship with silence.

In the previous chapter I discussed how silence surrounds, permeates, and inhabits all reality (Panikkar, 2014; Ross, 2014; Sardello, 2008; Valle, 2019). As indicated in that chapter, there are several ways of naming this silence, and various religious traditions, even humanistic and atheistic ones, use different terms to do so. Yet regardless of how silence is named, entering this experiential domain usually results in a relatively universal outcome: people who encounter silence typically emerge with a deep feeling that everything, *absolutely everything*, is interconnected (e.g., Panikkar, 2014; Sardello, 2008). In

Chapter One I indicated that McGilchrist wrote of this phenomenon as a prime example of right-brain dominant ways of engaging the world (McGilchrist, 2021). For McGilchrist, Indigenous approaches to life are paradigmatic in this regard. Karen Barad (2007) and Judith Butler (2020) also write of such interconnectedness as characterizing both quantum physics and feminist ontologies (see also Keller, 2015). Furthermore, Panikkar's (2014) articulation of how silence is closely related to a person's embodiment of the cosmotheandric principle approaches this same ontological reality from an inter-religious and/or inter-spiritual perspective. Describing silence as a phenomenon that surrounds, permeates, inhabits, and connects all that is thus draws upon the insights of several human and scientific fields, all of which seem to be growing into a shared understanding of reality.

What differentiates spiritual perspectives from some of these other domains, however, is spirituality's capacity to engage this ontological interconnectedness experientially (see e.g., Parameshwaran, 2015; Panikkar, 2014; Ross, 2014). Specifically, people typically need to mobilize their spiritualities to integrate their relationships with interconnected reality into their behaviors, actions, attitudes, interactions, and interpersonal dynamics. Within these pages, people typically do this by drawing upon their awareness, openness, neutrality, freedom, wisdom, and contentment, all for the purpose of moving toward overall manifestations of flourishing. Specifically, experiential engagements with silence produce concrete behavioral and relational dynamics within a person's inner life that similarly render behavioral and relational dynamics that are readily observable to others; many mindfulness or contemplative approaches to psychotherapy have documented this phenomenon (Siegel, 2013; Loizzo, Brandon, Wolf, & Neale, 2023). Flourishing in this context is therefore the concrete outworking of a person's relationship with the ontological reality of silence. This relationship is the foundation for any person's inner dynamic, which then conditions how that person relates to the realities they share with others (Panikkar, 2014; Ross, 2014). As a result, there is an emerging correlation between a person's experiences of flourishing and their relative spiritual health. In my experience, outward expressions of flourishing are rarely sustainable long-term without the inner traits of spiritual health described in these pages.

Practices like prayer or meditation are thus often necessary for people like Judy's senses of overall spiritual health and wellbeing. Such practices are necessary because they are capable of producing the deep feelings of interconnectedness that integrate the ontological dimensions of spirituality into a person's conscious experiences. It is also for this reason that Spiritual Care Practitioners are typically required by their certifying bodies to continue nurturing their personal and spiritual development well after their CPE has ended (e.g., CASC/ACSS, 2019). This book has therefore demonstrated how Spiritual Care Practitioners' intentional work with their clients' spiritualities, as well as their own relative spiritual health, can contribute to the clients' overall manifestations of flourishing. This is true regardless of whether flourishing is measured using VanderWeele's approach or not.

CONCLUDING THIS BOOK'S ARGUMENT

By systematically articulating how clients can manifest specific traits associated with spiritual health, this book has shown how each of these traits is readily identifiable in clinical settings. As such, these traits can be both assessed and informally measured by skilled Spiritual Care Practitioners. Practitioners also possess tools that can assist clients to grow into greater spiritual health and flourishing. Because Spiritual Care Practitioners have worked to develop their own spiritualities and spiritual health during their CPE, they have first-hand knowledge of how—and how not—to build spiritual health in their own lives. Through their CPE learning, Practitioners furthermore learn how to expand their own experiences so they might assist their clients to grow into greater spiritual health. Such first-hand knowledge consequently grounds Practitioners' caregiving practices in their own spiritualities, and hence brings an authenticity to their interventions that is often not required by other healthcare professions.

Spiritual Care Practitioners therefore provide a holistic kind of care that is grounded in and integrated into their own senses of personal and professional identity. This caregiving orientation enables Spiritual Care Practitioners to engage their clients in the depth of their humanity, precisely because Practitioners have engaged their own humanity to its depths. Awareness, openness, neutrality, freedom, wisdom, and contentment all serve as the foundations for Practitioners' own manifestations of flourishing. Practitioners can thus walk their clients into greater manifestations of these traits, because they, too, have walked this path and are intimately familiar with its numerous snares and pitfalls as a result.

While Spiritual Care Practitioners might draw upon concepts and techniques from various psychotherapeutic modalities, these concepts and techniques are often housed within a broader understanding of what makes people human. Again, a Practitioner's work with their own frame for reality is crucial here. Whereas other helping professionals like counselors, psychologists, and social workers might rely upon the teachings of their specific modality to guide them in their caregiving, Spiritual Care Practitioners can draw upon the techniques of multiple modalities depending on the needs of their clients. Practitioners can do this because they are able to assess the discrete dynamics of their clients' frames for reality very quickly, and then with similar speed mobilize interventions that promote a client's overall spiritual health, precisely due to the Practitioner's acute attunement to the dynamics of their own and their clients' frames. There may be some similarities between this approach and psychodynamic and/or psychoanalytic approaches to therapy, yet it is Practitioners' attention to the onto-logical and/or metaphysical dimensions of their clients' lives that makes their profession unique in the caregiving world.

As articulated in these pages, spiritual health is measured according to a person's capacity to build, maintain, and enhance their relationships with all that is. While space has not permitted a comprehensive engage-ment with this topic, I have indicated at several points that much of good spiritual health relies on a felt emotional and intuitive connection to the ontological interconnectedness of all reality. This interconnect-edness is implied and described by Panikkar's *cosmotheandric* principle, McGilchrist's prioritization of the traits associated with the human brain's right hemisphere, and the scientific and feminist ontologies articulated by Barad and Butler. This interconnectedness is also described by numerous religious traditions, often captured in the lan-guage of wisdom (Judaism and Christianity), bliss, nirvana, and non-duality (Hinduism and Buddhism). As established by my analysis of the consensus healthcare definition of *spirituality*, a person's spirituality is that *through which* they construct and experience their relationships with everything in life. A person's intentional work to grow the traits described herein will therefore often result in increasing measures of flourishing in their life. Increased flourishing is a result of this work because the traits described herein are the inner foundation for enhanced relationships with all of interconnected reality.

Ultimately it is a person's fuller participation in the interconnectedness of all reality that is the goal of spiritual care work. Within this approach, religious, secular, and cultural concepts, symbols, practices, teachings, and vocabularies all contain numerous understandings of how to build, maintain, and enhance a person's relationship with all that is. It is for this reason that teachings and practices from all these shared domains can play significant roles in frontline spiritual care. However, the specific area of interest for Spiritual Care Practitioners is how their clients integrate these various practices, teachings, symbols, concepts, and vocabularies into their own internal dynamic. This book has offered several examples of how clients can do this in both helpful and unhelpful ways. Spiritual Care Practitioners are therefore oriented toward determining the extent to which their clients' religious, secular, and cultural beliefs, practices, rituals, teachings, and vocabularies are helping them participate more fully in the interconnected nature of reality—and this is regardless of whether a client considers themself religious or not.

Accordingly, the term *religion* in these pages has *not* been used exclusively to refer to the teachings, practices, rituals, concepts, and vocabularies of established faith traditions. Rather, *religion* has been used broadly to designate any cultural system of belief and/or practice that can provide conceptual and/or practical content for a person's relationship with the rest of reality. Atheists and humanists, as well as the so-called "spiritual but not religious," can therefore also be described as having a "religion" in this sense (see Blankholm, 2022; M. C. Taylor, 2007), yet I fully acknowledge that debating this finer technical point with a client would *not* be advisable clinically. Regardless, Spiritual Care Practitioners are explicitly concerned with the overlap and intersections of religion and spirituality, while also maintaining some important distinctions between the two. To pigeonhole Practitioners into solely religious frames of reference therefore does an injustice to the complexities of their profession, as does reducing their work down to yet another form of psychotherapy. There is much here that remains to be articulated, but my hope is this book will have gone at least some way toward making the character of spiritual care more intelligible to others.

ENDING WHERE THIS BOOK BEGAN

To conclude, I began this book by describing some events surrounding the elimination of spiritual care's funding in my Canadian province of Saskatchewan. While, at the time of this writing, Saskatchewan had yet to restore its funding for spiritual care, it is clear that the justifications offered for that elimination of funds in 2017 were not grounded in a good understanding of the nature and purpose of spiritual care as a profession. This book has therefore attempted to present spirituality, spiritual care, and spiritual health in ways that draw upon the wisdom of various faith traditions, as well as several secular disciplines. As a result, this book has worked to show that spiritual care is a much broader practice than what is typically embodied by faith- or denomination-based chaplains or community clergy.

At this point, therefore, it is reasonable to conclude that spiritual care is unique as a profession, drawing upon the concepts and techniques of several psychotherapeutic schools while also integrating millennia of faith-based reflection and contemplation. Furthermore, because spiritual care is a relationally oriented and driven profession, it strives to meet care-receiving clients in the fullness of their humanity. If its caregiving potential is maximized, then, spiritual care can add an intensely human-focused dimension to holistic, client-centered care in healthcare and other caregiving environments. This is in contrast to other caregiving professions that can often struggle to embody such focus on care receivers' humanity, largely due to time constraints and the technicalities bound up with the care they provide.

In articulating all this, my hope has been that spiritual care might move into a position of greater flourishing as a profession. I am very aware that what unfolded in Saskatchewan in 2017 is somewhat unique. However, I am also aware that spiritual care positions are under threat in other jurisdictions in Canada and that chaplains in other countries are also working to articulate the nature and purpose of their profession for similar reasons. It is an honor to contribute to this ongoing work through this volume. I have done so in the hope that, through this book, those who function in spiritual care and chaplaincy roles might be better able to articulate how they fit professionally within the many interconnected realities relevant to them in their own jurisdictions and workplace contexts.

Reflection Questions

- How have you experienced flourishing in your life? How do your experiences align with the descriptions of flourishing in this chapter?
- How do you understand the overall trajectory of this book's argument? Is there anything in particular that stands out for you as you recall reading these pages?
- How might your frontline practices change as a result of reading this book? How might they stay the same?
- How do you see spiritual care/chaplaincy moving into a position of greater flourishing as a profession? How might this book contribute to moving the profession in that direction?

REFERENCES LIST

American Psychiatric Association (2013). *Diagnostic and statistical manual of mental disorders: DSM-5* (5th ed.). Washington, DC: American Psychiatric Publishing

Aurobindo, S. (2001). *A greater psychology* (A. S. Dalal, Ed.) New York, NY: Tarcher/ Putnam.

Badiou, A. (2006). *Being and event* (O. Feltham, Trans.). London, UK: Continuum.

Barad, K. (2007). *Meeting the universe halfway: quantum physics and the entanglement of matter and meaning.* Durham, NC: Duke University Press.

Blankholm, J. (2022). *The secular paradox: on the religiosity of the not religious.* New York, NY: New York University Press.

Bourgeault, C. (2016). *The heart of centering prayer: nondual Christianity in theory and practice.* Boulder, CO: Shambhala.

Butler, J. (2020). *The force of nonviolence: and ethico-political bind.* London, UK: Verso.

Canadian Association for Spiritual Care/Association canadienne de soins spirituelle (CASC/ACSS) (2019, May 2). *Competencies.* Retrieved September 24, 2024, from Canadian Association for Spiritual Care/Association canadienne de soins spirituelle: https://spiritualcare.ca/cascacss_competencies/

Höltge, J., Cowden, R. G., Lee, M. T., Bechara, A. O., Joynt, S., Kamble, S., ... VanderWeele, T. J. (2023). A systems perspective on human flourishing: exploring cross-country similaries and differences of a multisystemic flourishing network. *Journal of Positive Psychology, 18*(5), 695–710.

Keller, C. (2015). *Cloud of the impossible: negative theology and planetary entanglement.* New York, NY: Columbia University Press.

Keyes, C. L., & Haidt, J. (Eds.). (2003). *Flourishing: positive psychology and the life well lived.* Washington, DC: American Psychological Association.

Koenig, H. G. (2008). *Medicine, religion, and health: where science and spirituality meet.* New Brunswick, NJ: Templeton Press.

Koenig, H. G., VanderWeele, T. J., & Peteet, J. R. (2023). *Handbook of religion and health* (3rd ed.). New York, NY: Oxford University Press.

Lasair, S. (2020). A narrative approach to spirituality and spiritual care in health care. *Journal of Religion and Health, 59,* 1524–1540. doi:10.1007/s10943-019-00912-9

Loizzo, J., Brandon, F., Wolf, E. J., & Neale, M. (Eds.). (2023). *Advances in contemplative psychotherapy: accelerating personal and social transformation* (2nd ed.). New York, NY: Routledge.

Lynch, G. (2012). *The sacred and the modern world: a cultural sociological approach.* Oxford, UK: Oxford University Press.

McGilchrist, I. (2021). *The matter with things: our brains, our delusions and the unmaking of the world.* London, UK: Perspectiva Press.

Panikkar, R. (2014). *Mysticism and spirituality* (Vol. 1). Maryknoll, NY: Orbis.

Parameshwaran, R. (2015, Jan-Mar). Theory and practice of chaplain's spiritual care process: a psychiatrist's experiences of chaplaincy and conceptualizing trans-personal model of mindfulness. *Indian Journal of Psychiatry, 57*(1), 21–29.

Pargament, K. (2007). *Spiritually integrated psychotherapy: understanding and addressing the sacred.* New York, NY: Guilford Press.

Pattison, G. (2024). *A philosophy of prayer: nothingness, language, and hope.* New York, NY: Fordham University Press.

Przywara, E. (2014). *Analogia entis: metaphysics-: original structure and universal rhythm* (J. R. Betz, & D. B. Hart, Trans.). Grand Rapids, MI: Eerdmans.

Ross, M. (2014). *Silence: a user's guide* (Vol. 1: Process). London, UK: Darton, Longman, and Todd.

Sardello, R. (2008). *Silence: the mystery of wholeness.* Berkeley, CA: Goldenstone Press.

Seligman, M. E. (2011). *Flourish: a visionary new understanding of happiness and wellbeing.* New York, NY: Free Press.

Siegel, D. (2013). Therapeutic presence: Mindful awareness and the person of the therapist. In D. Siegel, & M. Solomon, *Healing moments in psychotherapy* (pp. 243–269). New York, NY: Norton.

Taylor, C. (2007). *A secular age.* Cambridge, MA: Belknap Harvard University Press.

Taylor, M. C. (2007). *After God.* Chicago, IL: University of Chicago Press.

Trungpa, C. (2018). *The future is open: good karma, bad karma, and beyond karma* (C. R. Gimian, Ed.). Boulder, CO: Shambhala.

Valle, R. (2019). Toward a psychology of silence. *The Humanist Psychologist, 47*(3), 219–261.

VanderWeele, T. J. (2017). Religion and health: a synthesis. In M. J. Balboni, & J. R. Peteet (Eds.), *Spirituality and religion within the culture of medicine: from evidence to practice* (pp. 357–401). New York, NY: Oxford University Press.

VanderWeele, T. J. (2020). Spiritual well-being and human flourishing: conceptual, causal, and policy relations. In A. B. Cohen (Ed.), *Religion and human flourishing* (pp. 43–54). Waco, TX: Baylor University Press.

VanderWeele, T. J., Long, K. N., & Balboni, M. J. (2021). Tradition-specific measures of spiritual well-being. In M. Lee, L. D. Kubzansky, & T. J. VanderWeele (Eds.), *Measuring well-being: interdisciplinary perspectives from the social sciences and the humanities* (pp. 482–498). New York, NY: Oxford University Press.

Volf, M. (2015). *Flourishing: why we need religion in a globalized world*. New Haven, CT: Yale University Press.

Volf, M., & Croasmun, M. (2019). *For the life of the world: theology that makes a difference*. Grand Rapids, MI: Brazos Press.

Appendix A

Building Valid Assessment Measures

Initially it is worth acknowledging that assessment is somewhat controversial among spiritual care professionals. While it is generally understood that Spiritual Care Practitioners need to be assessing their clients for such phenomena as spiritual distress, there is little consensus regarding what approaches to assessment fit best within Practitioners' frontline practices. Currently the literature is divided between those who argue that some formal quantitative assessment measure ought to be used and those who argue that informal qualitative measures are sufficient.

While I see merits in both positions, I also believe that the interpersonal and relational dynamic that is characteristic of spiritual care interactions ought not to be disrupted for the sake of administering formal assessment measures. Therefore, spiritual care assessment practices need to be embedded within spiritual care interactions, using an assessment framework as a guide when engaging clients. As a result, the approach to spirituality and spiritual health articulated in these pages can serve as a conceptual apparatus that can help to illuminate clients' relative spiritual health within the context of spiritual care interactions. Yet to do so, there will need to be some further development of the framework, specifically in connecting the theory's broader concepts with specific client behaviors (some initial groundwork in this regard has already occurred in these pages in the documented clinical cases). By making such connections explicit, researchers will enable Practitioners to connect this book's theory systematically to concrete and observable client behaviors.

To approach this question of validating this book's theory, I suggest the following process:

1. Develop a consensus-building exercise regarding the overall approach to spirituality and spiritual health developed in these

209 **Appendix A**

pages. The outcome of this exercise need not confirm the theory articulated herein in all its details. Rather, it is the approach to spiritual health as the inner foundation for flourishing that needs validation. Some clarification of the concepts and traits of spiritual health would be needed, particularly when considering concrete client behaviors that can be connected with the theory's concepts and identified traits of spiritual health.

2. Once consensus has been built regarding the overall approach, it will then be necessary for a panel of experts to identify specific client behaviors that could be associated with the concepts and traits of spiritual health. While there may be overlap between the specific behaviors identified and the traits toward which they point, there would also need to be consideration of when and how these behaviors emerge in client interactions. Such consideration would be necessary because contextual and relational factors can also illuminate the traits that are evident in clients' behaviors, since their behaviors and traits emerge within the context of interactions with Spiritual Care Practitioners. As a result, it would be necessary to account for this interactional dynamic when constructing the methodology by which the specific behaviors would be identified.

3. A broader spectrum of experts would then need to confirm what the previous panel of experts identified as behaviors connected to the various traits of spiritual health. For this, a modified Delphi process combined with qualitative interviews might serve to validate the connections between this book's theory and concrete client behaviors. While there would likely need to be some education provided for participants regarding the conceptual apparatus constructed during earlier phases of this validation process, this preliminary step would only serve to orient participants to the overall approach previously developed. Nevertheless, it would also be necessary to mitigate against biasing participants toward simply confirming what was developed during the previous stages of this process—if such mitigation were absent, the validation process would likely be undermined, potentially to the point of rendering it invalid.

4. Finally, a study of the psychometric properties of the assessment framework would need to be conducted, comparing it with other approaches to assessing spiritual health and wellbeing within clinical contexts.

In many respects, the process outlined in this appendix is similar to many of the established processes used to create valid measures of various phenomena that can emerge in clinical settings. As a further step, it might be necessary to consider how the overall assessment framework could be integrated into Practitioners' frontline practices without disrupting the relational dynamic that is so characteristic of spiritual care.

Consequently, there are some further questions regarding how best to educate Practitioners into using an assessment framework like the one proposed in this appendix. In Canada, at least, spiritual care education practices are undergoing some significant changes. As a result, thought is being given to how best to integrate conceptual academic knowledge into education practices like CPE that in many ways are better for training students in the skills and attitudes that contribute to Practitioners' overall competence than in conceptual or cognitive knowledge.

For Practitioners to integrate a framework like what is being proposed here into their clinical settings, it would therefore be necessary to provide some conceptual training, balancing it with training in how to use the concepts without distorting the ethos of spiritual caregiving practices. It could be that specific approaches to teaching this framework could be developed for CPE didactic sessions. Yet it is also possible to imagine that training in this framework could be developed as a stand-alone module for already-certified professionals, in addition to what might be delivered in CPE. Much would depend on the priorities of the organizations sponsoring the education. Developing this assessment framework, as well as specific training in how to mobilize it clinically, would therefore be one way of further enhancing spiritual care's frontline caregiving practices while also making these practices even more intelligible for other professions, employers, and funders.

Appendix B

Adapting the Theory for Long-Term Care

Of central concern when considering how to adapt this book's theory for long-term care is that this book assumes most clients have at least some capacities to reflect on their experiences and enter into neutral and free interior spaces in relation to them. Because these capacities are central features of the trajectory toward spiritual health articulated in these pages, it can be questioned whether people with limitations in their cognition, caused either by dementia or developmental or intellectual disabilities, can experience spiritual health in the same ways as described in the preceding chapters. However, because spiritual health in this book prioritizes a person's emotional and intuitive connections with all reality, it is also true that in some cases a person's cognitive capacities and apparatuses can negatively affect their spiritual health, as demonstrated by Bonnie's case in Chapter Four.

So, to recall the discussion of my experiences in long-term care at the beginning of Chapter Three, Practitioners' abilities to construct trusting emotional connections with clients living with cognitive limitations is of crucial importance. Such ability draws upon Practitioners' skills to build secure therapeutic alliances with their clients in any caregiving setting. The main difference in long-term care lies in how Practitioners need to use both verbal and non-verbal communication to engage their clients in these contexts.

In long-term care, language can still be used to build, maintain, and enhance clients' relationships with all that is, but in many cases the level of engagement with clients' frames for reality is deeper, drawing upon historical events and how those might affect clients' experiences in the present. Yes, Practitioners engage some of these dynamics in other settings as well, as mentioned in several chapters above. In those other settings, these historical dynamics often surface in response to something a client says, or through a concrete interpersonal challenge. However, as discussed in Chapter Three, in long-term care it is necessary to engage clients differently than in other caregiving contexts. Specifically, in long-term care, it is often necessary for Practitioners to rely more heavily on information provided by clients' family members or loved ones. As indicated by Scottish practical theologian John Swinton (2012), when clients' capacities for speech or cognition are inhibited by dementia or some other disease process in their brain, families and other loved ones become the bearers and communicators of clients' memories. In this way, families can explain clients' behaviors, while also assisting Spiritual Care Practitioners to understand better what has changed and what has remained consistent for the client while the client has been living through their brain's particular disease process.

Therefore, because Practitioners are sensitized to the dynamics of clients' frames for reality, a skilled Practitioner can hypothesize how a client might be experiencing their current realities based on historical and contextual information provided to the Practitioner by the client's family and/or loved ones. These hypotheses can be further substantiated when the Practitioner assesses the client themself, paying attention to the client's cognitive capacities, as well as to the client's awareness of their current situation and personal history. All this information can then be used to construct spiritual care interventions that support a client's overall quality of life, even when the client is living through progressive limitations in their cognitive and communicative abilities.

When Practitioners nurture sustained relationships with clients in long-term care, then, they can easily assess how the client's frame for reality remains consistent or changes over time. This information is crucial for Practitioners, because it can help them adjust their interventions as needed, while also assisting them in liaising with clients' families regarding clients' care plans. Furthermore, because caring for families and loved ones can also be a high priority for Spiritual Care Practitioners in long-term care, tracking the consistencies and changes in a client's frame for reality can similarly help Practitioners offer effective care for clients' family members as well. Practitioners' sensitivities regarding frames for reality can also assist them in understanding how family members might be framing their experiences of any given client and of the care delivered at the Practitioner's site. A skilled Practitioner can also therefore engage potentially challenging dynamics in family members' frames and help to mitigate any interpersonal difficulties that might be produced by these dynamics.

The specific traits of spiritual health articulated in these pages, then, are not as important for Practitioners working in long-term care as they might be for Practitioners working in other contexts, except perhaps in relation to clients' family members. Instead, Practitioners in long-term care can use narrative information provided by family and loved ones to assess a client's overall manifestations of flourishing. This narrative information can then be used to address any areas of a client's life that could be improved by engaging them in topics and/or activities that might connect them to various things that have remained consistent for them over their lifespan. In doing so, Practitioners and other caregiving staff can honor and engage the long-term dynamics of a client's frame for reality, particularly those dynamics that have brought positive benefit to the client over time.

Here are some questions that can guide Practitioners' assessments of clients in long-term care:

- To what extent is the client aware of their circumstances and able to articulate this awareness to others?
- To what extent is the client able to communicate verbally?
- What are some of the key events in the client's life? To what extent is the client able to recount these events?
- How did these key events affect the client's senses of self and identity? To what extent is the client able to express the meaning of these events for themself?
- How do the client's family members and/or loved ones remember the client over their lifespan? To what extent does the client's current presentation align with how the client's family and loved ones remember them?
- How has the client's experience of progressive cognitive and/ or physical limitations affected their relationships with family members and/or loved ones?
  - What kinds of emotional and spiritual support might the client need as they are living through these changes?
  - What kinds of emotional and spiritual support might the client's family and loved ones need as they are living through these changes?

- What has given the client meaning and purpose in the past? How have these things remained consistent or changed in light of the client's disease process?
- What spiritual care programs and interventions might help this client to feel meaningfully engaged in life and connected to others?

REFERENCE LIST

Swinton, J. (2012). *Dementia: living in the memories of God.* Grand Rapids, MI: Eerdmans.

Appendix C

Adapting the Theory for Mental Health Contexts

Over twenty years ago John Swinton (2001) made an initial and significant contribution to the literature on how best to provide spiritual care to patients in mental health settings. While there has been some growth in this body of literature since that time, including some further publications by Swinton (e.g., 2020), my purpose in this appendix is neither to review this literature, nor to contribute to it in any significant ways. Rather, my goal is, like in Appendix B, to discuss briefly how this book's theory can be adapted for a context where individuals' perceptions and cognitions can be significantly altered due to a disease process in their brain.

Given the voluminous literature on various psychiatric conditions (e.g., American Psychiatric Association, 2013), it is impossible in these pages to give a systematic or comprehensive account of how this book's theory can be adapted for mental health settings. However, it is worth noting that a key concept when considering how to bring this theory into these contexts is the competing forces of consistency and change (see Chapter Two). As discussed in several of the preceding chapters, assessing how a client has lived through these competing forces can render crucial information regarding how well-equipped they are for living through life's various ups and downs. When acute mental illness has been part of a person's experience, this can add several complexities to how that person might experience consistency and change in their life. Furthermore, when a person's diagnosed psychiatric condition is connected to historical experiences of trauma, it is necessary for Practitioners to tread carefully into territory that is often emotionally and spiritually fraught because of how trauma can affect how a person encounters changes in their life. Practitioners thus ought only to venture into such territory with clear understandings of their roles and scopes of practice.

First, it is worth noting that in mental health settings Practitioners often work closely alongside other professionals whose scopes of practice overlap their own. Psychologists, psychiatrists, and social workers all have various ways of connecting with individuals' frames for reality and therapeutically engaging parts of those frames that might be causing individuals difficulty or distress. While each of these professions uses different concepts and treatment modalities to assess their clients and engage what their assessments reveal, there are clear areas of overlap between how these more-established mental health professions might engage clients and how Spiritual Care Practitioners might. Indeed, some Practitioners in mental health settings have received specialized training in modalities like acceptance commitment therapy or internal family systems therapy to directly treat the causes and symptoms of clients' mental health concerns.[1] Yet these modalities address concerns different from those explored in this book, thus they do not engage clients' *spiritual* health in the same way as has been described in these pages.

Similar to long-term care, then, in mental health settings it is not feasible for Practitioners to begin by assessing a client's manifestations of spiritual health as discussed herein. This is especially true when a client is in the acute phases of their illness, regardless of whether that illness has psychotic features or not. Instead, Practitioners need initially to focus on building relationships with their clients in mental health settings, using their own capacities to generate a calming and peaceful diffraction pattern between themselves and their clients as the foundation for whatever conversations might follow. These initial relational phases help to build the trust needed so that Practitioner and client can engage in more sustained integrative work as the client's acute symptoms begin to resolve.

During this integrative work, Practitioners' holistic concerns for clients come to the fore. Specifically, the Practitioner's ability to engage clients' narratives in their totality enables Practitioners to pay attention to how clients might or might not have been able to build, maintain, and enhance their relationships with all reality. If there is evidence of trauma in a client's narrative, the Practitioner can refer the client to a psychologist or social worker who might be able to help the client address the trauma's legacy. Yet when a client might be struggling to make sense of their identity in response to their experience(s) of acute mental illness, this is where a Practitioner's skills are likely best utilized. As discussed in Chapter Seven, Practitioners specialize in helping clients engage the ontological and metaphysical dimensions of their relationships with reality. Skilled Practitioners can therefore assist clients in reconstructing their relationships with all reality as part of their healing journey after an acute mental health crisis.

Now, because many mental health contexts specialize in treating illnesses with psychotic features, like schizophrenia or some forms of bipolar disorder, it is worth including a brief discussion of religious delusions and how Practitioners might engage them. In fact, there is a growing body of literature regarding ways in which Practitioners might consider how a mental health client's perceived religious or spiritual experiences might be genuine manifestations of these domains or more rightly understood as symptoms of their illness (e.g., Lucas, 2017; van Holten, 2021). There is not space in this appendix to resolve this very complicated question.

However, recalling my discussions in Chapters Two and Three regarding Downes' (2011) perspective from the cognitive science of religion, religious terms and concepts are often used to express everyday realities, even when clients are not experiencing acute mental health challenges. As a result, it may be helpful for Practitioners to consider that in some cases clients may use religious terms and concepts to make sense of perceptual changes they are experiencing because of their disease process. As neuropsychiatrist Iain McGilchrist (2009) points out (and as discussed in Chapter Three), the realities a person perceives are the realities they experience.

Part of a Practitioner's role in mental health settings, then, is to grapple with how clients are making sense of their experiences and to come to a shared understanding with the client regarding those experiences' meanings. This is how Practitioners can become familiar with the contours of mental health clients' frames for reality, even during the acute phases of their illness. As the client begins to return to normal functioning, a skilled Practitioner can then assist the client in reconstructing their frame for reality. Specifically, a Practitioner can help a mental health client explore how working to regain their cognitive and emotional health can also contribute to their overall spiritual health and wellbeing.

When considering this book's theory, then, like in long-term care, the specific traits of spiritual health identified by this book are not immediately relevant in mental health contexts, especially during the acute phases of a client's illness. However, as a client regains their normal functioning, strategically attending to specific traits of spiritual health can contribute to a client's cognitive and emotional recovery, even from psychological, psychiatric, and social work perspectives. That spiritual health is the inner foundation of flourishing is crucial to recall here (see Chapter Seven). While psychologists, psychiatrists, and social workers are very skilled in engaging the specific symptoms and etiologies of numerous mental health conditions, Spiritual Care Practitioners are uniquely positioned in mental health environments to help clients build within themselves practices and insights that can contribute to their flourishing over long-term timespans.

Consequently, Spiritual Care Practitioners should also be available for mental health clients in the community, mainly to follow up on initial interventions provided in acute care settings. Yet in many cases such community-based interventions are hard to begin and sustain, primarily due to lack of both human and financial resources. Nevertheless, Practitioners who work in acute mental health contexts can introduce clients to the integrative work discussed in this appendix, with the understanding that when the client is discharged their Practitioner should also provide them with various tools that can help them continue this work in the community, regardless of whether spiritual care follow-up is available or not.

Here are some assessment questions Practitioners can use when engaging clients in mental health contexts:

- To what extent are the client's perceptions of reality shared by others?
- What kind of emotional and interpersonal dynamic is being created by the client?
- What effect does my own emotional and interpersonal dynamic as Practitioner have on the client?
- What kinds of terms, concepts, symbols, and metaphors does the client use to describe what is going on for them?
- How are the client's words connected (or not) to their overall emotional and interpersonal dynamic?

- How receptive is the client to exploring the meanings of their experiences?
- To what extent do I, as Practitioner, need to focus on building my relationship with the client in this encounter, in contrast to engaging in collaborative meaning making?
- What are the emotional needs of this client in this moment?
- Are religious and/or spiritual themes helpful or harming for this client in this moment?
- What ideas, symbols, metaphors, and concepts—religious, spiritual, or otherwise—will be most helpful for this client as they work toward regaining their normal functioning?

NOTE

1 Personally, I have attended spiritual care conferences where Spiritual Care Practitioners working in mental health contexts have presented on these and other modalities that they use in their clinical contexts, sometimes even following the modality's manuals to guide their clients through a standardized and validated therapeutic trajectory.

REFERENCES LIST

American Psychiatric Association (2013). *Diagnostic and statistical manual of mental disorders: DSM-5* (5th ed.). Washington, DC: American Psychiatric Publishing.

Downes, W. (2011). *Language and religion: a journey into the human mind.* Cambridge, UK: Cambridge University Press.

Lucas, S. (2017). Assessing transcendental experiences vs mental illness. *Journal of Pastoral Care & Counseling, 71*(4), 267–273.

McGilchrist, I. (2009). *The master and his emissary: the divided brain and the making of the Western world.* New Haven, CT: Yale University Press.

Swinton, J. (2001). *Spirituality and mental health care.* London, UK: Jessica Kingsley.

Swinton, J. (2020). *Finding Jesus in the storm: the spiritual lives of Christians with mental health challenges.* Grand Rapids, MI: Eerdmans.

van Holten, W. (2021). A chaplain's view on religious delusions (and other extraordinary experiences): toward a theological framework of understanding. *Journal of Pastoral Care & Counseling, 75*(1), 4–12.

Anticipation: A person's act of considering how they might move into the future, actively evaluating how their desires and understandings of the good (morals) might inform this movement (see also **Desire** and **The good**).

Apparatus: All the numerous interconnected phenomena that contribute to how different components of reality are revealed. In these pages this term is used in conjunction with physics experiments; it is also treated as largely synonymous with a person's frame for reality (see also **Frame for reality** and **Mental model**).

Awareness: The extent to which a person can consciously name and integrate different aspects of their frame for reality (see also **Openness**).

Coherence: The inner logic that a person ascribes to their personal narrative, particularly when recollecting the past (see also **Memory** and **Recollection**).

Contentment: A person's awareness of their inner dynamics, capacity to see and accept these dynamics as part of their identity, and ability to work with these dynamics creatively through engagement with the silence that surrounds and inhabits all that is (see also **Awareness** and **Silence**).

Cosmotheandric principle: The idea that all people simultaneously participate in the physical (*cosmos*), divine/transcendent/ultimate (*theos*), and human (*aner/andros*) domains by virtue of their very being in the world.

Countertransference (see **Transference/countertransference**)

Desire: That which a person considers beneficial as they consider their movement into the future through anticipation. Typically, a person's desires are explored in tandem with their notions of the good (morals) (see also **Anticipation** and **The good**).

Discernable entity: A single component of an overall phenomenon. For such entities to become discernable, it is often necessary for the person studying an overall phenomenon to possess an apparatus that reveals these entities. This idea is true both in physics experiments and in human settings (see also **Intra-action** and **Overall phenomenon**).

Flourishing: A person's relative capacity to live in full relationship with all reality. Specific measures have been established for flourishing. Of particular note is the measure devised by Tyler J. VanderWeele and colleagues.

Foreclosure: A person's conscious or unconscious act of limiting the potential meanings a specific event or experience can have within the context of their life's narrative at any given time.

Frame for reality: A person's fundamental apparatus for engaging and understanding their lived realities. A person's frame for reality is constructed through their notions of the good, their experiences of pursuing the good, the effects of these experiences on their perceptions of their identity, and the extent to which elements of their identity have become embodied in their way of being in the world, specifically their behaviors, actions, interpersonal dynamics, attitudes, and body language (see also **Apparatus** and **Mental model**).

Freedom: The extent to which a person is not constrained by their automatic tendencies in perception and projection (see also **Perception**, **Projection**, and **Neutrality**).

Interpolation: A phenomenon that occurs when a large portion of a person's existence becomes defined by a cognitive, conceptual, social, or institutional apparatus that pre-exists them.

Intra-action: An entity's act of changing the dynamics of an overall phenomenon by altering the nature of its entanglements with other discernable entities within the phenomenon's overall makeup. This kind of agency can be seen in physics experiments, in a person's internal dynamic, as well as in broader interpersonal or social phenomena (see also **Discernable entity** and **Overall phenomenon**).

Memory: A person's conscious or unconscious act of invoking the past within the context of the present, typically when recollecting prior events or experiences. Memory and a person's perceptions of coherence in their personal narrative are bound together in their acts of recollecting the past (see also **Coherence** and **Recollection**).

Mental model: The neurological components of a person's apparatus or frame for reality (see also **Apparatus** and **Frame for reality**).

Metaphor: A use of language that cannot be explicitly connected to empirically verifiable entities or phenomena, but which reveals different aspects of reality or experience regardless.

Moral Aims: The good around which a person orients their life (see also **The good**).

Neutrality: A person's capacity to view their perceptions and projections without getting "hooked" by any emotional or bodily responses to these automatic tendencies. Neutrality typically emerges when the reciprocal relationship between a person's awareness and openness is well-established (see also **Awareness**, **Openness**, and **Freedom**).

Openness: A person's capacity to receive and derive insight from the emotional and intuitive fullness of their experiences in relation to all reality, both inside and outside them (see also **Awareness**).

Overall phenomenon: A complex entity composed of numerous subsidiary entities, some of which are discernable, many of which are not. The dynamics and composition of an overall phenomenon can be significantly altered through various kinds of intra-action between its entangled subsidiary entities (see also **Apparatus** and **Discernable entity**).

Perception: A person's act of receiving and making sense of events or experiences. A person's tendencies in perception are often influenced by their prior experiences, temperament, personality, and neurobiology. Perception can occur either consciously or unconsciously (see also **Projection**).

Procedural secularism: An organization's, institution's, or society's choice not to invoke any divine or transcendent or sacred entities within its decision-making policies or procedures.

Programmatic secularism: An organization's, institution's, or society's choice to require that individuals must conform to an explicitly positive secular norm to become and remain one of its members.

Projection: A person's act of imposing their perceptions on realities outside themself, regardless of whether those realities actually conform to the person's perceptions or not (see also **Perception**).

Recollection: A person's act of revisiting the past through their memory while also ascribing a sense of coherence upon it (see also **Memory** and **Coherence**).

Religion: A cultural storehouse of symbols, ideas, concepts, teachings, practices, rituals, and/or behaviors that help people connect to Ultimate Reality and make sense of their daily realities. Typically, the term *religion* has been understood to refer to specific faith traditions, but current research suggests that secular, social, and cultural traditions can have religious dimensions to them as well.

Secular$_1$: The understanding that enchantment and the sacred do not permeate all reality; the sacred and the secular are distinct domains.

Secular$_2$: The understanding that purely religious (in the traditional sense) and purely secular understandings of reality are two, often competing, options for people in any social or cultural setting. The numerous debates between the so-called "New Atheists" and their religious counterparts during the first two decades of the third millennium are often cited as examples of secular$_2$ phenomena.

Secular$_3$: The understanding that reality cannot be defined with any reference to transcendence or metaphysics. Reality in this approach is defined according the purely immanent frame of empirically verifiable entities. Secular$_3$ is also most often associated with programmatic secularism.

Silence: An experiential absence of words that often conveys feelings of transcendence, vastness, depth, and resonance. Various religious traditions use various terms to name this silence, among them "God," "*brahman*," "*ein sof*," "emptiness," and "Absolute" or "Ultimate Reality" (see also **Contentment** and **Truth**).

Spiritual care: A form of care that mobilizes the resources of religion, culture, or tradition to assist clients in modifying their internal spiritual processes. This modification is done so clients can build, maintain, and enhance their relationships with all of reality. Spiritual Care Practitioners prioritize the affective, intuitive, and relational aspects of life.

Spirituality: The specific processes a person uses to connect to Ultimate Reality and make sense of their life. Because spirituality is an embodied phenomenon, religious rituals, behaviors, and practices can be important for a person's individual spirituality, yet spirituality is also connected to a person's neurobiology, prior experiences, and so on. A person's frame for reality is the most fundamental expression of their spirituality.

Spiritual struggle: Any struggle where a person's frame for reality is revealed to be inadequate to account for the experiences through which they are living. Spiritual struggles can therefore be religiously oriented, but they can also emerge when a person can no longer make sense of their realities without invoking religion. Such inability to understand or make meaning can emerge in response to the overwhelming magnitude of an experience or because the person does not have the cognitive, emotional, or intuitive resources to properly engage with whatever they are living through (see also **Spirituality**).

The good: Notions of what is desirable or beneficial within any macro-cultural context. The good may include such things as wealth, various kinds of material objects, social or interpersonal realities, lifestyles, political realities, religious or spiritual principles or practices, and so on. Notions of the good are often portrayed in mass media, advertising, public and/or political discourses, all of which are mediated at the level of the family and appropriated (or not) by individuals to become embodied in their moral aims (see also **Moral aims**, **Desire**, and **Anticipation**).

Third eye: A complex metaphor to express a person's capacity to perceive seemingly contradictory realities as part of a unified, yet at times paradoxical, vision of reality. In several religious and/or spiritual traditions, the third eye is understood to be the organ of metaphysical/spiritual perception.

Transference/countertransference: Terms originating in the psychoanalytic tradition to refer to the concrete feelings that a therapist evokes from their client and that a client evokes from their therapist. When engaged skillfully in therapeutic contexts, transference and countertransference can be mobilized to significantly benefit clients. Yet when left unattended, transference and countertransference can contribute to unethical crossings of boundaries that often result in psychological, professional, and personal harm to both therapist and client.

Truth: A person's intuitive, emotional, and cognitive understandings of their embodied relationship to silence (see also **Contentment** and **Silence**).

Wisdom: A person's relative capacity to choose a course of action based on what they have experienced as beneficial in the past, in contrast to what they have experienced as not beneficial. A person's capacities for wisdom are dependent on their manifestations of neutrality and freedom, in addition to a well-established reciprocal relationship between awareness and openness in their inner life. A wise person also draws upon the truth of who they are with contentment when assessing how best they can move into the future (see also **Awareness**, **Openness**, **Neutrality**, **Freedom**, **Anticipation**, and **Contentment**).

Index

For Product Safety Concerns and Information please contact our EU
representative GPSR@taylorandfrancis.com
Taylor & Francis Verlag GmbH, Kaufingerstraße 24, 80331 München, Germany

9 781032 677873